THE WAY IT WAS

OTHER BOOKS BY THE AUTHOR

King of the Tulares
Land of the Tules
Visalia, Her First Hundred Years
Jim Savage and the Tulareno Indians
Sites To See

THE WAY IT WAS
The Colorful History of Tulare County

by
Annie R. Mitchell

Panorama
West Publishing
Fresno, California

Copyright © 1976
by
Annie R. Mitchell

Library of Congress Card Catalog Number 76-41499
ISBN 0-944194-07-9

First printing 1976
Second printing 1987

Panorama
West Publishing
Fresno, California

Manufactured in the United States of America

Preface

This is a book which will delight San Joaquin Valley history buffs and collectors of Californiana generally. It relates specifically to Tulare County, the very heartland of the state's agricultural empire, and it deals with circumstances and events which residents of this county and others, far and near, need to know about.

It represents the most recent and best effort of Annie Mitchell, a wise, sensitive and scholarly researcher and author. Her distinguished professional career was in education, but her avocational lifetime has been spent, in addition to fields of community service, in the study of Tulare County and San Joaquin Valley history. Miss Mitchell's grandfather was a pioneer merchant, hotel owner, and community leader in Tulare County in the 1850's. The Mitchell family has been well known and respected in the county for more than 120 years.

Miss Mitchell has long been the ultimate authority — the one to consult — on events and people of the past in the county in which she has spent her productive lifetime. She has been generous in sharing her knowledge with responsible colleagues in the field. For this reason, and because of the warmth of her personality, she has received information, either requested or volunteered, which might have come to other historians less easily, or not at all. She genuinely likes people. She spent many years as dean of girls at Redwood High School in Visalia, and in the early mornings and late afternoons her office was often filled with laughing, chattering girls. These girls had no disciplinary problems; they had come to visit with someone they knew cared.

This book is not Annie Mitchell's first venture into historical writing. She is the authority, because of two books, on Major James Savage; her delightful *Land of the Tules* is a joy to young and old alike. She has done many, many articles and several special editions. Her writing style has matured, and she tells her story well.

Her readers will especially appreciate the thorough coverage of the valley's Spanish and early American exploration era, as well as the exciting chapter on badmen, the intensely informative discussion of the development of our agricultural resources, and the final chapter on the growth of the communities themselves.

This, then, is a book for students, for scholars, for those who like to know what happened in the past, and for those who just enjoy good reading.

Joseph E. Doctor

Acknowledgements

I am indebted to many people who, over the years, have written letters, furnished family histories and diaries, and granted interviews. Their lives and experiences re-emphasize that history is the essence of biographies. Pioneers were seekers, and to them the golden days were always ahead. For that belief we are all indebted, as this cavalcade of the past reveals.

Special acknowledgement must be given to Jeff Edwards, who furnished most of the pictures. Through his skill as a professional photographer and his interest in history, he is preserving the pictorial history of Tulare County for the future.

My thanks to Charles Browne, Harold Schutt, the National Park Service, Cecil Berkley, Katherine Green, Lucinne Bennett, Emily McCain, and Tom Rivers for their help in locating and loaning pictures.

I am deeply grateful to Jospeh Doctor, who has encouraged and helped me in researching the history of Tulare County for so many years. Special mention is given to Harold Schutt, who ably edited *Los Tulares* from 1948 until his death in 1985.

I am grateful for the help given to me by Mrs. Rosemarie Rose of the Tulare County Recorder's office and to Miss Mary Ann Terstegge of the Tulare County Library.

A.R.M.
August 1987

Contents

	Preface	v
	Acknowledgements	vii
1.	The County of Versatility	1
2.	The Yokuts	4
3.	The Turbulent Tulares	15
4.	Long Rifles and Sharp Dealers	21
5.	Tulare County Comes of Age	25
6.	Home on the Range	35
7.	Visalia Saddles	45
8.	Robin Hoods or Hoods Who Robbed	49
9.	Experimenters and Innovators	63
10.	The Land of Milk and Money	83
11.	Fleecy Fibers	91
12.	Cotton	97
13.	High Adventure	101
14.	Towns of the County	117
	Bibliography	157
	Index	159

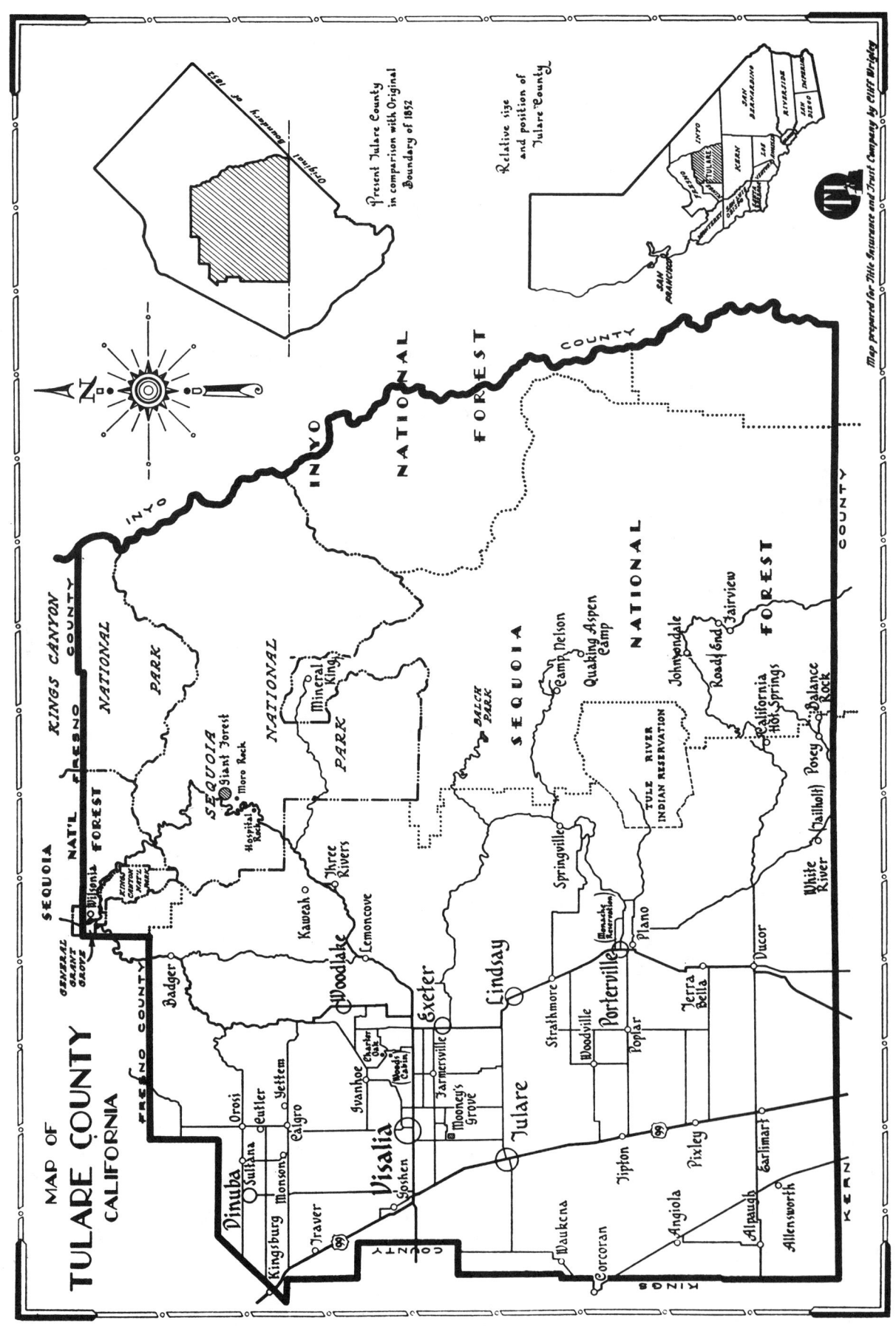

CHAPTER 1

THE COUNTY OF VERSATILITY

In some dim geologic time, according to Indian legend, an inland sea broke through the surrounding hills and flowed into the ocean of the West. The space that it left is our own San Joaquin Valley.

Thousands of years ago violent upheavals of the earth's crust moved an immense block upward. This block, some 430 miles long and 40 to 80 miles wide, tilted westward with its eastern edge raised to form a towering crestline. After many geological thrusts, streams flowed westward and, aided by glaciers and floods, gouged out canyons and river beds. The water carried soil from the mountains, and the soil spread out in rich alluvial fans on the valley floor. Later on the Spaniards named these mountains Sierra Nevada, an appropriate name for the eternally snow-clad crestline.

Our valley remains a geological laboratory. It is veined with earthquake faults. Berg-like hills remind us that they are but buried mountain peaks. Inactive volcanos are plainly discernible in the Sierra Nevada. Lakes, rock basins, and scarred rocks reveal past glacial action. Fossilized clams and mussels as well as sharks' teeth are found on the valley floor. Over the years floods have not only changed the earth's surface, but have dug out new channels for rivers and sloughs.

The interior of California is an elongated trough divided into the San Joaquin and Sacramento Valleys. These valleys are named for their principal rivers, which converge to flow into Carquinez Strait and then into the Bay of San Francisco. The delta formed by their convergence separates the two valleys.

The San Joaquin Valley is approximately 250 miles long and 50 miles wide. It is isolated by the Coast Range Mountains on the west and by the Sierra Nevada on the east. These ranges merge on the south as the Tehachapi Mountains.

The first white man of record to see the San Joaquin was Pedro Fages, first *commandante* and fourth governor of the Californias. The history of California is peppered with accidental discoveries. Don Pedro Fages made one of them in 1772, when he was searching for army deserters. He left San Diego with a detachment of soldiers. The trail of the deserters took Fages through what is now the Imperial Valley, Cajon Pass, and the Mojave Desert. They went on to a pass (Tejon) where Fages looked out over a vast valley which he described as a labyrinth of lagoons and tulares. Smoke rose from the campfires in many *rancherias*. Tall, tangled tule patches, tree-lined rivers, and marshy lakes provided hiding places for the deserters. Fages knew he would never find them, so he went back forever unaware of his historic discovery.

By 1776 the name *Valle de los Tulares* was applied to the southern end of the valley. More properly it covered the drainage basin of Tulare Lake. *Tulares* is derived from an Aztec root, *tullin,* used to describe the common cattail or tule. Today the name is commemorated in Tulare County, the City of Tulare, Tulare Lake, and Tule River.

Father Juan Crespi saw and named the large river of our valley on March 30, 1772, when with Fages he was trying to reach Point Reyes. He named it San Francisco, for Saint Francis of Assisi. In 1805 Gabriel Moraga reached the San Francisco on Saint Joachim's feast day (March 20), and he renamed it the San Joaquin. From then on, various sections of the river had different names, but by 1810 the whole river was generally called the San Joaquin. However, *Tulares* remained in use and on maps until shortly after the American conquest of California.

The eight counties which make up the San Joaquin Valley constitute one of the most productive areas on earth. The original Tulare County was the heartland of the valley.

When Tulare County was created on April 20,

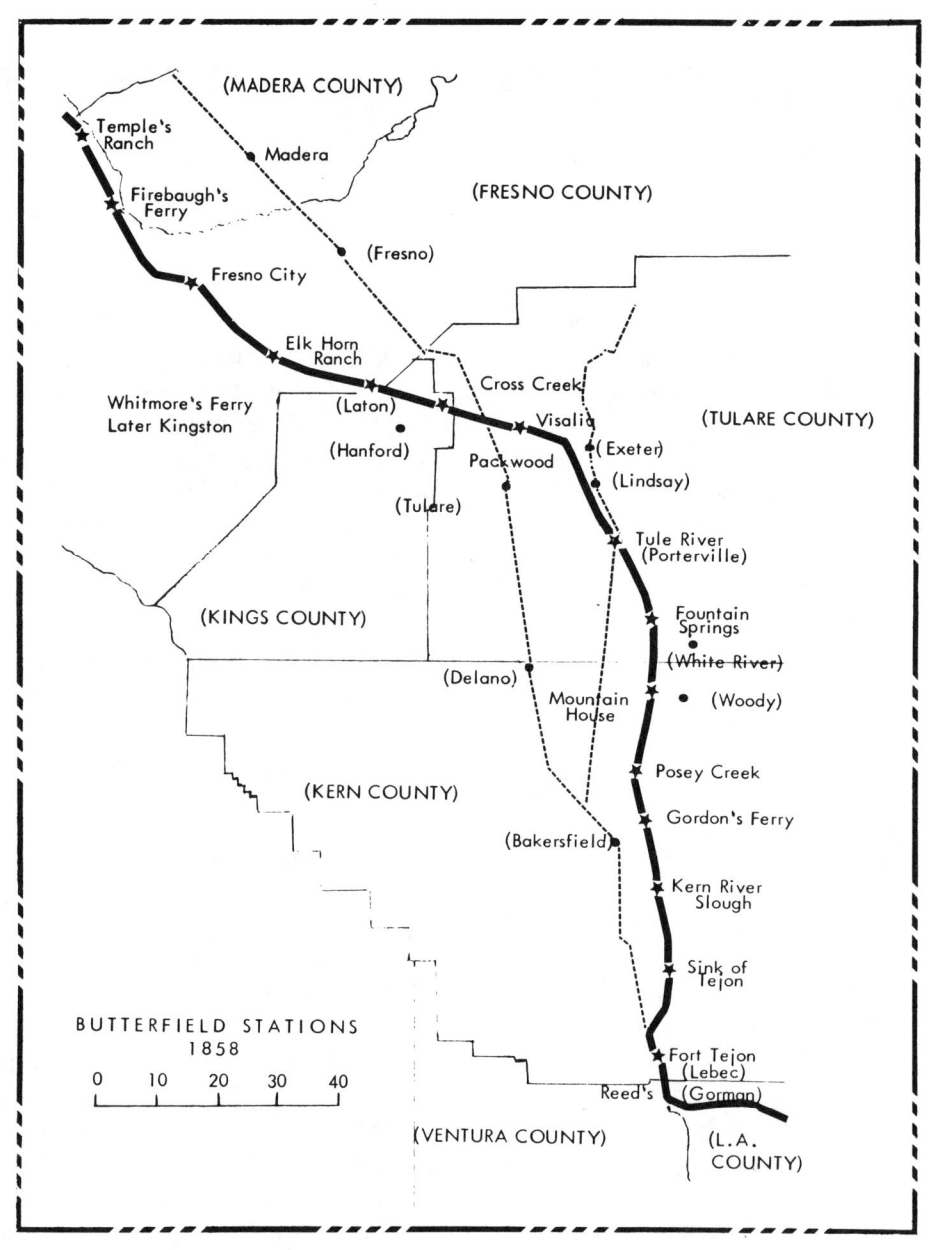

Butterfield Stage route through the San Joaquin Valley. The trip took 41 hours. Visalia was the only town along the way. Present towns are shown in parentheses. (Courtesy of Los Tulares)

1852, its boundaries stretched from Mariposa County on the north to Los Angeles County; from the Coast Range Mountains to the Utah Territory on the east. Out of the original boundaries have come all or part of these counties: Fresno County, 1856; Kern County, 1866; Inyo County, 1866; Kings County, 1893.

Tulare County is still a big county and ranks seventh in size among the 58 counties of California. It is truly a county of versatility. Geographically it is made up of distinct but merging areas. About one-third of its 4,935 square miles is the valley floor. The rest of the county is composed of foothills, timbered slopes and high mountains. This topography accounts for contrasts in soil, rainfall, climate, vegetation, scenery, recreation, and density of population. Elevations range from 270 feet on the valley floor to 14,495 feet at the top of Mt. Whitney. There are more than 110 mountain peaks in eastern Tulare County. They range in altitude from 8,000 to 14,495 feet and furnish a backdrop of scenic wonder.

Sequoia and Kings Canyon National Parks and Inyo and Sequoia National Forests comprise 1,371,020 acres altogether. The Tule River and Strathmore Indian Reservations total 49,040 acres, and the county-owned parks total 120,000 acres. The parks and forests provide diverse recreational areas. Mountain resorts, winter sports of all kinds, fishing, boating, back-packing, hunting, hiking, and water skiing attract thousands of visitors. The two national parks contain the largest redwoods in the world, including the famous General Grant Tree and the General Sherman Tree.

The climatic conditions vary according to elevation. The average rainfall on the valley floor is about 10 inches, most of which falls during the winter months (November through February). Summers are long, hot, and dry, and farmers may expect an average growing season of about 270 days.[1]

The first County Directory was published in 1888 and made this candid comment on our weather.

Tulare County is not builded upon climate, but on soil and water, and production. There are two seasons, dry and rainy. Dry hits the nail squarely on the head. The term rainy season is unfortunate. Our so called rainy season is merely that portion of the year in which it sometimes rains. The general health of the County is excellent. People do die here occasionally, but the death rate is low. If Tulare County had neither dust nor heat to contend with, her climate would be faultless and all of the people of the world would want to live within her boundaries.[2]

Economically the county developed in stages. The early settlers were stockmen attracted by water and abundant feed in the mountain meadows and on the plains. Grain farming came when the railroad made it feasible to transport grain in bulk. Irrigation and pumped wells made it profitable to raise deciduous fruits, citrus, and alfalfa on small farms. The same factors made dairying a major industry. Irrigation changed viticulture from the family grape arbor to a leading income crop. In the 1920's cotton culture began on a large scale. None of the major new crops eliminated the preceding ones.

Agriculture still remains the most important factor in Tulare County's economy, although there is a marked trend toward increased industrialization and tourism. Today's top sources of agricultural income are grapes, citrus, cattle, alfalfa, cotton, and dairy products. For many years the county has ranked among the top four counties in the nation in terms of agricultural income.

With all our natural bounties, we are faced with the problems common to growth: destruction of prime farm land, water and energy shortages, waste disposal, pollution of air and water and land, urban sprawl, and rapid growth in population. The Federal Census figures describe this growth:

Year	Population	Note
1860	4,638	
1870	4,533	
1880	11,281	
1890	24,574	
1900	18,375	Kings County formed in 1893
1910	35,440	
1920	59,031	
1930	77,442	
1940	107,152	
1950	149,364	
1960	168,403	
1970	188,322	
1990	245,500	Projected population[3]
2000	362,206	Projected population'

---

1. Tulare county Chamber of Commerce.
2. *Directory* of Tulare County, 1888.
3. Tulare County Chamber of Commerce.

CHAPTER 2

THE YOKUTS

The Indians who lived in the Tulares occupied one of the world's most beautiful and productive valleys. The Coast Range Mountains and the Sierra Nevada provided both isolation and sustenance. The grass-covered valley floor was interlaced with rivers and sloughs bordered by thickets of tules, wild berries, and grapevines and shaded by willow, cottonwood, and alder trees.

Valley oak trees dotted the plains, and an oak forest spread from the foothills to Tulare Lake. The foothills provided a habitat for deer, elk, antelope, bear, small animals and game birds. The rivers and lakes provided fish, shellfish, terrapin, and water fowl. Variations in diet were found in edible roots such as tule and yucca, bulbs, berries, seeds, nuts, sweet clover, mushrooms, certain insects, and of course salt. If one source of food failed, there was always another. The Yokuts' staple food was the acorn. The Yokuts were true conservationists and never took more than they could use. They learned to live in harmony with their environment, an example modern man could well emulate.

The Yokuts, the Tularenos of the Spaniards, were a remarkable people. Compared to the eastern tribes, the Indians of California were certainly less advanced and less sophisticated, but they were not "digger Indians." That derogatory label was given by white men who saw the Indians digging roots for food, yet the same white men enjoyed eating carrots, turnips and beets!

Kroeber described the Yokuts as the only true tribe in California in that they had tribal names, tribal dialects, and tribal territory.

The Yokuts derived their name from their word "Yokoch," meaning peoples. They were divided into some 50 recognizable tribes, and it was estimated that they numbered 20,000, thus making them one of the largest tribes in California. They held territory from the Stockton delta to the Tehachapi Mountains, and the lower foothills south of the Fresno River.

The Yokuts belonged to the large Pennutian linguistic family which in California also included the Maidu, Miwok, Wintun, and Costanoan tribes. On the eastern and southern sides of the valley the Yokuts came into contact with tribes from the Shoshonean linguistic family. The tribes directly east were the Monos or Monaches, and directly south was the Tubatulabal tribe of the Kern River drainage basin.

Early visitors recorded that the Yokuts were a friendly, peaceable people. The tribes could communicate in spite of different dialects. The Yokuts also developed a smoke "telegraph" that disseminated news rapidly. Different tribes co-mingled on trading expeditions and when they prospected for minerals. Old-timers said that the valley and hill Indians did not get along well with each other, but there are few references to open warfare. Tribal feuds arose when Shamans (medicine men) exorcised evil spirits. Nevertheless, each tribe kept within its own territory and guarded its identity. This was to create many problems when they were herded into reservations.

We should not imply that the Yokuts were a docile people. They were able hunters and also fierce fighters when the need arose. Primitive people fight over food and territory, but neither of these caused problems in the Tulares. Tribes which came into early contact with white men, such as the Tachi and Chowchillas, became aggressive. So did the Miwok and Maidu, the first Yokuts to feel the force of the gold rush invasion.

The local Indians were not to bear that burden for some time. In the 1820-1840 era, valley Indians changed their tactics from defensive to offensive attacks on coastal settlements. In the Tule River Indian War of 1856, Indians armed with bows and

Headquarters Building at the first Tule River Indian Reservation, taken about 1900. The reservation was a few miles south and east of Porterville in what is now the Alta School District. The adobe brick buildings have all disappeared.

arrows held off armed white men for six weeks. One wonders what might have happened if the American occupation of California and the gold rush had not occurred so close together.

There is a correlation between food, climate, and geography. Because of that correlation, three different cultures emerged among the local Yokuts. These have been labeled lake culture, river culture, and plains culture.

Little is known about the Indians on the semi-arid west side of Tulare Lake, for they had disappeared before the pioneer settlers came. Their disappearance was not a mystery. These were the people who were taken to nearby missions to be Christianized and civilized. The only known tribes on the west side were the Tachi and Tulamni.

The lake people were distinctive. Tulare Lake was the home of the Wowol, Tachi, Chunut, and Nutunutu people, who also roamed up the rivers which flowed into the lake. There they came in contact with the river culture. The lake Indians were migratory because of geography and climate. The Tulare Lake bed is shallow, and stiff winds could blow water out for several miles onto the plains. Homes had to be made so that they could be dismantled quickly as their inhabitants fled. The use of tules for house covering, mats, boats, clothing, and food set the lake people apart.

Many times over the years Tulare Lake has been alternately dry, full, and at flood stage. It covered 760 square miles at flood stage, and even when it was holding a normal runoff, there were stretches of marsh around the lake for several miles. Indians and pioneers found Tulare Lake literally teeming with fish, shellfish, and terrapin. Elk, deer, antelope and wild horses lived there, as did wild predators. Game birds and waterfowl fed there. As the water level fluctuated, five islands rose from the

These unidentified Indian women were still wearing old-style clothing in 1910, but the children were wearing "white man's clothes." Taken at Tule River Indian Reservation.

Mrs. Mary Pohut making acorn mush.

lake, providing a refuge for both Indians and waterfowl.

Tule mats were an indispensible part of life. They were used to cover the framework of the house, for beds, and for rafts. The remarkable tule rafts were sometimes large enough to carry several people, and sturdy enough to stay on the water for days while men fished.

The lake people had a communal apartment house not found elsewhere. The long structure was built by setting notched poles in a line. Ridge poles were placed in the notches, and the frame was covered with tule mats. Some of these apartments had tule awnings over a sort of front porch to protect people from the sun. Each family had its own section and entrance.

The river people were affluent and lived amidst beautiful surroundings. They had permanent houses and sweat houses and did little traveling except to trade or gather food in the mountains. Since they had a good deal of leisure time, they were able to design beautiful baskets and develop an imaginative folklore.

The plains people lived on the valley floor, between the rivers. They were hunters and wanderers but stayed within their tribal boundaries, which ranged up into the foothills. Since they were primarily hunters, they were more aggressive than the people of the other cultures.

Dress varied little among the three cultures. In our mild climate clothes were minimal. Women wore a short two-piece skirt that was really like a modern mini-skirt. It was usually made from skins, and fashion-conscious ladies painted designs on the dress or fringed it. The women wore their hair long, and most had bangs. Men wore little except a breechclout. Both sexes wore fur blankets around their shoulders in cold weather. Men wore their hair long, sometimes braided or held back with a headband. Moccasins were not in general use in the valley, although men going on hunting trips did wear a sort of sandal made from thick skin. During religious rites both men and women painted their bodies and faces, and facial tattoos among women were not uncommon. Some pioneer reminiscences refer to "war paint," but these usually resulted from confusion between religious ceremonies and warfare.

The Yokuts were omnivorous eaters, but the acorn was their staple food. The acorn of the valley oak is larger, but the Yokuts preferred acorns from

Francisco Emeterio was 104 years old when this picture was taken in 1905 on the Tule River Indian Reservation. The woman behind him is not identified.

the mountain oak, which they said were sweeter and more nutritious. Harvesting acorns was hard work for the women. When the acorns began to fall they were scooped up in gathering baskets. Then they were dumped into a large cone-shaped carrying basket which could hold up to 200 pounds. The women carried these baskets by head and back straps to their camp, where the acorns were stored in family granaries. Each family used about 2,000 pounds of acorns every year. Preparation of the acorns was also arduous work. They were hulled and ground into a coarse meal. Bedrock mortars still help us visualize long-gone campsites where women went about the task of preparing acorns for their families.

Acorns contain a high percentage of tannic acid which must be leached out before the meal is useable. The women scooped out shallow depressions in sand or well-drained soil and lined the hole with leaves or fine brush. The acorn meal was poured in and doused repeatedly with hot water. When the bitter taste was gone, the meal dried and was broken into cakes. Acorns have a high fat content and contain more calories than wheat. Their chemical composition is 21.3% fat; 5.1% protein; 62.2% carbohydrates, and the rest is ash, water and fiber.[1]

Acorn meal was used in many ways. Sometimes the dried cake was eaten by itself, but usually the meal was boiled to make a gruel. The gruel could be eaten plain or it could be varied by adding fish, meat, seeds, berries or salt.

Salt was a precious item to primitive people. In this area the salt was gathered laboriously from salt grass. This salt has a sour taste, somewhat like that of a dill pickle. The Yokuts also obtained sea salt in trade with tribes living near the ocean.

Primitive people have proscribed foods. Tradition endowed certain animals with magical powers, which gave rise to taboos. It is interesting that the Yokuts ate dog meat, which was absolutely taboo in other tribes. The Yokuts proscribed bear and coyote because of their belief in the magical attributes of those animals. Like most primitive peoples, the Yokuts avoided reptiles, birds of prey, and skunks. However, when it became a choice between surviving or not eating some of these foods — they ate these foods. Long before health foods became so popular, Indians were eating succulent roots, nuts, seeds, and sweet clover. It is easy to see why the Indians in this valley of plenty were hunters, fishers, and gatherers, and not agriculturists.

In addition to a variety of tools — soaproot brushes, hot rock lifters, bone needles and awls and digging sticks — the Yokut housekeeper had basic baskets such as the conical burden basket, seed beater, collecting basket, winnowing tray, and sieves. Steatite cooking vessels were obtainable, but most of the cooking was done in watertight baskets. The cook lifted hot rocks from the fire and dropped them into water in a cooking basket. The Yokuts' method of cooking small animals was not particularly attractive — they cooked the whole animal and then skimmed off the fur and other inedible parts. Mountain men who used the same method said it improved the taste.

The lake Indians found an ingenious way to cook shellfish. Clams or mussels were placed on tules, which were set afire and doused with water. The steam opened and cooked the shellfish.

The Yokuts gathered tobacco, which still grows wild in the county. Pedro Fages, that keen observer of Indian lifestyle in the Californias, left an excellent description of the use of tobacco:

Hospital Rock. This glacially split boulder overhangs in such a way that a circular room is formed. It was named by Hale Tharp and was the tribal meeting place for nearby Indians. One side of the room is covered with Indian pictographs.

..the common Indians wear a small cloak which reaches to the waist; in their hair they interweave cords or bands with beads; among the folds of which they bestow the trifles which they need to carry with them. The most common of these small articles is a small horn of the antelope containing tobacco for smoking, wrapped in leaves. They gather great harvests of this plant, and grind large quantities of it mixed with lime, from this paste forming cones or small loaves which they wrap in tule leaves and hang up in the house until quite dry. They assert that as a food it is very strengthening, and that they can sustain themselves on it for three days without other nourishment; they usually partake of it at supper.[2]

The Yokuts were canny traders. They traded skins, furs, food, fiber, salt, clay, paints, and steatite for such items as obsidian, juniper wood, sea salt, pigments, asphaltum, moccasins, and shell beads. The trade trails to the Monaches, to the coastal Chumash, to the Coalinga country, as well as to neighboring rancherias, were well worn. One trail along the eastern foothills was followed by white "pathfinders" who explored the valley. Parts of these trails have been incorporated into our modern highway system, for example, Highway 65 from Lindsay to Porterville.

The Yokuts were observant miners. It was necessary for them to know the physical properties of rocks and minerals, such as color, hardness, cleavage, and thermal index. As they hunted or traded, the Yokuts came to know every useable outcropping within their territory. Any discovery made belonged to the whole tribe, not just to the individual who made it. Some people have wondered why the Yokuts did not find gold when it lay right on top of the ground in many places. The answer is, the probably did find some gold, but they ignored it because they had no use for it.

Obsidian was used universally for arrow points, spearheads, and knives. The Yokuts obtained obsidian in trade with Indians living in what is now Inyo County. Steatite was another valuable mineral. Steatite, or talc, will not break when it is heated. It was used for pipes, cooking utensils, arrow and spear shaft straighteners, ornaments, and money. One of the best sources of steatite is about four miles east of Lindsay. Indians worked the mine for years, and white men mined the site up until a few years ago.

Besides the steatite deposit near Lindsay, there is some evidence that the Yokuts were familiar with

Left: Sally Sweatheal carrying an acorn gathering basket. Taken at the original Tule River Indian Reservation. Above: Mrs. Maggie Ichow making a basket.

the magnesite deposits near Porterville and the jasper or chrysoprase deposits east of Visalia.

Asphaltum was used to waterproof baskets, to fasten points to shafts, and to waterproof the backs of bows. It was a trade item from the area around Coalinga and from the tar springs on Posey Creek.

The Indians also traded pigments. For example, the principal trade item of the Indians who lived in the Yokohl Valley was pigment from a white soil found on the north ridge of Rocky Hill. Pigments were mixed with milkweed juice or vegetable oils. Paint was used by war parties, during religious ceremonies, for pictographs, and by shamans. The colors in the baskets came from native fibers and not from pigments.

The Yokuts did not depend upon barter entirely, for they were developing a simple monetary system. The unit of exchange was a string of beads made from shell or steatite. The unit having the least value was made from the small bi-valve, *olivella biplicata*. There were several in-between denominations, and the highest value was placed on discs made from the Pismo clam. Abalone shell was also valued highly both as money and for ornaments. Steatite had a high value and the edges were milled as are our coins.

Artifacts left by primitive people can help us reconstruct their lifestyle. Tools, points, money, fish hooks, baskets, shell mounds and campsite refuse leave their own interpretative story. Rock mortars, grinding stones, and pottery are tangible reminders. Baskets tell another story. Pictographs and petrographs still need a key to unlock their secrets. There are places where an observant person may still see circular depressions on which an Indian house once stood.

The Yokuts were noted basket makers. In general they made baskets by coiling, although twining and weaving techniques were also used. Dozens of stitches per inch were sewn with a bone needle. What patience it took to split a root fiber into several threads! Commonly used materials were bunch grass, caladium roots, redbud bark, bracken fern roots, black sword fern roots, tule, cottonwood and willow shoots. Designs were both symbolic and abstract. One can see deer tracks, the skin pattern of king snakes and rattlesnakes, quail, water skaters, wild geese, flying ants, trees, sun, moon, stars, and other imaginative designs in these baskets.

Collectors have valued Indian baskets for their aesthetic qualities. The Indians valued them for their practical use. Besides the household baskets, there were gaming trays and baskets in which to keep treasures. Some were used as caps. Shamans had special baskets in which they kept their magic.

The Wukchumnes, who lived along the Kaweah River, were noted for their square-necked baskets decorated with topknots from male quail. Baby cradles were lovingly made, and are always favorites in modern museum exhibits.

Just as some women are famous for their cooking or handiwork, certain Indian women were famous for their baskets. Within the settlement of Tulare County, Maggie Ichow, Molly Lawrence, Mary Pohut, and Dinkey Wilcox made baskets which are now collectors' items. Each of the ladies left a legacy of tribal history.

Maggie Ichow, whose Wukchumne name was Wah-nom-kot, was the granddaughter of Chief Chappo, a Pahdwisha. She and her husband, Henry Ichow, were both born at the Wukchumne village at Terminus Beach, which is now covered by Terminus Lake, Henry Ichow's mother, Milly, died in 1928 at well over 100 years of age. Her family saw Jedediah Smith when he came through the valley. She remembered Jim Savage, the Woods party, and the Tule River Indian War of 1856. Much of this remarkable woman's history was recorded by Frank Latta.

Molly Lawrence's skill in basketry was well known. Her husband, Henry Lawrence, was a Yowlumne Indian born near Bakersfield. His Indian name was Wah-hum-cha. Molly Lawrence died in 1928 before much of her history was recorded. Henry Lawrence lived until 1959. He was one of the last to remember the mourning ceremonies, songs and dances of his people. In 1948 he helped reconstruct an Indian village in the Kern County Museum Compound.

Dinkey Wilcox (Mrs. Jim Wilcox) lived in Drum Valley. As a small child she was taken to the Tule Reservation, and in the 100-year span of her life her tribal connections were forgotten. People who collected baskets ordered them from her for years, and her handiwork is in many well-known collections.

When Mary Garcia Pohut died in 1960, the old art of basketry died with her. Mrs. Pohut was a Wukchumne born in 1865 at a village near Venice Hills. She married Joe Pohut, whose ancestry was both Wukchumne and Pahdwisha. He was well known for his horsemanship. The Pohuts' home place was on Dry Creek, and they also had a place near Woodlake. Mrs. Pohut was a valuable informant not only for Indian history, but for local history in general. Like Mrs. Ichow, Mrs. Lawrence, and Mrs. Wilcox, she was known for her singing, and fortunately many of her tribal songs were recorded. The Pohuts, like the other families, have descendants living in the county.

Mr. Henry Cow, father of Henry Lawrence, taken at the first Tule River Indian Reservation.

A tangible legacy left by the Indians is disappearing through natural erosion, vandalism, and "progress." This legacy is the petrographs cut into rocks and pictographs painted on rocks. At one time there were so many along the foothills that the rocks could have been described as a picture book.

We do not know when Indians first came into the valley. Recent discoveries have pushed the time back thousands of years. The Indians who lived here when white men came could not interpret the pictures. When Chief Chappo invited Hale Tharp into the Pahdwisha camp in 1858, he showed him the pictographs at Hospital Rock. According to Indian legend a man would come some day and be able to read the pictures. Of course, Tharp could not, for only the artist knew what they meant. The story told by the Indian paintings will always be in the eye of the beholder. The paintings may have something to do with hunting, or perhaps they show game trails, or perhaps they are calendars or even just doodles. The more logical explanation is that the paintings are linked in some way to Shamans and religious practices.

Since the Yokuts did not have to fight for food or territory, they had time to develop creative ex-

Bob Tisto, a Tachi Indian medicine man and rainmaker, in his medicine man dress.

periences. Their folklore sprang from a universal desire to know and understand the world about them. Their myths involve history, moral conduct, and the conflict of good and evil forces. Many stories revolve around a creator and a destroyer. All tribes told stories of a flood, of obtaining fire, and creation. The principal relator was always an animal who assumed the attributes of people. Ki-you, the coyote, was deceitful and tricky. Tro-kud, the eagle, was said to be one of the creators of the Yokuts. Lim-ik, the Prairie Falcon, was a hero as was Mih-kit-tee, the bear, found in a spring by his grandmother, Mrs. Lim-ik.

Prayer was an essential part of an Indian's life. White men overlooked this because the prayers were expressed so simply. Before eating an Indian might say, "I wish to eat, good Father." When a relative died an Indian might say, "You are going to another land. You will like that land. You shall not stay here." The first lines of an Indian version of the 23rd Psalm are wonderfully expressive:

The Great Father above a Shepherd Chief is. I am His, and with Him I want not. He throws out to me a rope, and the name of the rope is love, and he draws me to where the grass is green and the water not dangerous, and I eat and lie down and am satisfied.

Each tribe had its doctors whose duty it was to cure the sick and conduct ceremonies such as the elaborate annual mourning ceremony, puberty ceremonies, jimson weed rites, dances, and the rattlesnake ceremony. Indian doctors worked under trying conditions, for too many non-cures or deaths made the doctor answerable to the close relatives of the deceased.

One of the relevant experiences of western Indians was the world renewal concept, expressed through the Kukus cult and the Ghost dance. The Kukus cult was widespread among the tribes of northern California. It had little acceptance in the valley, but the Yokuts were caught up in the frenzy of the Ghost Dance. That concept began with the northern Piutes about 1870. It took 20 years before it was accepted by tribes east of California.

The essence of the Ghost Dance was the promise that there would be no more death, and that all dead relatives would return. By inference, the good days would come back. It is not difficult to understand why the Indians were affected by such concepts. Secularization of the missions, American occupation of California, the gold rush, and rejection of the treaties of 1851-52 left California Indians with little hope.

The instigators of the Ghost Dance said the dead would return if they were appeased through dancing, prayers, and singing. In this locality the largest Ghost Dance was held in Eshom Valley in 1870. It was also the first social intermingling of the Yokuts and Monaches. Smaller dances were held in Farmersville, near Tulare Lake, and near Tule River. Two recollections of the Eshom Valley Dance show how little the Indians and white men understood each other's customs, even though the white men were friendly toward the Indians.

Enos Barton, a pioneer of Three Rivers, was one of the white men who saw the Eshom Valley Ghost Dance. His recollections were recorded in 1921.[3] The white men had heard rumors that Indians from all sections of the valley were going to Eshom.

Although women and children were seen going to the valley, the white men decided that war was imminent. When signal fires were seen, a few white men decided to investigate. Mr. Barton recalled:

When we got there we found the lower end of Eshom Valley swarming with Indians and six or eight other white men there for the same purpose we came for. The fandango was in a small cove off to one side of the main valley. It was in a perfect circle with an opening about twenty feet wide on the side facing the main valley...This circle was about 300 feet across as near as I could estimate. About every two rods, just inside the shacks was a fire, and a large fire in the center of the circle was kept burning night and day...Just inside the circle of fires was a circle of Indians, reaching clear around, some places just a single file of Indians, and some places they would be three or four thick, but the circle of Indians was never broken while I was there. All would hold hands and all would move slowly to the right with a sort of hitching sidewise step, all keeping perfect time to the music of a song furnished by a band of about twenty-five or thirty Indians that went in a bunch going around with the rest. They changed songs once in a while but never missed time for a second.....There was not much difference in the dress of the choir and the rest of the Indians except their hats, some of which were the most beautiful I ever saw. They were made of hawk tail feathers standing straight up, all perfectly matched, not entirely rigid, but so they would wave around a little as the Indians danced.

We white men that were there did not want the Indians to know we suspected anything was wrong, so we just got in and played Indian along with the rest. Every once in a while we would get in the circle and dance a round or two with the rest of the Indians.

There was an unprincipled scamp of a white man there by the name of Tom Love who owned a whiskey joint over on Mill road. He was there with plenty of whiskey to sell but I do not think he made much money for there was not a drunken Indian during the fandango.

Mr. Barton was asked to estimate how many Indians were in Eshom Valley. He said it was hard to estimate since some were sleeping, and those who had horses were dragging up wood to keep the fires going. He counted 742 dancing at one time and estimated that five or six thousand were in the valley.

Four of the white men went home for provisions, and hurried back since they thought that if anything were planned, it would happen early in the morning. Nothing happened. The dance went on all day and another night. As the sun rose on another day, we pick up the story in Mr. Barton's words:

...An old chief out in the center gave a whoop; then every Indian there just instantly started for that opening. It put one in mind of a flock of sheep rushing through a gap in a fence. It was a good thing they were barefoot or

Joe Ely (1869-1911)
He was the last identifiable member of the Indian tribe which lived in the Yokohl Valley near Exeter. Mr. Ely was a barber in Exeter for many years.

there would have been a lot of crippled Indians for they ran right over the ones that fell down; then when the main rush was over the ones that were down began to get up and limp off toward the creek where they all jumped in and had a much needed bath for the dust was two or three inches deep where they danced, and that was the great fun they had talked about. The Indians now began to straggle back to camp and said, "Fandango over; Indian now go home."

However, it was not over. Rumor had it that some white men were coming to Eshom Valley, so the Indians fled. After a couple of days, Bill Osborn and Dave De Masters went after the Indians to tell them that there was not to be an attack. They found many Indians in a small canyon leading into Kings

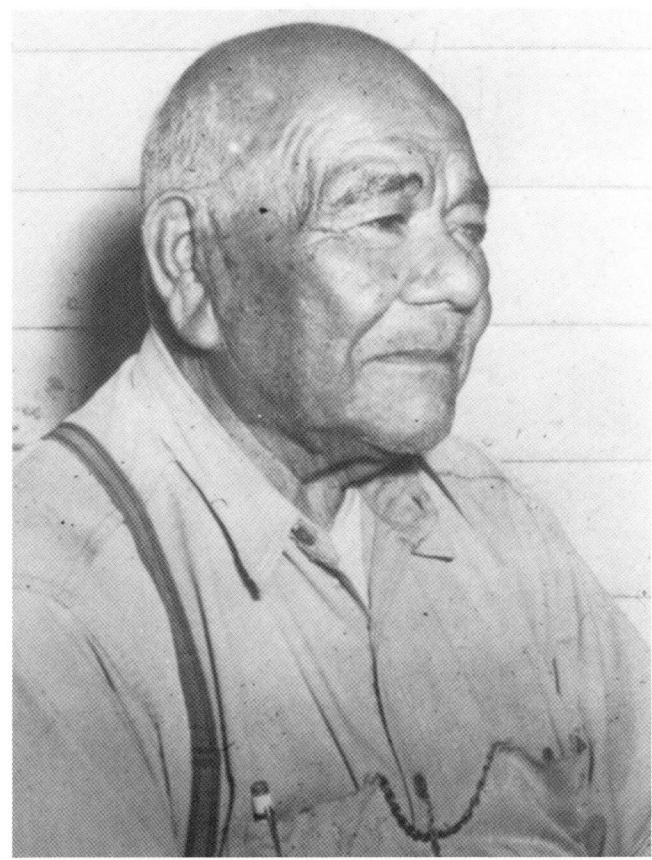

Jose Vera (1867-1963) was born on the first Tule River Indian Reservation.

River, scared and very hungry. They were persuaded to go back to their own homes.

Frank Latta recorded the story of the same Ghost Dance as it was told to him by Yoi-mut, the last survivor of the Chun-ut tribe.[4] Her version follows Mr. Barton's story, but it shows the religious concept as well as the fear the Indians had of white men.

Yoi-mut said many Indians were dying and the doctors were not able to stop the sickness. Some doctors came from the Mono country and talked with the local doctors. The Mono doctors told them the dying would stop, and the dead would return if the Indians would have a new kind of dance. There was no thought of war. They wanted to see their dead relatives.

Eshom Valley was selected because there was plenty of water and fine clover fields. The doctors told them they must be kind to each other, dance all night and day, and bathe each day. Yoi-mut estimated that 1,000 Indians came. They danced six nights and most of the days. There were paid singers and musicians to accompany the dancers. When the dance was almost ended, white men came and said other white men were coming to kill the Indians.

We were afraid of the white people all of the time, so we ran away into the timber, and into the mountains. This was the last night of the dance. We left without either our clothes or our grub. We found a good place to hide in a canyon this side of Kings River. We stayed there a week until we almost starved. Some people killed a little game and one bear. We ate the bear meat. That was all we had even the little children. After we had been hidden almost a week, some white people came and told us no one would hurt us. So we came back to our own camp and got ready to go home. We never finished the Eshom Valley dance. We had a good time at Eshom Valley, but we were sorry we did not see our dead people. Lots of people had been dying and we wanted to see them, but we never did.

A few months later another Ghost Dance was held at Farmersville. The Indians believed the dead did not come back because the Eshom Valley dance was not finished. They danced six days and nights at Farmersville. The dead did not come back, and the Indians said the Mono doctors had fooled them.

The destruction of the Indians of California is a sorry page in the state's history. The grim facts are revealed in the population figures. When white men arrived in 1769 the Indian population of California was estimated at 300,000. A century later it had been reduced to 20,000. Much of the early history of the Tulares revolved around those figures.

The role of the missionaries in California was to Christianize and civilize the Indians. All missions would become parish churches, and the missionaries would then move on to other fields. One of those fields was to be a chain of missions in the Tulares. The plan had worked well in other parts of the New World, but for many reasons it did not work in Alta California. The Indians were no more fitted for that responsibility after 65 years of mission life than before. Furthermore, records show that from 1779 until 1833 there were 62,600 deaths at the missions and 29,100 births.[5] The American policy was in direct contrast to that of the missionaries. As white men came west, the Indians were pushed further west. When the white men reached California, there was no place else to push the Indians, and a war of extermination began. Governor Peter Burnett said in his annual message:

That a war of extermination will continue to be waged between the two races until the Indian race becomes extinct, must be expected; while we cannot anticipate this result with but painfull regret, the inevitable destiny of the race is beyond the power and wisdom of man to avert.[6]

Within two decades after the gold rush began, miners and settlers had overrun the Indians' food

Indian Rock basins in Mt. Home State Forest. Joseph Doctor is in foreground. These basins are found in groups at elevations ranging from 4,000 to 9,000 feet and are always near redwood trees. They may be man-made or made by glacial action. (Courtesy of Harold Schutt)

sources. Before the white men came, the Indians had suffered principally from rheumatism, eye diseases, sprains, fractures and wounds. White men gave them venereal diseases, tuberculosis, typhoid, smallpox, malaria, cholera, measles, and a variety of fevers. As a result, germ warfare killed more Indians than bullets did. Epidemics of cholera, measles, and malaria killed thousands of Indians in the valley. Not only was there disease, there were also social problems. An act passed by the State Legislature in 1850, *For the Government and Protection of Indians,* provided for the indenture or apprenticeship of Indians, and opened the door to slavery and the kidnapping of Indian children. Indians were forbidden to buy liquor, but unscrupulous white men sold it to them anyway. Anyone could pay the fine of an Indian jailed for drunkenness and make him work it out. Under California law, an Indian had no rights. He could not vote, he could not testify, and he could not defend himself in court.

Indians were eventually taken to reservations without regard to tribal affiliation or cultural differences. Some effort was made to care for them, but in reality they received little help. Reservations were aptly termed little better than almshouses.

1. R. F. Heizer and M. A. Whipple, *California Indians,* University of California Press, 1960, Page 241.
2. A Historical, Political and Natural Description of California by Pedro Fages, written for the Viceroy in 1775. Translated by Herbert I. Priestly, Ballena Press, Ramona, California, 1973.
3. Republished in *Los Tulares #14,* March 1953. Publication of the Tulare County Historical Society.

4. Frank Latta, *Handbook of Yokuts Indians,* Bakersfield, 1949, page 244.
5. Sherburne F. Cook, "The Conflict Between the California Indians and White Civilization," *California Monthly,* December, 1968.
6. *California Senate Journal,* 3rd Session, 1852, page 714.

CHAPTER 3

THE TURBULENT TULARES

Don Pedro Fages looms large in California history both as a soldier and as an administrator. In 1767 he came to the New World from his native Catalonia to serve on the frontier. In 1769 he was ordered to join the expedition organized by Visitador General Jose de Galvez. That two-pronged expedition came by land and by sea to occupy Alta California because of the Russian advance down the Pacific coast. Fages sailed on the *San Carlos* in command of the Catalonian soldiers. The land and sea expeditions, decimated by illness and other misfortunes, met at San Diego on July 1, 1769. General Gaspar de Portola, commander of the expedition, had been ordered to occupy the Bay of Monterey which Viscaino had discovered and glowingly described in 1602. When Portola started for Monterey, "of the 300 men who had originally started on the expedition (to Alta California) less than half remained alive, and many of the survivors were wholly prostrated, some half disabled, and others on foot without strength."[1]

Fages was with Portola on the ill-fated trip to Monterey in 1769, and on the successful trip the next year. When Portola returned to Mexico, Fages became *commandante*. He had less than 50 soldiers to protect the Province. In November 1770 Fages explored from what is now Monterey to Alameda. In March and April 1772 he and Father Juan Crespi explored from the Bay of San Francisco to the mouth of a river they called San Francisco (the San Joaquin River). They actually saw part of the great central valley. In the fall of 1772, Fages entered the great central valley through what is now Tejon Pass.

Fages had many problems to face in Alta California. He and Father Serra quarrelled over who was responsible for what. Father Serra did not think the military should tell him where and when to found missions. The fact that there were not enough soldiers to protect the existing establishments did not bother Father Serra, for patience was not one of the zealous Father's virtues. Eventually he managed to have Fages recalled to Mexico, but in 1782 Fages returned as Governor of the Californias, a post he held until 1791. History records him as one of the ablest administrators during the Spanish period.

Fages' domestic life was far from blissful. His wife, Eulalia, was a member of an aristocratic family living in Mexico. When she married Don Pedro, she was in her early teens and he was 45 years of age. It took five years of pleading by her family and Fages to get her started toward Alta California. She finally set out with a retinue of servants, trunks of clothes, and wagons of baggage. Fages rode horseback to meet her at Loreto. He had never seen his son, Pedrito, and the indulgent father let him ride with him most of the 1,200 miles back to Monterey.

The family received the honors due the Governor along the route, but Senora Fages complained loudly and at length all the way to Mission San Gabriel. A contemporary account stated that when she arrived at the Mission she was wearing a green velvet riding habit, a plumed hat, chicken skin boots, and a sour expression.

In the years that Fages had expected her, he had furnished the Governor's House with silver service, linens, dishes, painted chests and wall sconces. He had also trained Indian servants. She took one look at the adobe house and wailed that she would not live in a mud hut, but she did. She also started plotting and scheming to get her husband to take her back to Mexico. When that failed she tried to have him recalled. Her tantrums set tongues wagging over the Province and on to Mexico. When she threatened to divorce Fages, the exasperated padres threatened to excommunicate her. Finally a reconciliation was worked out. In 1791 the old soldier sailed to Mexico with his family. He left with a place in history. She left California with its first scandal.

The distinction of exploring the valley for the first time goes to Father Francisco Garces, one of western history's giants. His story, as it relates to Tulare County, begins when he was assigned to San Xavier del Bac (nine miles south of Tucson, Arizona) in 1768. From that frontier mission he found his role in history as a missionary, explorer, and chronicler. In 1768 he explored as far as the Gila River. He returned again a year later, and in 1771 went as far as the junction of the Gila and Colorado Rivers. He was the first white man of record to cross the Yuma and Colorado Deserts. His journal supplies a wealth of scientific and geographical data. With all his exploring, he never neglected his role as a missionary and spiritual leader.

When Capitan Juan Bautista de Anza planned his overland expedition into Alta California, he asked that Father Garces be assigned to go with him. The first expedition arrived at Mission San Gabriel in 1774. The second expedition left Tubac in 1775, and it was on that trip that Father Garces left the main caravan. He was accompanied by just one companion, the Indian Tarabel. When Father Garces was in Antelope Valley, he made this interesting comment in his journal. "According to signs Senor Faxes had been near this same rancheria."

Father Garces was in the Tulares in April and May 1776. Place names he gave help us follow his trail. On May 1st, with the help of some Indians, he swam a river he called Rio de San Felipe (Kern River). He went on to Rio de Santiago (Posa Creek), and on May 3rd was on Rio de Santa Cruz, now White River. In that area he recorded several noteworthy items. An Indian asked him for paper to make cigars, which indicated that at some time the Indian had been at a mission. Father Garces was told that a Spanish soldier was living with an Indian woman, and that two other soldiers had been killed because of their behavior. The most poignant entries in the journal came near White River. The Indians asked him to baptize a dying Indian boy. Today that baptismal site, 16 miles northeast of Delano, is designated by a State Registered Marker.

Some place around White River Father Garces turned back and left the valley through Tehachapi Pass. He was later assigned to the Colorado missions. On July 1, 1781, the Yuma Indians along the Colorado revolted, and among those massacred was Father Garces.

There is no available record of another trip into the Tulares for a quarter of a century, although it is hard to believe that none were made. Father Juan Martin's trip bears this out. He came to Mission San Miguel Arcangel a month after its founding in 1797 and remained until his death in 1824. Some of the mission Indians told him that the Tularenos wanted instruction. Father Martin, indefatigable in temporal as well as spiritual affairs, met the challenge. He made the trip into the Tulares in 1804, without permission, and did not write an official report until 1815.[2]

Father Martin left San Miguel in November 1804 and reached the rancheria of Bubal, on the southeast shore of Tulare Lake, in three days. He called the main settlement La Dolorosa and an outlying settlement, La Salve. These were probably inhabited by members of the Wo-wol people. He also visited Sum-Tache, a Chun-ut village. In his report Father Martin wrote:

> Their favorable disposition will continue if the fugitives from the north do not set them against us. Thus the most recent mission Indians had arrived on horseback from the north saying that the fathers were simply going to kill the Indians. Satan will do his utmost to gain possession of more than 4,000 souls who will be started on the road to salvation if a mission is established in the nearby Tulare Valley.[3]

Father Martin wrote that about 200 children were brought to him for baptism, but when the Chief arrived he railed against it and the people ran away. He made a strong request for a mission. He had sufficient cause:

> What I regret is that so many heathen are dying not only in continuous warfare but also from the many diseases, especially syphilis. Therefore, if a mission is not placed among them soon, when one is established, there will be no one to convert.

In the first decade of the nineteenth century, the history of the Tulares revolved around expeditions sent to locate suitable sites for an inland chain of missions, to apprehend runaway Indians, to recover stolen livestock, and to arrest deserters from the army.

There were expeditions in 1805, but the decisive year was 1806, when four expeditions came into the Tulares. Two of them were important in the county's history.

On July 19, 1806, Lt. Francisco Ruiz, Father Jose Zalvidia and a detachment of soldiers left Mission

Santa Barbara for the Tulares. Several days later they stood in a great oak forest near present-day Visalia. Although the surrounding area was almost arid in the summer heat, the delta and the oak forest were deemed suitable for a mission. On the return trip, Lt. Ruiz named Tejon Pass for a dead badger he found there.

In September 1806 Lt. Gabriel Moraga, Father Pedro Munoz, and a detachment of soldiers left Mission San Juan Bautista for the Tulares. Although Father Martin was the first Spaniard of record to see Tulare Lake, Moraga is credited with discovering it in 1805 and naming it Laguna de los Tulares. In that same year Moraga had found and named Rio de los Santos Reyes, or Kings River.

Moraga was the son of Lt. Jose Joaquin Moraga, a member of Anza's expedition, and the founder of the pueblos of San Jose and San Francisco. Gabriel Moraga was an outstanding soldier with 46 forays against Indians on his service sheet, but his ability as a soldier would be overshadowed by his explorations. He renamed Rio San Francisco the San Joaquin River, which in turn became the name of the entire valley. On his trip in 1806 he named the Mariposa country for swarms of small yellow butterflies. He also named these rivers: Rio de Neustra Senora Merced (Merced River), Rio de Neustra Senora Dolores (Tuolumne River), Rio de Neustra Senora Guadalupe (Stanislaus River), and Rio de la Passion (Calaveras River). In 1808 he explored northward and gave the name Sacramento to a large river there. The name was later applied to the Sacramento Valley.

When Moraga was camped on Rio de la Passion, the Indians told him that 20 years before, soldiers had come from the east and fought with them. He heard the same story a few days later from other tribes. On October 18, 1806 the men were in the great oak forest. Father Munoz' diary tells the story.

...We went into a village which might contain 600 souls where twenty-two were baptised. (The village was Telamne on the site of present-day Visalia.)

October 20. This day seeing that the oak forest was full of arroyos without water we went in search of their origin. After traveling a league we came upon a big village but all of the people were hidden in the nearby willow thickets. From here we continued eastwardly and at about a league and a half we encountered another village named Cohochs, its Chief called Chumueu. We were received with much satisfaction by these poor people. All of them, after being instructed concerning God and the welfare of their souls, want to be baptized and have a mission. Following the direction of the mountains we

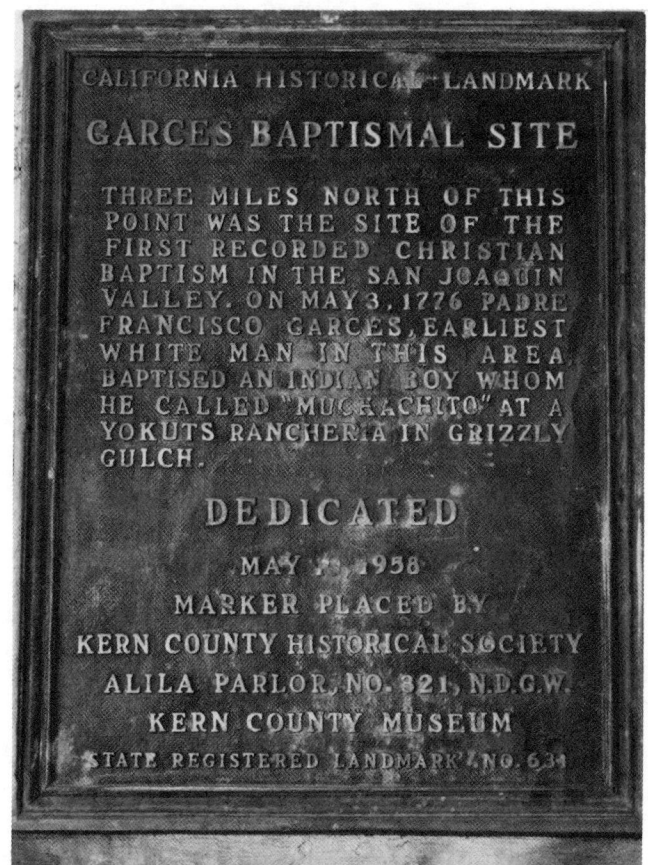

On May 3, 1776, Father Francisco Garces baptised a dying Indian boy. This was the first Christian baptism in the Valley.

came upon a fine river, already discovered by the other expedition made at the end of April in this same year. The great extent of sand which it has is damaging in its effect, for only at the time of melting snow or in the rainy season does water copiously fill all the stream beds in the oak forest.

Never the less it would be easy to get water if a mission were established. For this oak forest, which contains about 3,000 souls who want baptism and a mission, is the place most suitable for a mission of all that we have explored. There are fine land for cultivation and great meadows in many parts of the oak forest which are green all the time. There are also spots of salt peter and alkali. The river is known as the San Gabriel (Kaweah River). It divided into two branches, one of which is called San Miguel, and the latter sends its waters into several branches.

Moraga sent a scouting party south of the oak forest and the diary recorded "...they found a river already discovered by the expedition of the month of April already mentioned. It was called the San Pedro (Tule River). Because that portion which was examined was found to be without water we were forced to move the camp to the village of 600 souls mentioned above called Telamne, where water was scarce but good pasturage was obtainable."[4]

The party stayed at Telamne waiting for supplies from Mission San Miguel. When they arrived, Moraga marched southward. The men followed Rio San Pedro upstream and Father Munoz wrote that it was a fine river, that the land was good, and that there were pine and redwood trees in the mountains. As they went south, Moraga crossed the streams which today we know as Deer Creek, White River, Posey Creek, and Kern River. He left the valley through Grapevine[5] Canyon and Tejon Pass, arriving at Mission San Gabriel after 43 days.

There is a blank space in the record books until 1814. In the fall of that year, Father Juan Cabot was in Bubal where he found "700 souls ripe for the missionary harvest." He baptized 24 natives and went to Sum Tache, where he found the Indians fighting among themselves. Father Cabot tried to be a peacemaker but, as peacemakers often do, he failed. The Indians attacked his party and he chastised them. He went on to Telamne and some rancherias on the Kings River before going back to Mission San Miguel.

By 1815 a change was noticeable in the attitude of the Tularenos. They were openly hostile to the Spaniards and, in some areas, to other tribes. Much of this was due to the struggle for independence in Mexico and its impact on Alta California. Father Miguel Hidalgo set off the Mexican Revolution in 1810. For the next 10 years Mexico was torn by war, disorder, and intermittent peace. Supply ships stopped coming to Alta California. Soldiers were not paid and government in the Province was tenuous. It would be correct to say that the missions supported the Province. Soldiers deserted, and Indians not only ran away from the missions but also took livestock and firearms. Many returned to rob the settlements of cattle and horses. Missionaries urged immediate establishment of an inland chain of missions, and many expeditions came into the Tulares. Some were posses led by civilians, and some were military; few were ecclesiastical. It is just as well that many of these expeditions went unrecorded. A brief account of some of the expeditions between 1815 and 1824 will show what was happening in that decisive decade.

In November 1815 Father Juan Cabot and Sergeant Juan Ortega left San Miguel to hunt runaway Indians. As they neared Tulare Lake the diary read:

Realizing that it was useless to fall upon the village of Tache in the daytime, for the sun was already up, I decided to remain hidden all day in a low area formed by a bend in the river. We managed to catch two old Indians who were coming to fish, who before they went back to their village of Tache, told us its correct location...At dawn I attack the village of Tache although considerably discouraged by my suspicion that the two Indian fugitives had given word during the night of our arrival. As a matter of fact, I found the village deserted.[6]

Ortega found or heard about Christian Indians everywhere he went. He found the once populous village of Telamne decimated by disease and hunger. He visited a Choinok village on Deep Creek and found the same condition. At Tulare Lake he warned the Indians not to protect fugitives. While they were camped at the lake they met Father Jaime Escudo and Sergeant Jose Pico, who were also searching for runaway Indians. Pico had caught many natives and had also found numerous stolen horses. Most of the villages they visited were deserted, but in one village the Spaniards counted 238 dead horses, 16 live horses, and a quantity of butchered horsemeat.

In 1816 Father Luis Martinez, accompanied by soldiers, visited the Tulares. He reported that the people he visited were so unreasonable that they preferred their unhappy condition to any benefits they might obtain away from their present home. At Tulare Lake the party was fired upon. The next day the soldiers burned the village "because the people in it had taken up arms against the people who treated them so well."

In 1819 Lt. Jose Estudillo was in the Tulares. The Indians, as usual, knew every move his party made. They told him Gabriel Moraga was also in the valley.

Augustin Iturbide proclaimed Mexican Independence in 1821. Governor Pablo de Sola made the proclamation official in Alta California in 1822. The missionaries' frustration in not being able to build missions in the Tulares was well summed up by Father Mariano Payeras in his report of 1821-1822.

The object of our ministry being the propagation of the faith among the gentiles, and the gentiles no longer existing among the coastal mountains, the padres of the various missions have attempted to baptize those living in the district called the Tulares. They have, however, never succeeded. The Tulare Indians are inconstant. Today they come, tomorrow they go, not on foot as they came but on horseback. With such guests no horse is safe in the northern valley and the mountains that surround it. They kill the horses and eat them.

The Government has not been neglectful in pursuing such deadly enemies, but little has been effected because great lagoons surrounded by green tules furnish them shelter from our horsemen. For this reason, the padres

Garces Baptismal site, located 16 miles east of Delano, May 3, 1776.

and more intelligent officers think it needful to form in the valley of the Tulares a new chain of missions with presidios. If this not be done, the time will come when the existence of the Province will become threatened, and a region that up to a recent time has been the center of tranquillity will be changed into an Apacheria.[7]

In 1824 the Indians at Missions Santa Ynez and La Purisima revolted, with some casualties and considerable damage to mission property. The rebellion was crushed, but not before the news reached Santa Barbara, where the Indians also revolted. Although the rebellion was put down, many Indians fled into the Tulares, gathering in San Emigidio Canyon and around Buena Vista Lake. Surprisingly, the reports tell us that a Russian was at Buena Vista Lake showing the Indians how to use certain firearms.

Lt. Narcisco Fabregat followed the Indians and met them near Buena Vista Lake, killed a few, and took a number of stolen horses. He reported that the Indians had forgotten their teaching in a short time, for they did not pray; they played cards, gambled, and drank wine. After a few months, Captain Pablo de la Portilla persuaded most of the runaways to go back to the missions. By that time, Father Payeras was calling the area around Telamne a republic of hell and a diabolic union of apostates! He appealed emotionally for missions in the Tulares.

The friars were now grown old and the task of expansion was a dangerous one, yet they, and especially himself would willingly go there to found the much talked of missions in the tular and stay there until death should bring release.[8]

The situation in the Tulares was demoralized. It was impossible to tell stolen stock from wild horses, and no attempt was made to distinguish good Indians from bad Indians. The Indians who fled from the coast brought firearms, stock, and the vices and virtues of white men.

The Yokuts began to plan well organized attacks led by such men as Estanislao. Much of the fighting was in Miwok territory, but tribes around the larger rivers and lakes were also involved. In 1833, with secularization of the missions certain, with mountain men invading the Province, with Indians on the offensive, Brigadier-General Jose Figueroa issued this decree:

Being so serious and so scandalous the damage caused frequently by horse and cattle thieves throughout the entire territory, and it being desireable to cut out the roots of this regrettable evil, which in addition to devastating the country is demoralizing our customs and promoting indolence, I have circulated to the military commanders the following order.

The order proposed that each presidio would send out a monthly military expedition. The missions and citizens of the Province were to help by providing the necessary horses. Excerpts from the lengthy order fully show the effect of the invasion of mountain men, the Indian problem, and the results of contact between Indian and mountain man.

All horses encountered which have not been sold or disposed of through any other procedure which demonstrate their legal acquisition shall be repossessed from any party and shall be returned to their owners.

All the trappers who shall be met, shall be informed if they are foreigners, that they are enjoined from hunting and shall immediately remove themselves; if they are Mexican or naturalized citizens they cannot hunt without previously obtaining a permit and pass from the government.

All infractions will be severely punished. All the livestock found in the Tulares and the desert will be regarded as stolen and their possessors will be treated as thieves, they being also responsible for any damage done by wild Indians whom they may incite to evil.

Any trapper who disregards these regulations and who is encountered in the wilderness will be regarded as a smuggler. His effects will be impounded and he will be brought before a court of competence which will confiscate his goods if occasion requires.

The natives will be treated with gentleness and charity. They shall be caused to realize that it is delinquency to steal cattle. Those who persist shall be taken to the presidios for punishment.

Furthermore, I direct likewise not only to the alcaldes but also the military commanders, the private owners of ranchos and haciendas and their agents to pursue all cattle thieves and capture them when they encounter them in the act or upon proof of crime.[9]

The last paragraph gave almost anyone *carte blanche* to organize a posse. It is just as well that we pass over the next few years in the turbulent Tulares, for most of the reports of that period are hearsay and speculation.

---

1. Robert G. Cleland, *History of California 1542-1900*, New York, 1944, page 63.
2. Fr. Zephyrin Engelhardt O.F.M., *San Miguel Arcangel*, Acoma Books, California, 1971.
3. Sherburne F. Cook, "Colonial Expeditions to the Interior of California Central Valley, 1800-1820," *Anthropological Records*, Vol. 16, #6, page 243.
4. Sherburne F. Cook, Ibid, page 252.
5. Fages had noted the wild grapes in 1772. Cajon de las Unvas was named on July 29, 1806. Gudde, Erwin G., *California Place Names*, University of California Press, 1962, page 119.
6. Sherburne F. Cook, Ibid., page 271.
7. Irving B. Richmond, *History of California Under Spain and Mexico*, Boston, 1911, page 221.
8. Charles Chapman, *A History of California, The Spanish Period*, New York, 1916, page 134.
9. Sherburne F. Cook, "Expeditions to the Interior of California's Central Valley, 1820-1840," *Anthropological Records*, Vol. 20, #5, University of California Press, 1962.

CHAPTER 4

LONG RIFLES AND SHARP DEALERS

Free trappers were a motley breed. They roamed the West dressed in dirty, greasy buckskin and fur, armed with long rifles and knives. They lived off the land and were often hungry. By their standards they were free, uninhibited, and beholden to no one. As we see them, they were in constant danger from the elements, from wild animals, from sickness and hunger, from Indians, and from each other. Most were illiterate. The proceeds from a year's trapping often evaporated in the fumes of liquor at the annual bacchanalian rendezvous. Many were cheated by unscrupulous agents and fellow trappers. Most left for the wilderness in debt for staple food and trapping gear. Unknowingly, they were the instigators of the doctrine of Manifest Destiny.

The most famous mountain man was Jedediah Smith, who did not fit into the usual characterization of a free trapper. He was literate, a good businessman, and an outspoken, Bible-carrying Christian.

Furs have always been a luxury item. The basic cause of the long struggle between the French and the English in North America was furs. Sea otters brought Russia to the Pacific coast and as far south as the Bay of San Francisco. Beaver brought a good price, ranging from $2.00 to $5.00 a pelt pound. Competition between fur companies was so keen that it was constantly necessary to find new fields and keep their location secret. Jedediah Smith's responsibility to his partners was to explore for new fields.

In 1826 he started west with 17 men. When they reached the Colorado River, Indians told them of settlements in Alta California. On November 26, 1826, Smith reached Mission San Gabriel and received a joyous welcome from the padres. It is not likely that anyone realized the effect that expedition would have on history. Smith was the first American to cross the Sierra Nevada, and in so doing had broken the eastern barrier of California.

Smith and his men stayed at the Mission for some weeks, and from his journal we may deduce that he and the padres had much to talk about, including some lively discussions on religion.

California's politics were chaotic at the time of Smith's arrival. Governor Jose de Echeandia ordered Smith to backtrack out of the Province. He started out, but once away from the Mission Smith turned north and entered the Tulares through Tehachapi Pass. He found good beaver country. Smith noted that the Indians were friendly, and that the Tulares Valley was exceptionally fertile. He named a large river for the Wimilchi tribe which lived there. This was the Kings River.

In April Smith was ready to recross the Sierra Nevada but was driven back by a heavy snowpack. He set up a winter camp on the Stanislaus River. It was imperative that someone get to the rendezvous near Salt Lake, so Smith and two volunteers left the camp. They reached Salt Lake, and on the return trip he brought 19 men and supplies for two years. Coming back, they were surprised by the Mohaves and Smith lost 10 men, his supplies and his horses. Courage, speed, and stamina helped the rest to cross the desert and reach the camp on the Stanislaus.

This time the Governor was adamant. Smith was detained but finally released through the intervention of an American ship captain. The men who had wintered in the valley had had a successful trapping season. Smith sold 1,568 pounds of beaver to the captain for $2.50 a pound. He bought supplies and horses and set off for the Oregon Territory. He again was attacked by Indians, but managed to get to Fort Vancouver. Dr. John McLaughlin, Chief Factor of the Hudson Bay Company, treated the men kindly and managed to recover Smith's stolen equipment. Smith and his men eventually joined his partner, Sublette, on the Snake River. Later on he returned to the Company's headquarters in St. Louis.

Jedediah Smith stayed in St. Louis for some time, but the lure of the wilderness was too strong for him to stay too long. He started for Santa Fe with a large party of trappers. He was only 32 years old when he was ambushed and killed by Indians on the Cimmarron River in 1831. An impressive list of achievements is his monument. He was the first to recognize that South Pass was a natural road for wagon trains. He was the first American to cross and recross the Sierra Nevada. He was the first American in the San Joaquin Valley, and he was the first American to enter the Oregon Territory from California.

Better than any man of his day, native or foreign, Smith understood California, its attractions, and its drawbacks. He had visited no fewer than seven and perhaps nine of the early missions, three of the presidios, and two principal pueblos. He had met many of the officials, the Governor, the alcaldes, and generals. He had come in close contact with both the mission Indians and the Tularenos. He had traveled the length of the great central valley, along three important segments of the coastline and was the first white man to cross the Sierra Nevada. He had traded with the ranchos both in Southern California and about San Francisco Bay. Unwittingly, his enforced detention provided him invaluable information. His reports exploded the myth of an aggressive Spanish government, and pointed the way for an easy Spanish conquest.[1]

If Jedediah Smith was the most famous mountain man, Christopher Carson became the most publicized. Kit Carson was very familiar with the San Joaquin Valley. He made his first visit in 1829 as a guide for Ewing Young and his trappers. When they reached the Kings River they found Peter Skeene Ogdon and a party of Hudson Bay trappers. Young went on to Los Angeles. He not only had trouble getting a trapping license, but his men celebrated the delights of civilization so boisterously that they almost were detained in the local calaboza.

Carson trapped and traded in the Rocky Mountains for the next 12 years. John C. Fremont hired him as a guide in 1842, and Carson was also a guide on the second and third Fremont expeditions to California. During the American conquest of California, Kit Carson led 25 men who guarded Tejon Pass to prevent Indians from driving stock out of the valley. Much to his delight he was chosen to carry the news of the conquest to Washington. On the way he met General Kearney and the Army of the West. Kearney needed a guide, so he ordered Carson to lead them into California and sent the news East with a soldier.

Carson returned to his home in Taos, where he was appointed Indian agent. He guided several wagon trains to California during the gold rush. When the Civil War began, Carson helped repulse Confederate raids into New Mexico. He was commissioned a Brevet Brigadier General in the Union Army for distinguished services. He was probably the only General at that time who could neither read nor write. Even if he could not write, others could, and Carson became a folk hero in books, stories and eventually movies and now television.

Carson had a personal interest in Tulare County, for two of his daughters lived here. Their names were Carmelita and Melcaldie. One of them, a Mrs. Simmons, lived for a time in Tailholt.

Jedediah Smith's enthusiastic description of the valley while he was in Oregon undoubtedly added impetus to the explorations of the Hudson Bay fur trappers. Their familiar trade beads are found throughout northern and central California. By 1841 their activities were extensive enough to be granted a "post" in San Francisco.

American, French, and English trappers were involved in many of the skirmishes between Mexicans and Indians. Since the trappers did not favor either race, circumstances dictated which side they took. Most of the trouble involved stolen horses. For example, in 1833 a party of Mexicans was in the valley to recover their stolen stock. They met Ewing Young who finally "gave back" 27 horses, but insisted that he had bought the rest in Southern California.

Mountain men needed horses, and there is no doubt but that they planned raids made by Indians on coastal settlements. Neither is there doubt that mountain men rounded up wild horses in the Tulares, and also raided the ranchos for domesticated horses.

The famous scout Joseph R. Walker knew the Tulares well. He was guide for Captain Benjamin Bonneville, who was sent West in 1832-33 to gather information for the War Department. Bonneville's real orders are still a mystery. He sent Walker to scout around the Great Salt Lake, but Walker kept on going and reached California. If he and his men had had an inclination to explore a deep canyon in November 1833, they would have been the first white men to actually enter Yosemite Valley. Walker wintered in the Tulares and traded furs for horses before going to the Great Salt Lake. His name is commemorated in Walker's Pass, and his role in Fremont's expeditions will be related later. Walker was a professional guide during the gold rush, and later on settled in California. He is buried in Martinez, where the inscription on his headstone reads: "Camped at Yosemite November 13, 1833."

Lebec, another valley place name, commemorates Peter Lebec, a Hudson Bay trapper, although he probably spelled his name Pierre Lebeque. In 1904 a piece of bark was accidentally knocked from an oak tree on the grounds of Fort Tejon. Carved into the bark and into the tree were the words: "I H S Peter Lebec, Killed by a bear Oct. 17, 1837." The town of Lebec on the Ridge Route carries his name, the only other thing we know about him.

Another mountain man who left a trail of sorts was Thomas "Peg-Leg" Smith, of dubious fame. He was a typical mountain man, prodigal of the present and heedless of the future. He lost his leg in a fight with Indians, and his wooden leg became a formidable weapon when he used it as a club during brawls. He was probably in the Tulares in 1829 to take wild horses, which he sold on the Santa Fe Trail. With the help of the Yokuts, he supposedly masterminded the biggest of all the raids on the coastal settlements. He said he took 3,000 horses, but had to fight the Spanish all the way and lost some Indians. During the gold rush he set up camp on the Bear River, where he sold horses to immigrants for a bottle of whiskey or a pound of powder. There he lived happily, waited upon by his Indian wives. After the glamor of the gold rush wore off, Peg-Leg came back to San Francisco, where he lived on the charity of his friends. Peg-Leg could have been the prototype for the white horse thieves described by Governor Figueroa:

> Scattering over various regions they identify themselves with the wild natives, following the same kind of life. They live in a wandering fashion with them and in this way become familiar and gain their confidence. From this has come rapidly one positive evil, namely, that influenced by these adventurers, the natives have dedicated themselves with the greatest determination to the stealing of horses from all the missions and towns of the territory. The object is to trade the animals for intoxicating liquors and other frivolities.[2]

It would be impossible to name all the mountain men who came into the Tulares. Some left letters or were interviewed in later years. Their greatest pleasure was to sit around a campfire and spin incredible yarns which were probably true. Jim Bridger once told an interviewer, "They said I was the damnedest liar that ever lived. That's what a man gets for telling the truth." For better or for worse, the mountain men left a legacy, for they, more than any other group, started the stream of migration that made the acquisition of California inevitable.

That acquisition was proceeding smoothly through diplomatic channels when John C. Fremont intervened. His contributions to western history cannot be minimized, but he was an aggressive opportunist and his role in California politics is open to scrutiny. He was a member of the elite Corps of Topographical Engineers which took an important part in exploring and mapping the West. Between 1842 and 1854 Fremont made five trips west, and became known as "The Pathfinder," which was a misnomer for he found few paths by himself. On each trip he had with him well known western guides and competent Indian trackers. His own driving ambition was augmented by that of his wife, Jessie Benton Fremont, and her father, Senator Thomas Benton. Fremont became a famous, glamorous, and persuasive national hero.

Fremont's second expedition reached Sutter's Fort in March 1844. On his way south he traveled the length of the San Joaquin Valley. Rainfall that year was heavy; rivers were running bank to bank; and Tulare Lake was overflowing into the San Joaquin River. The lush grass and wild flowers turned the valley floor into a floral carpet. Fremont loved nature and was a facile writer. His official report became a best-seller — some 10,000 copies were printed by the Government Printing Office. His appreciation of the valley may be gleaned from this paragraph.

> One might travel the world over without finding a valley more verdant and fresh, more floral and sylvan, more alive with birds and animals, more bounteously watered than we had left in the San Joaquin.[3]

Fremont started west in 1845, when war with Mexico was imminent. There were men with him who were, or would be, famous in California history: Kit Carson, Joseph R. Walker, Theodore Talbott, Richard Owen, Edward Kern, and Alexis Godey, as well as 60 armed men. When they reached Walker's Pass the party divided. Fremont went to Sutter's Fort and left the rest of the men under Talbott's leadership. Walker was to lead them to a rendezvous with Fremont on the Kings River. Because of a misunderstanding, Walker camped on the Kern River. Their subsequent meeting and involvement in the conquest of California is really not part of valley history. The place names they left did make valley history. We find Kern River, Kernville, Kern County, Owens Lake, Owens River, and Owens Valley; and Carson is commemorated by Carson River, Carson Pass, and Carson Valley. Fremont was also honored, but as his glory faded, Fremont County was changed to Yolo County and Fremont Peak became Gavilan Peak. Schools and parks still bear his name, as does Fremont Peak in San Bernardino County.

Fremont's purchase of the property known as Las Mariposas, with its ruinous litigation, is a matter of history. His partnership in San Emigidio, in what is now Kern County, is not as well known. San Emigidio, southeast of Maricopa, was the site of an Indian village whose roots go back into unrecorded history. Pedro Fages was the first white man to visit the village. Chumash Indians lived there when settlers came into the area.

Fortunately, the southern San Joaquin Valley was not carved up into Mexican Land Grants. San Emigidio was one of the few such grants. In 1842 Governor Alvarado granted four square leagues to Jose Dominguez. Dominguez died in 1853, leaving many heirs. His wife sold a half interest to Fremont for $10,000. This was during the time the Federal Land Claims Commission was in California examining all land grants. In 1855 the Commission ruled that Fremont and the Dominguez heirs each owned one-half of the grant. Fremont visited the ranch but did not live there. Before Fremont eventually disposed of his partnership, Alexis Godey became involved with the property. He had been living at Pueblo San Emigidio, and was believed to own it. We know now that he was hired as an overseer either by Fremont or Edward Beale.

The Dominguez heirs sold to David Alexander and F.P.F. Temple. In 1860 Fremont deeded his half to his daughter, Frances Porter. She then sold to Edward Beale, whose acquisition of other land grants gave him ownership of much of the southern end of the valley. Beale eventually sold to L.F. Fox. After several subsequent sales, the property became part of the famous Kern County Land Company, now part of Tenaco.

1. *Pacific Historian,* University of the Pacific, Stockton, May 1958, page 1.
2. Sherburne F. Cook, *Expeditions to the Interior of California, 1820-1840,* University of California Press, page 185.
3. John C. Fremont, *Memoirs of My Life,* New York, 1887.

CHAPTER 5

TULARE COUNTY COMES OF AGE

President Millard Fillmore signed the bill admitting California into the Union on September 9, 1850, and news of that event reached the new state on October 8, 1850 — in record-breaking time. One of the first acts of the California Legislature was to divide the state into 27 counties. One was Mariposa County.

By 1952 a few stockmen were in the southern part of Mariposa County, centering their activities around Tulare Lake and the Four Creeks.[1] William Campbell and John Pool had a ferry and trading post on the Kings River. The ill-fated Woods Party had built a cabin on the Kaweah River, near Dr. Thomas Payne's toll bridge. Dr. Erasmus French, who had served with General Kearney, had a cabin near Tejon Pass. There were doubtless other toll bridges and ferries in the valley, for they were very profitable.

The main "road" through the valley was the old Indian trail along the axis of the Sierra Nevada. El Camino Viejo, on the west side of the valley, was used by Indians and Spaniards, but not by people on their way to the mines. There was definitely no grass roots movement to create a new county when Tulare County was cut from Mariposa County on April 20, 1852, although the additional county did provide more opportunities for citizens to seek county office.

It was an unsettled time. The federal Treaty Commissioners had made treaties with the Indians calling for the Indians to surrender their land in exchange for reservations, goods, and services. Through misinformation and their own ignorance of geography, the Commissioners had set aside reservations which included traveled roads and potential new gold fields. Most Californians were infuriated. To them Indians were a labor force easily exploited, and not groups to be placed on some of the best land in the state. They were also disgusted with the heavily padded claims submitted for care of the Indians, who saw little of the food or other goods.

However, the Mariposa Indian War of 1851-52 was over. The miners returned to the diggings, and Major James Savage was once more in control of the Tularenos. Only a naive person could believe that peace and serenity had come to stay.

Indicative of the tension was an event that occurred on the Kings River Reservation the first week of July 1852. Chief Watoka went to Campbell and Pool and told them they were on Reservation land and would have to leave. He showed them a paper signed by Major Savage. The white men jumped to the conclusion that war was imminent and went for help. A posse, led by Walter Harvey (who would be elected Tulare County's first judge a few days later) attacked the main rancheria. A white man was wounded and a number of Indians were killed. Indian Agent Dr. Oliver Wozencraft wrote to the Governor to "...join with me in maintaining the supremacy of the law." The Governor did not answer. Dr. Wozencraft then went to San Francisco, to the U.S. District Attorney, to get warrants for the arrest of the white men. He was stunned to be told he "was not aware of the existence of any law that would apply in this case, the Federal Court having no jurisdiction in cases where life was taken."[2] Since the leader was elected County Judge, Dr. Wozencraft did not think it would be worthwhile to prosecute him in his own county.

The unexpected result of the unwarranted attack was the unfavorable publicity it received. In an unparalleled action the white men defended themselves in open letters to newspapers.

The Legislative Act which created Tulare County read in part: "The Seat of Justice shall be at the log cabin on the south side of Kaweah Creek near the bridge built by Dr. Thomas Payne, and shall be

25

Charter Oak or Election Tree. One of the two polling places in the organizational election of Tulare County, July 10, 1852. Located eight miles east of Visalia.

called Woodsville until changed by the people as provided by law." The same legislation named James Savage, John Bowling, M.B. Lewis, and W.W. McMillan commissioners to carry out the election. They met, set July 10th as election day, and selected Campbell and Pool's Ferry and Woods' cabin as polling places. Over 100 men set out from Mariposa County to vote. Many had taken part in the raid a few days before. William Campbell was Inspector at the ferry, and he moved to the safety of a sand bar in the river called Grand Island. William Dill was Inspector at the cabin. It was a hot day so he moved to the shade of an oak tree, Election Tree, now a State Registered Landmark. Fifty-eight votes were cast at the ferry and 51 at the cabin.

That evening a rousing political caucus was held at both places. John Marvin was at Woodsville and so was Phillip Herbert, Democratic nominee for the State Assembly from Mariposa and Tulare Counties. Marvin, who was State Superintendent of Public Instruction, was elected delegate to the Democratic Convention to be held at Benicia. Both men addressed the voters in a "neat and forcible manner." The voters at Woodsville elected F.H. Stanford and Dr. Thomas Payne as Democratic delegates. History did not record which man attended, but we may be certain someone went. A voter present on July 10th wrote a letter which bears out the latter inference:

All the officers of the new County are Democrats except Mr. Davis who is a Whig. The County may, therefore, be set down as Democratic. It is but fair, however, to state that politics did not enter into the election; the voters being chiefly Democrats elected as a matter of course, Democrats to fill the various offices.[3]

Most of the voters went back to Mariposa County, and Commissioner Lewis reported that he traveled from July 12th to July 27th in order to locate and administer the oath of office to the newly elected officials.

Criticism of the raid on the reservation Indians intensified, and Indians began to gather in the Four Creek country. Dr. Wozencraft called a grand tribal meeting in the Four Creeks for the middle of August. He asked Major Savage to come, and so did the Indians. It was rumored that a company of soldiers was on the way to investigate the raid.

Major Savage stayed in the Four Creeks after the July 10th election, meeting with the Indians. He

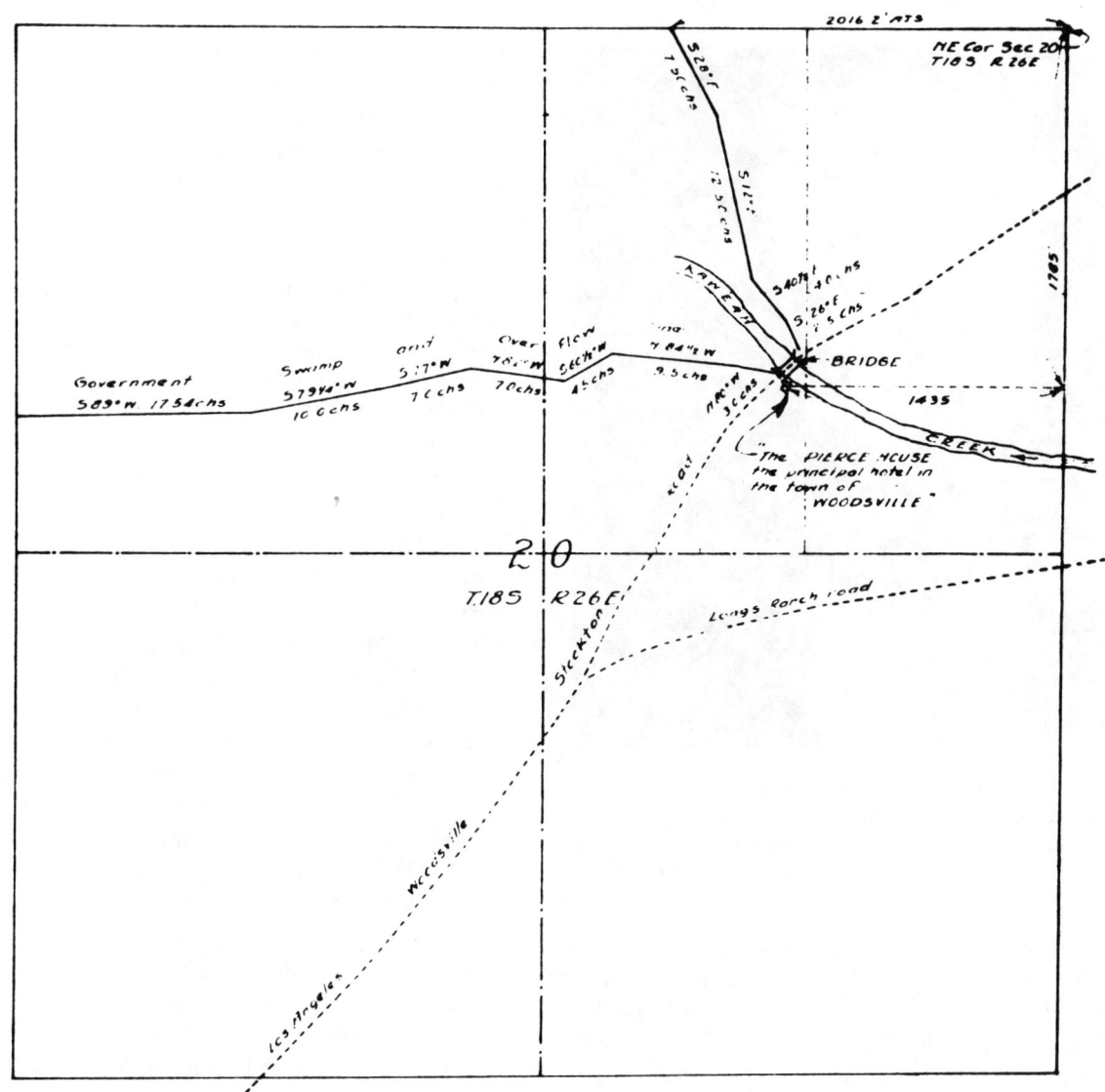

Plat of Section 20, T 18 S., R 26 E M D B & M From the field notes of the Government Survey dated 1855.

Site of Woodsville, first county seat of Tulare County.

then returned to his headquarters on the Fresno River. A few days before the scheduled tribal meeting, he and John Marvin left to talk with the tribes before the convocation. At Campbell and Pool's Ferry they met Walter Harvey, and Savage advised him to give himself up. Harvey agreed. Savage then said to Harvey, "I understand Major Harvey that you say I am no gentleman." Harvey said that was his opinion, and Savage knocked him down. Marvin separated them, but they continued fighting. Savage wore his pistol in his waistband, and it fell out. Whether Harvey saw that happen was not determined, but he fired at Savage and killed him. The date was August 16, 1852. News of his death aroused both the Indians and the press, which expressed regret since Savage would have been better able to keep peace than treaties, troops, or agents.[4]

Joel Brooks, Justice of the Peace, heard the case brought against Harvey at Woodsville on September 3rd. Testimony indicated that Savage hit first, so Justice Brooks dismissed the case.

Harvey was later appointed Sergeant at Arms of the California Senate, and in 1861 was appointed Superintendent of Immigration for the Port of San Francisco. The records of the County Treasurer show that Walter Harvey was paid $213.70 for the three months he served as Tulare County Judge.

The men who settled at Campbell and Pool's Ferry antedated the Woods Party by a few months. That trading post and ferry lasted until 1855 or 1856, when James Smith's ferry proved to be in a better location for travelers crossing the Kings River. John Pool moved to Mendocino County, and William Campbell went into the cattle business in Tulare County.

Thomas Baker (1810-1872)
He helped organize both Tulare and Kern counties and founded Bakersfield. Served as Tulare County Judge in 1853, was elected State Assemblyman in 1854 and State Senator in 1861.

The first real settlement in Tulare County was Woodsville, the village which grew up around Woods' cabin. In some old records the name is also spelled Woodville. John Woods, the man for whom it was named, came to California in 1849 with a wagon train led by John Hudgins. The train broke up in Los Angeles, where Hudgins and 16 men were hired by the Merchants' Association to improve the road into the San Joaquin Valley. They were to be paid $750, tobacco, and provisions. In an interview in Visalia in 1902, Hudgins said they were misinformed as to distances. Once in the southern valley they bridged the principal rivers, including the Kaweah, in March 1850. They continued to the northern mines.[5]

In the fall of 1850 Woods and 14 men were back in the Four Creeks. What they were hired to do was and is a mystery, for they began to clear land and laid foundations for five cabins where the Los Angeles-Stockton Road crossed the Kaweah River. Only one cabin was completed before the men were killed by Indians. Joel Brooks later testified that Dr. Wozencraft, John Marvin, M.B. Lewis, and Major Savage planned to plant 1,100 acres of wheat and barley in the Four Creeks if they could prevent the formation of a county in the southern end of Mariposa County. In the same case, Brooks gave much incorrect evidence, and apparently tried to implicate several men, principally Savage, in false claims submitted to the Government.

Another possible explanation might be deduced from this advertisement in the *San Joaquin Republican* November 16, 1850:

NOTICE TO TRAVELERS: The subscriber takes this method of informing the traveling community that his ferries and bridges over Kings and Kern Rivers and the Four Creeks, which furnish the chain of bridges and ferries on the road from Stockton to Los Angeles, are in process of building and will be completed by the time high water demands their use. This will make this the best road in California. For Particulars see hand bills. T. PAYNE.

Toll bridges and ferries were profitable business ventures, so there must have been enough travel through the valley in 1850 to warrant building them. In May 1850 Lt. Derby noted that he had met a Mr. Shumway on his way to the Kern River to build a ferry.

It is certainly possible that the men Joel Brooks mentioned, or even Dr. Payne, hired Woods to clear land and plant grain. That is all conjecture, for Woods did not live long enough to really begin the work. His arrival in the Four Creeks coincided with an uprising of Indians in the valley. The first attack was made on Major Savage's trading post on the Mariposa, and another attack was made December 17, 1850 on his Fresno River store. Contemporary accounts stated that Woods was attacked December 13, 1850. Chief Francisco of the Kaweahs had told the men they had 10 days to get out of the Four Creeks. Surprisingly, they agreed, but made no effort to leave until the last day.

They were in the field burying tools and utensils when the Indians came. Two men escaped, Woods reached the cabin, the rest were killed. Woods killed at least nine Indians before running out of ammunition. The same account stated that Woods was skinned alive by the Indians, but that was more of a gory cliche than a physical possibility.

News of the attack was carried by one of the men who escaped, and later soldiers were sent down from Fort Miller. They started to build a fort, but were recalled to take part in the Mariposa Indian War. On February 4, 1851, Dr. Payne came to the scene and found that his toll bridge had been destroyed. He reported 13 bodies near the cabin. The bodies were interred by the soldiers in what is marked as Lone Oak Cemetery, the oldest cemetery in the southern valley.[6]

The next record of the Wood Cabin being used was in an interview with Abraham Hilliard in 1860.

*Nathaniel Vise
(1810-1882)*

*Matilda Vise
(1813-1890)*

He brought his family to the Four Creeks from French Gulch in April 1853 and lived in the cabin for several months. Fifteen people were living in Woodsville then, but the only women were Mrs. Hilliard and Mrs. Orson K. Smith. The official Government map of 1854 showed that Woodsville had Billy Smith's Hotel and William Dill's Saloon. A post office was granted October 13, 1853, with Orson K. Smith as postmaster. Orlando Barton wrote that when he came, in 1865, the village of Woodsville stood in the northeast corner of the Goad field, and that five cabins were still standing. They were built of logs with shake roofs and faced the river.[7]

The same day that the Legislature created Tulare County, it passed *An Act Prescribing the Mode of Maintaining and Defending Possessory Action on Public Land in the State.* Stockmen had been running cattle in the county before 1852, and although it was the day of the open range, they began to file under the Act. The first few pages of claims and surveys contain many familiar names in county history: C.R. Wingfield, Alfred Wingfield, P.A. Rainbolt, J.S. Meckley, Jacob Lambert, W.C. Deputy, Nathaniel Vise, John C. O'Neil, Thomas McCormic, A.H. Fraser, Reuben Shoufler, Loomis St. John, W.H. Ewing, Daniel Haynes, John Fancher, Elisha Packwood, Almerin Morrow, W.A. Peterson, J.B. Hatch, J.M. Ball.

The quarter sections filed on were near or adjacent to the Kaweah River and its tributaries. Much of the surveying in July was done by M.B. Lewis. Some claims were never completed, and some were not recorded for several years because cattlemen did not necessarily stay in one place. In addition to these pioneers, and the people who lived in Fort Visalia, records show that other well-known settlers were in the Four Creeks in 1852-3:[8] Glenns, Deans, John Patterson, Hazelton, Mayfield, Rhodes, Orton, Akers, Baker, Barker, Murphy, Blakenship, Goldstein, Harrell, and Hartley. Others who came during that period can only be listed through family tradition.

By law the governing body in California counties was the Court of Sessions, which combined legislative and judicial duties. It was made up of the County Judge and two associate judges elected by their fellow justices of the peace. The first Court of Sessions included Judge Walter Harvey and Justices William J. Campbell and Loomis St. Johns (for whom the St. Johns River was named). It met for the first time in the Woods Cabin, which had been designated the official County Court House in the Legislative Act of April 20, 1852. All members were present, and Sheriff William Dill acted as Bailiff. The agenda was typical of the time:

Thomas McCormic was appointed County Assessor as James Davis had failed to perform his duties. P.A. Rainbolt was appointed to finish the term of County Treasurer L.C. Frankenberger who had died.

J.M. Ball was granted permission to operate a ferry on Kings River. The license fee was $75.00. The Court of Sessions set all ferry rates at 50 cents for a man on foot, $1.00 for a man and a horse, $1.00 for each wheel of a wagon, $1.00 for pack animals, and 5 cents a head for loose stock.

For similar license fees, William Dill was to operate a toll bridge at Woodsville, and E.P. Edmunds to operate a ferry on Kings River. County Recorder A.B. Gordon was granted a license backdated to July 1852 to sell goods and liquors at his ferry on Kern River.

The County tax rate was set at 50 cents per $100.00. The State tax was 30 cents per $100.00. Voters also paid a poll tax.

The County of Tulare was divided into three election precincts: #1 at Visalia, #2 at Campbell's Ferry, and #3 at Woodsville.

When the Court met for the second time, on June 6, 1853, the Associate Justices were the same and William Dill was Bailiff again, but Colonel Thomas Baker had replaced Walter Harvey as County Judge. The meeting reflected the transient life of stockmen, for the offices of County Clerk, Treasurer, and Assessor were declared vacant. Aneas Gordon, Charles Wingfield, and J.B. Hatch were appointed to fill out the terms of these offices. The Court then called the first Grand Jury to meet at the next session, on July 5, 1853. That day was to be a milestone in county history. Samuel C. Brown and D.W.C. French were admitted to the Tulare County Bar. Both were college-trained lawyers, as was Judge Thomas Baker. Judge Baker then convened the first Grand Jury. Since the panel included so many men of historical importance to the county, their names should be recorded here:

Josiah Turner	Abner Vise
Charles Hayden	William Scott
Daniel Haynes	Henry Burrough
Henry Kinder	Richard Glenn
Sam Jennings	C.V. Walker
George Young	Louis Van Tassel
A.J. Lawrence	I.W. Hunt
Jonathan Mitcham	Robert Goodburn
Abraham Hilliard	Almerin Morrow
Warren Matthews	William Finley

Bailiff Alexander Cameron

The Grand Jury brought in a true bill against Samuel Logo on two counts, larceny and assault with intent to commit murder. The Court met August 22nd in Dill's Saloon to hear the first criminal case in county history. The saloon was about 80 yards north of the Courthouse and was larger. Samuel C. Brown served as District Attorney. D.W.C. French defended Logo, and Judge Thomas Baker presided. The three men represented the entire bench and bar of the county. The case was tried in the morning. The jury deliberated in the afternoon and brought in a guilty verdict. Logo was sentenced to two years in state prison. The verdict was extraordinary, for the victims were Indians. The men who served on the jury sat within sight of the graves of the Woods Party. Their verdict was a tribute to their integrity and respect for law — a concept which has continued to permeate the history of Tulare County.

In 1853 the State Legislature set up procedures for electing Boards of Supervisors to take over the legislative duties of the Courts of Sessions, and to gradually eliminate that court. In Tulare County the election was held September 7, 1853, the same day as the general election. It turned out to be one of the more hotly contested elections in our history — that is, until the same issue came up a quarter of a century later. The bone of contention was the selection of a Seat of Justice. Thomas Baker, running for County Judge, campaigned for moving it to Visalia. Dr. John Cutler, running for the same office, spearheaded a move to keep the Seat of Justice at Woodsville. Dr. Cutler won the office, but the adherents of Colonel Baker took comfort in winning the issue.

The supervisors were elected at large and not by districts. Twenty-six votes were cast at Woodsville, 20 at Campbell's Ferry, and 48 at Visalia., The men elected to the first Board of Supervisors were: Henry Burrough, John Pool, A.J. Lawrence, Warren Matthews, and Alexander Fraser. They met October 3, 1853 in Visalia and elected Mr. Burrough Chairman. The Court of Sessions met the same day and continued to meet irregularly until 1859.

The immediate problem before the Supervisors then is still a problem today. They had to find the money to conduct the government. In 1853 land had little value, and most individual incomes came from livestock. The tax rate was set at 35 cents per $100.00. There is an apocryphal story that the first assessment roll was written on a single sheet of paper. The Tax Collector had his problems, for after several names he had noted "skipped the country" or "dead," and after one name was the note "gone to hell."

In 1854 the county fared a bit better financially,

Tulare County Courthouse, built in 1876 between Court and Church Streets in Visalia. The building was damaged in the 1952 earthquake and was razed. The new courthouse on West Main Street was dedicated in 1957.

for the records show an assessed valuation of $193,137 and $676.00 in taxes was collected. The money was augmented by license fees and the sale of lots in Visalia. Orson K. Smith was hired to survey the original quarter section of Visalia into lots, for which he was paid $1.00 for each platted lot. Block 21 was set aside for public buildings, Block 18 for a school, and Block 6 for a cemetery. The Matthews Brothers were given a site for their grist mill, and Phillip Wagy was offered a site if he would build a grist mill within a specified time. At the December meeting the Board of Supervisors changed the name Visalia to Buena Vista and thus kicked up a storm of protest. Petitions were filed asking the Board to rescind their action, which they did in March 1854.

There was no money for public buildings, so the Board of Supervisors rented a house on what is now the corner of Oak and Bridge Streets in Visalia for $75.00 a year. It was the Courthouse and also served as a jail for model prisoners. Those who did not behave were chained to a tree and their cases were heard in the outside courtroom. Buildings were rented until 1857, when a contract was let for $1,000.00 for a building on Block 21. Four hundred dollars was to be paid in cash and the rest in county scrip. The building was inadequate, and in 1858 another contract was let for a courthouse and jail. The site was the same. The financial condition of the county may be indicated by quoting from the Minute Book:

The payments for the Courthouse are to be made as follows: $2,500.00 to be paid upon completion, provided there were sufficient funds in the treasury at that time belonging to the building fund, then $3,000.00 to be paid down, and the remainder to be paid in two equal installments, twelve and twenty-four months after the said day of December next."

The structure had six cells on the lower floor, lined with boiler plate in which to house desperate criminals. The local editor, carried away with civic pride, described the second floor as commodious enough to accommodate a thousand persons.

The Board of Supervisors was the governing body for Visalia as well as the county from 1853 until the City of Visalia was incorporated in 1864.

Woodsville was located on the main road from Los Angeles to Stockton, but it was not a good site for development as a town. In the fall of 1852 a group of families came into the Four Creeks to settle. They bypassed Woodsville, went west about eight miles and made camp in an oak grove on the north bank of a creek. These families, with the help of cattlemen already in the area, built a log stockade that became known as Fort Visalia. The wagons were placed inside the Fort, and people lived there during the winter. Most of the families came from Iowa. Mrs. Osee Matthews kept a diary and the last entry reads:

September 12, 1852. Brother Reuben (Matthews) and Evennen arrived with the stock and we stopped at this place, four miles from Stockton until October 12th when we started with the Baker families and Stevenson family for Tularee Valley, an unsettled part of California.[9]

In letters to this writer Cecil Matthews, grandson of Osee Matthews, wrote that his grandfather had selected a site for a grist mill in the Four Creeks in 1849. That is family tradition, but it was a fact that the Matthews, who had been millers in Iowa, brought milling equipment with them in 1852. They also brought seed corn and 200 bushels of wheat. During the winter the people in Fort Visalia used 50 bushels of wheat for food. In 1969 the site of the Matthews mill was excavated, and two of the original millstones were found. One remained intact, and is now housed at the Tulare County Museum.

By the spring of 1854 a village had grown up around the Fort. The Matthews planted wheat and corn and hired Indians to dig a ditch from the creek to their mill built east of the Fort. The Indians also dug a mill race to power the mill. They hired their nephew, Edgar Reynolds to provide meat for the Indians at $5.00 a day. He later said it was not a hard job since deer, antelope, and game birds were plentiful.

Nathan Baker established a general store south of the Fort (present corner of Bridge and Main Streets), and planks were placed across the creek so people could get to the store.

Three cities in Tulare County were named for or by individuals. These are Visalia, Porterville, and Lindsay, and each person contributed more than just a place name.

Nathaniel Vise was born in 1810 in Mayesville, Kentucky. He brought his family to California in 1849. He was a typical restless frontiersman and had moved his family to Indiana, Mississippi, Missouri, and Texas. His livelihood was just as varied, for he had been a preacher, horse trader, gambler, owner of restaurants, wagon master, and fur trader.

In 1830 he married his childhood sweetheart, Matilda Jarbeau, and six children were born to the couple. Vise lived in San Diego before settling in El Monte. He soon succumbed to wanderlust, and we find him in San Francisco and Stockton. In San Francisco he operated a restaurant which featured a menu of bear meat. Many years after Nat Vise was in Visalia, this letter appeared in the *Alta California* from someone who knew the colorful Nat Vise:

VISALIA: This thriving town derives its name from Nathaniel Vise, an eccentric but good hearted individual well known in the latter part of 1849 and beginning of 1850 to the residents of San Francisco. I recollect well his having a fashionable restaurant on Kearney Street which was frequented by the Haute Ton of the place. To his advertisement in the papers his name was always exhibited thus: Nat Vise, Alias the Bear Hunter.

I feel somewhat confident that he hailed from Texas, and I can at this distant day see him distinctly through my mental vision, issue from his house of a morning in his shirt sleeves, sans coat on his way to market, ever an anon giving a peculiar yell in imitation of a Comanche or some wild quadruped. Nat was a Devil me care, happy go lucky, generous character and in that great rush to these Pacific shores and great influx of people to San Francisco, he was soon lost sight of....[10]

Nat Vise was a wanderer. Relatives said he probably never stayed in any one place more than a year. We do not know why he was in the Four Creeks in 1852, but he voted at the organization election at Grand Island on July 10th. Old timers said he was accompanied by a Cal O'Neal, who was hiding from the authorities. The fact that Vise and a J.C. O'Neal had land surveyed in what is now Visalia in October 1852 would show he was not hiding. However, O'Neal did not vote in the election, and aside from the survey, he has disappeared from history. To add an intriguing sidelight, an Abner Vise served on the first Grand Jury. In later interviews the Vise family stated they had no record of an Abner Vise.

The main issue in the election of 1853 was the proposal to move the Seat of Justice from Woodsville to Visalia. Tradition has it that Vise swung the election by a promise to donate a quarter section if the people voted for Visalia. When that happened, the story goes, the happy voters named the new town for Nat and his wife Salia Vise. That story still pops up even though the election issue was "to stay in Woodsville or move to Visalia," indicating that the name was already in use.

Through the research of the late A.W. Frost,[11] the derivation of the name was authenticated. Visalia, Kentucky was named about 1820 for the Vise family. Nat was familiar with the name, and in a short role as a land promoter named Visalia for his family. That is substantiated in an article in the *Alta California* December 11, 1852.

Nat Vise, the Bear Hunter, who is located at Visalia on

PROGRAMME!

FUNERAL OBSEQUIES.—The Committee, appointed by the citizens of Tulare County, to make arrangements for an appropriate funeral service, in honor of our late and lamented President, Abraham Lincoln, have adopted the following:

Procession to form at 1 o'clock, P. M., to-day, in front of the Court House, in the following order:
1st. Military from Camp Babbitt.
2d. Home Guards.
3d. Hearse.
4th. Pall Bearers—Nathan Baker, W. N. Steuben. L. W. Ransom, D. R. Douglass. S. C. Brown, Joshua Owen, H. Morrell, M. Baker, Stephen Davenport and A. Hadley.
5th. Officers and Members of the Union League.
6th. Children.
7th. Citizens.

Procession to move across the bridge down Court street to Acequia street, thence up Acequia street to Bridge street, thence up Bridge street to Main street, thence down Main street to Court street, thence to the stand in the grove near the School House.

Captain H. Noble is selected as Marshal of the Day.

Rev. Chevers is selected to deliver a funeral sermon.

The Military to meet at Camp Babbitt; the Union League at their Hall; the children at the Church.

Business to be suspended throughout the day.

By order of the Committee.
S. C. BROWN, Sec'y.

Tulare County was predominantly pro-Confederacy during the Civil War, but when news of Lincoln's death arrived people forgot their political differences. These hastily printed handbills were sent out so people could gather to honor President Lincoln. April 17, 1865.

the Four Creeks in Tulare County, furnishes the San Joaquin Republican with the following account of that interesting country: "On the first of November, Vise and O'Neal located and surveyed a new town called Visalia. It is in the finest section of that country...."

The rest of the long article is pure sales promotion, for Nat said there were 11 good hewn log cabins and a new school, and that a half interest in 160 acres on the townsite sold for $1,000. In reality, the people had barely had time to build the Fort.

Mrs. Vise and the children lived in El Monte. Their daughter Ellen married Thomas J. Wiggins and lived in Visalia for a time. Nat Vise went to Southern California where, in 1853, he helped organize the Los Angeles Rangers. In 1855 he was one of the organizers of the Monte Boys, a vigilante group. Nat evidently enjoyed the excitement of such organizations, for he had been a member of the Texas Rangers before he came to California. In 1856 he was running an eating house once more in Casa de Juan Rodriquez in San Diego. Again, he helped organize the San Diego Guards, who rode to protect the community from outlaws.

He may have returned to Tulare County during this period, but there is no record that he did. In the last years of his life, he was an agent for an eastern fur company. It was entirely fitting that this colorful man, who loved movement and excitement, should die the way he did. On a return trip in 1882 he stopped in Texarkana. He and others sought shelter in a brick building during a cyclone. The building collapsed, and Nat Vise was among those killed.

Visalia is the oldest community between Stockton and Los Angeles, and thus the site of many valley firsts. Before the people left Fort Visalia in 1853, a school and church had been organized. Nathan Baker had his general store south of the Fort. The Matthews brothers had a grist mill operating.[12] There were "firsts" of a personal nature too. The first white child born in the county was Commodore Murray, son of Mr. and Mrs. A.H. Murray. He was born August 7, 1853. The Richard Glenn family had three lovely daughters who did not lack beaus while the family lived in the Fort. The first wedding was solemnized December 20, 1853, when William J. Campbell married Louisa Glenn. On January 12, 1854 Margaret Glenn married Richard Chatten, and in the same year Rebecca Glenn married John Patterson.

Supplies were freighted in from Stockton. Freight rates were high, and so were retail prices. Most families raised a large portion of their food. Adequate transportation was a problem, since Visalia was eight miles away from the Los Angeles-Stockton Road. Communication was another problem. For almost a year Visalians had to go to Stockton for their mail. 1852 was an exceptionally wet year, and the round trip on horseback took almost a month. A request for a post office came through October 12, 1853, but it went to Woodsville and not Visalia. On June 2, 1855 the post office was moved to Visalia, with John P. Majors as the first postmaster. There is no available report for the first year, but from July 1, 1856 to June 30, 1857 Postmaster Majors' compensation was $83.96, and the net proceeds of the office were $54.11.

1. There were more than four creeks in the delta of the Kaweah River. Early settlers referred to the four creeks as St. Johns, Packwood, Outside Creek, and Deep Creek.
2. Senate Ex. Doc. #57, 32nd Congress, 2nd Sess., 1853.
3. *San Joaquin Republican,* July 21, 1852.
4. Annie R. Mitchell, *Jim Savage and the Tulareno Indians,* Westernlore Press, Los Angeles, 1957.
5. *Visalia Daily Times,* April 3, 1902. Interview with John Hudgins.
6. Plaque erected 1975 by Tulare County Historical Society and Alta Vista Chapter, Daughters of the American Revolution, at Avenue 324 and Road 168.
7. *Iron Age,* Visalia 1906, Orland Barton, Editor.
8. Annie R. Mitchell, *Visalia, Her First Fifty Years,* Exeter, California, 1963, page 4.
9. Letter from Cecil Matthews, October, 1957. *Visalia Daily Delta,* May 6, 1893. Mrs. Reuben Matthews and S.C. Brown were interviewed. She was visiting Visalia from her home in San Diego. She said that in the fall of 1852 the families of Colonel Baker, Dr. R. Matthews, Warren and Osee Matthews, Orson K. Smith, and Robert Stevenson left Stockton for the Four Creeks. They met S.C. Brown on the Kings River. Nat Vise was living in what is now Visalia. The Glenns, Reeds, Murray, Schipe, and Turner all came from Texas.
10. *Alta California,* February 6, 1866, signed Santiago.
11. A.W. Frost Papers, Tulare County Library, Historical Collection.
12. The Baker Store would be on the corner of Main and Bridge Streets today, and the Matthews mill at Main and Santa Fe Streets.

CHAPTER 6

HOME ON THE RANGE

Hispanic California's only industry was livestock. The economy of Southern California until the middle 1870's was based on livestock, as was the economy of the San Joaquin Valley. Livestock still makes up a large share of Tulare County's multimillion dollar agricultural income. In 1974 livestock returned $46,680,000 with an additional income of $90,802,000 from milk.

Spanish cattle differed little from the stock Columbus brought to the New World. They were long-horned range cattle, fleet of foot, and able to protect themselves from predators. Although beef was a staple food at the missions, ranchos, and pueblos, the commercial value of cattle came from hides and tallow. During the Spanish period there was no free enterprise, but as foreign ships appeared in ports or hove to off shore, an extensive trade developed. The American ships took hides and tallow in exchange for manufactured goods and luxury items. During the decade 1830-1840 "leather dollars" or hides were used as currency, and the period was called the era of hides and tallow. Dana's *Two Years Before the Mast* is the classic story of that time in California. Prophetically Dana wrote, "In the hands of an enterprising people, what a country this might be." During that pastoral era many American visitors stayed in California, became naturalized citizens and Catholics and married into Mexican families.

The gold rush transformed that pastoral paradise. Southern California was not touched by the gold rush per se, but the miners needed meat, and a fantastic market developed. Cattle that once sold for a couple of dollars a head sold as beef for $30.00 to $70.00 a head. For the first time in California, meat was sold by the pound in camps and towns. Herds north of San Luis Obispo were soon depleted, and cattle buyers began to bargain with cattlemen in Southern California.

The herds they bought were driven either up the coast or through the San Joaquin Valley. The cattle drives took about a month. There were losses from wild predators, rustlers, and Indians. Usually the cattle were allowed to rest as they neared market to recoup the weight they had lost on the drive.

Sheep practically disappeared after the secularization of the missions. The gold rush opened up a market for mutton and lamb and provided an incentive to drive sheep into California, where they brought from $9.00 to $16.00 a head. William Hollister, the father of California's sheep industry, drove thousands of sheep into the state in 1853. That same year, Solomon Jewett brought a large flock into what is now Kern County.

For many years westerns have dominated movies and television. Much of what we see is the writer's idea of what life was like during the boom market, when thousands of cattle and sheep were driven across the plains into California.

The real western cowboy was something else. His life was hard but never dull. There was nothing dashing in his appearance, clothes, or equipment. Unlike mountain men, the cowboys worked in groups, but like mountain men, they lived it up when they rode into town. Their habitats were the cattle camp and the saloon. The appeal of the cowboys came from their lifestyle. They worked in all kinds of weather; they had accidents; they were virile; they settled personal grudges with violence; they fought over water holes, grazing rights, and cattle brands. They were a breed apart, and probably will live forever in books, movies, and television. A strange sidelight is that the real legendary cowboys were Mexicans and blacks who do not appear in the media.

By 1860 the livestock market was deflated. The reasons are not hard to assess because census figures reveal a glutted market:

Cattle		Sheep	
1850	262,659	1850	17,574
1860	1,180,142	1860	1,008,002

When miners had a choice between tough stringy beef (which they called bull mahogany) and tasty mutton, they naturally chose the latter. When the market collapsed, both cattlemen and sheepmen were hurt, but the sheepmen were saved by the Civil War. The North was cut off from its supplies of cotton, and wool prices rose dramatically. The principal cargo carried by the river steamers *The Visalia* and *The Harriet* was wool. (The riverboats came down the San Joaquin River from Stockton to Sycamore Slough.) The principal freight carried over the new road (1861) from Tulare County to San Luis Obispo was wool.

Another factor in the financial upset was the business ineptitude of the native Californians. The era of hides and tallow was followed by a market which brought in more money than most of them had ever seen. They had always lived indulgently; now they lived extravagantly. The inherent courtesy and hospitality of the Spanish and Mexican people was demonstrated at every rancho. "Mi casa est su casa" ("my house is your house") was meant sincerely. They lived on leagues, not acres. Their herds and flocks could only be estimated. Money was borrowed easily. Interest rates were exhorbitant, and land and livestock were put up as security. Often friends co-signed notes. Suddenly men found themselves with debts they could not pay.

The terrible drought of 1864 almost wiped out the livestock industry. Rangeland was strewn with dead animals. Any price was acceptable as indicated in this item:

It is reported on good authority that the drought conditions on the plains are getting worse. 60,000 head of cattle were sold in Santa Barbara for 37½ cents a head. It is estimated that cattlemen have lost many times that many by thirst and starvation.[1]

These factors coincided with the arrival of the land-hungry Americans. The first land grant in Alta California was issued by Pedro Fages in 1784 to an army veteran. During the Spanish period, fewer than 30 land grants were issued, but many were for 11 leagues, or 48,712.4 acres. During the Mexican era, almost 500 land grants were issued. It has been estimated that at the end of Mexican rule in California, 200 families owned 14,000,000 acres of land. Only a few land grants were in the southern valley. They were Laguna de Tache, El Tejon, San Emigidio, and Castaic. Each was to play an important role in legal history.

The Treaty of Guadalupe-Hidalgo guaranteed land titles which were legitimate, but the only area of California not overrun by squatters was southern California.

In 1851 a Federal Land Claims Commission arrived in California to examine land titles and untangle problems stemming from "squatters rights." In the next four years the Commission heard 800 cases and approved title to 520. Thus many Californians lost their property because their land grant was either illegal or improperly recorded.

The boom and bust cattle market, along with the examination of land titles, coincided with the formation of Tulare County in 1852. It is now evident that cattle were pastured in the southern valley as early as 1846. Most of them grazed on the land grants mentioned. The early arrivals in the Four Creeks were all cattlemen.

John Keener came to Visalia in 1852 with his family. After they left Fort Visalia they settled south of the creek in what is now the Keener Addition. Mr. Keener went back to Missouri and drove the first herd of American cattle into Tulare County in 1853. The drive took seven months. John Keener made five more cattle drives from the East to Tulare County. Like all stockmen, the family moved frequently. At different times they lived near Tulare Lake, Mariposa, Santa Rosa, and in the State of Washington, but their home was always in Visalia. John and Eleanor Keener were interested in schools, and all of their children had the advantage of higher education. In 1859 they donated the land for the Visalia Select Seminary (on the present site of the Kaweah Delta District Hospital).

Soon after John Keener drove in the first herd of American cattle, Elisha Packwood and his brothers-in-law, Jabes Smith and Joseph Prothero, drove American cattle into the Tule River Country. William Blankenship came into the Kaweah area about the same time. Since the economy of Tulare County for the next two decades was based on cattle, some of the early laws, cattle brands, and short biographies of the first cattlemen will let us slip back into that time.

The early industry centered around Tulare Lake, Visalia, and the Tule River Country. Tulare Lake was the center of the livestock industry. During the 1830-1840's it was used by horse thieves as a place to rest stock before the animals were driven out of the province. Early American stockmen grazed both hogs and cattle at the Lake. Frank Latta wrote that the earliest stockmen known to bring domestic stock to the Lake were the Rhodes and Murphy brothers, who came from Santa Clara. As Latta says:

Probably the earliest brand which remained permanently in the Tulare Lake country was the "Wine Glass" of

John Keener (1822-1902)
He brought the first American cattle into Tulare County in 1852-53.

Hale Tharp (1830-1912)
First white man in the Three Rivers area. Discovered Giant Forest in 1858.

James A. Crabtree (1829-1913)
He settled in the Tule River country in 1857. His discovery of the White Chief Mine in Mineral King in 1873 started a rush to that new mining field.

Charlie Wingfield. Wingfield was in the Lake country soon after the Woods massacre in 1850, and finally died there. Julius Orton, William Mayfield, Jack Gordon, John Fancher, Elisha Packwood, Thomas Baker, Joseph Harris, J.O. Rice, S.C. Brown, James Persian, Jasper Harrell, John B. Eshom, William Benware, Fielding Bacon, Henry Hartley, Nathan Dillon, Yancy Stokes, Foster de Masters, Richard Chatten, and half a hundred others almost as early and equally important.[2]

Hogs were brought in before cattle. The meat could be cured or smoked there, or the animals could be driven to the mines. The drives averaged about six miles a day, so the animals did not lose much weight. Many of the razorbacks escaped the roundups and gradually became the dreaded tule rooters. Hunting tule rooters became a favored but dangerous sport among pioneers, who trained dogs especially for that kind of hunt.

The first cattle brand registered in Tulare County was the JF of John Fancher. The date was December 17, 1852. Elisha Packwood's EP was the second registered brand (April 9, 1853). The first brands were usually the initials of the owner, or a recognizable design such as Jasper Harrell's Shoe Sole brand. By 1859, 100 brands had been registered in Tulare County.

By 1859 more attention was given to the design of a brand and counterbrand that could not be easily altered. The incentive for the change went back to a law passed by the State Legislature in 1851. *An Act to Regulate Rodeos* made it mandatory for each stockman to hold a yearly rodeo to brand his cattle. If he did not, anyone could hold it at the owner's expense. Another section unwittingly turned cattle rustling into a profitable enterprise. That section read, "All unmarked neat cattle, the mothers of which are unknown, shall be considered the property of the owner of the farm on which they are found." Men staked out range claims and at the yearly rodeos rounded up all the calves they could find. The lakes and sloughs surrounded by tules were especially hard to rodeo, and vaqueros who could work that territory were paid extra. A well known, prosperous stockman later said that his vaqueros "found" several thousand calves each year. Another said he owned only a steer until a trip to the lake country put him into the cattle business. Apparently, all one needed to be successful was a range claim, a branding iron, and alert vaqueros.

The yearly rodeos were held on large ranches and at fixed locations such as Tulare Lake, Elk Bayou, Tule River, what is now Mooney Grove, Bravo Lake (Woodlake), Dry Creek, Deep Creek, and Cross Creek. Each ranch group had its own grub wagon, and the cowboys slept in their bed rolls. In the late 1860's whiskey wagons began to show up. These refreshment spots created so much trouble that well known cattlemen not only forbade their appearance but were known to have personally smashed the whiskey barrels.

Mineral King Village

The 1851 *Act to Regulate Rodeos* provided for the appointment of Judges of the Plains, whose duty was to settle the endless disputes over stock ownership. That was done more easily than settling personal grudges, which usually ended up in fist fights. One of the more spectacular fights was between Tom Fowler and John Asbil and led to a well known county place name. The arena was present-day Woodlake, and as the fight went on, the bystanders yelled "bravo" so many times that the nearby body of water became Bravo Lake.

Most of the men mentioned by Latta became part of Tulare County's history. John Fancher, who registered the first brand, and Elisha Packwood are good examples. Fancher moved his herds northward and became identified with that part of the county which later became Fresno County. Fancher Creek was named for him. Mrs. Joseph Myer, whose family lived in Yokohl Valley, was a Fancher descendant.

Elisha Packwood stayed long enough to leave his name on Packwood Creek, Packwood Road, and Packwood Station on the Butterfield Stage Road. His story is typical of the financial ups and downs of all early stockmen. Elisha and his brothers, with their families, went to the Oregon Territory during the overland migrations of 1846. He brought his family to California just before gold was discovered. They settled near New Almaden and later moved to Mormon Island. After a stint in the mines, Packwood opened a general store at Colma, which proved successful. The family returned to Virginia and then came back to California driving several hundred head of Durham cattle. They settled in San Jose and sold both milk and dairy cattle. Elisha Packwood bought American cattle (Durhams) and pastured them in the Tule River country probably as early as 1853 or 1854. The country appealed to the families, and Elisha and his brother Samuel and their brothers-in-law, Jabes Smith and Joseph Prothero, used school warrants to buy land adjacent to the Tule River. Elisha built what was described as a "nice brick house" west of Porterville in what is now the Burton District. His holding of approximately 3,000 acres extended west, east, and north of present-day Porterville. The state map of 1855 showed the road from the vicinity of present-day Strathmore to Visalia as the Packwood Road.

Miss Ina Stiner, who researched records on the Butterfield Stage Road in the county, found interesting references to the Packwoods. Packwood Station has never been accurately located. It was said to be west of present-day Strathmore. It was also known as the Pike Lawless Station and the Lone Cottonwood Station, which would move it nearer to Farmersville. Later accounts confused it with an Eighteen Mile House. Miss Stiner also wrote:

In 1853 Elisha Packwood and A.H. Fraser went security on a $15,000 bond for Orson K. Smith, the first regularly elected Sheriff of Tulare County.

Cattle brands made by Clifford Witt in his Ducor blacksmith shop. The boards on which he burned these custom made brands are now in the Tulare County Museum.

His filings on land for which patents were obtained were near Tule River and Porterville and were dated in 1861 and 1863.

In the assessment for taxes in 1860 he and his brother Samuel Packwood were assessed for 2,900 acres of land. In 1862, besides his land assessment, his tax bill listed 36 American horses, 300 American cattle, one gold watch, 2 Spanish mules, 2 wagons, and household furniture.

The drought of 1864 was disastrous for stockmen. Packwood sold his cattle for $2.50 a head herd run. These were milk cows, not range steers. Eventually Dan Murphy bought the remaining stock, and the Packwood family went back to San Jose and the dairy business.

The brothers-in-law stayed. Joseph Prothero moved to Visalia, where his descendants still live. When his oldest son, Anastacio Prothero, died in 1941, his obituary stated that he was Visalia's oldest native son as he had been born in 1852* on the family ranch southeast of Visalia.

Jabes Smith built the first house on the site of modern Porterville, at Third and Putnam Streets. He was more interested in mining than ranching, and went to the northern mines several times. Eventually he settled in the Porterville area, and his descendants also live in Tulare County.

The history of the livestock industry in the county has been dictated by land usage, laws, and market conditions. It concerns more than just beef cattle, for hogs, horses, mules, and especially sheep have played their part. The level valley floor provided a vast open range where stock could roam unimpeded. The economic hub was Visalia, which was the source of supplies and mail, the medical and legal professions, and community activities. In the summer stock was driven to mountain meadows or stayed close to lakes, springs, or the larger rivers. Because water was so vital, the Tule River Country was ideal. Besides its branches, Deer Creek and White River were not far away. Fountain Springs, Elk Bayou and, in times of heavy rainfall, gulches provided water for the stock. Among the families who settled as stockmen in the Tule River Country before 1860 were Orton, Kirby, Hunsaker, Lewis, Monroe, Vincent, Blair, McGee, Callison, Murray, Murphy, Campbell, Williamson, Tyler, Sorrels, Manly, Rose, Coker, Martin, Hockett, Bond, and Wilcox.

Early stockmen on the White River included Biggs, Dunlap, Carver, James, Klein, Caldwell, Box, Slinkard, Guthrie, Ellis, Danner, White, Hawley, Peppers, and Hewey. In the 1880's flocks of sheep were brought into the southern end of the

*Mr. Prother's death certificate gives his date of birth as December 2, 1852. If that date is correct, he and not Commodore Murray, born August 7, 1853, was the first white child born in Tulare County.

Thomas Fowler (1828-1884)

John Patrick Murray (1836-1899) He ran cattle near Porterville and Tulare Lake as early as 1855.

county by Matt Flynn, Peter Norton, Henry Lubking, Harry Quinn, the Menne Brothers, and Henry and Adolph Zimmerman.

The first stockman on the upper Kaweah River was Hale Tharp, who settled on Horse Creek in 1856. He had come to California in 1852. Cloe Ann Swanson, a widow, and her four children were also in the wagon train. Tharp admired her spunk, and they were married at Mud Springs. The family lived for a time at Placerville, where Tharp mined. He came south in 1856, looking for a place to raise stock. A brother of Mrs. Tharp's first husband, John Swanson, was already living in the county near Farmersville. Tharp liked the mountains better, and moved his family to Horse Creek. He was good to the Indians, and in 1858 Chief Chappo invited him to visit the headquarters of his tribe. Tharp was the first white man to see the magnificent redwoods which John Muir later called Giant Forest. He visited the tribal meeting place, which was a natural cave formed when a huge boulder was split by glacial action. It was Tharp who called it Hospital Rock in 1873. Tharp's summer camp was a fallen hollow redwood log, which he first saw in 1858. For almost 40 years Tharp, his stepson George Swanson, and later his own son Norbert Tharp took horses and some cattle into what is now Sequoia National Park. Tharp's Log in Crescent Meadows is a Park landmark. John Muir visited Tharp and called the camp "a noble den." Besides naming Hospital Rock, George Swanson named Moro Rock for his favorite roan horse.

Other families came into what is now Lemon Cove, Woodlake, and Three Rivers. There was good feed in the watersheds, and the canyons were ideal places to run horses, mules, and donkeys. The mouth of the canyon could be barricaded in order to control the range area. There was a good market in horses, mules, and donkeys not only in sales to miners but also to replenish the worn-out stock of arriving settlers. Some of the earliest stockmen along the Kaweah and its branches were Works, Blossom, Homer, Van Gorden, Swanson, Lovelace, Palmer, Everton, Mehrten, Pogue, Blair, Wells, Ewing, Hambright, Bequette, Mitchell, Ragle, Hilliard, Balaam, Hamilton, and Rice.

The Homestead Act of 1862 allowed a settler to occupy 160 acres (320 for a man and wife). After he had fulfilled lenient legal requirements, the land was his. Land on the valley floor was soon proved up. The floods and dry years of the 1860's drove many out of the stock business and into farming. The age-old conflict between farmers and cattlemen flourished in the change-over. Cattlemen derisively called farmers "sand lappers" and "sky farmers." Farmers far too often found their crops and small trees eaten or trampled by wandering stock. Protests were met with, "Why don't you fence in your property?" That was easy to answer — it cost $2,240 to fence in 160 acres. When barbed wire came into use a century ago, it caused as many changes in farming as the cream separator did in the dairy business in the 1880's.

The first two decades of county history saw an economy based on livestock. From then on we may follow chronologically the history of what happened to that industry. Stockmen, led by State Senator Thomas Fowler, who represented Tulare and Kern Counties, opposed the construction of a railroad through the valley in 1872. They realized the value of better and faster transportation, but were astute enough to know that when the railroad came through, droves of settlers would come in and challenge the open range.

The election of 1874 was fought bitterly by men who opposed or wanted a "no fence" law. The Trespass Act forced the farmer to fence in his property. Tipton Lindsey, who opposed Fowler, won the election, and a law was passed making it mandatory for stockmen to fence in their rangeland. The law certainly was not obeyed quickly, but an influx of settlers, a switch in economy to grain farming, and one of the driest years of record in 1877 almost finished the livestock industry. Stockmen moved to homesteads in the foothills, or raised hogs on fenced land.

The southern end of the county was still sparsely

Vaquero cattle drive to the mountains east of Porterville.

Vaqueros driving longhorn cattle from Mexico to the county, 1890.

settled, and was taken over by sheepmen. Sheep grazed on the plains until summertime, when they were driven into the mountains literally by the thousands. Wherever they grazed they left bare churned earth, and in the mountains they ruined watersheds as well as meadows. John Muir, who hated sheep, called them horned locusts. Sheepherders had a practice which drove conservationists wild. They lit a circle of bonfires around the sheep at night to protect them from predators. Needless to say, the fires often "got away" and burned for days. Cattlemen, who opposed sheepmen as much as possible, borrowed a practice from the Indians which they did not advertise. The last man out each fall set fire to the brush in order to stimulate the growth of grass the next year.

Sequoia National Park was established in 1890. Soon cattle, horses, and sheep were allowed in by permit, and then sheep were banned entirely. At that time, an estimated 500,000 sheep were in the Park. As grain farming increased in the southern section of the county, sheepmen moved their flocks to the west side of the valley. The agricultural report now lists 20,000 sheep in the county.

The discovery that water could be pumped from an underground water table set off another economic change in land usage in the 1890's. With water, or irrigation water rights, a man could make a good living on a small tract. Citrus, deciduous fruits, alfalfa, and the growth of small dairies mark that era.

Scientific procedures began to slowly revitalize the livestock industry. Better breeds of cattle, horses, hogs, and sheep were introduced. They were fed better, and protected from common diseases. Corrals and cattle chutes were built along the railroads so stock could be shipped to market or to other areas for fattening.

In 1924 the dreaded hoof and mouth disease appeared in California, and many stockmen were wiped out before drastic measures controlled it. The only thing to do for infected herds was to kill the animals. Every highway had checkpoints where cars and people had to go through disinfectants, and for once the Tulare County Fair was cancelled.

The one factor that did the most to put the industry back on a sound basis was probably the establishment of feed lots. These are aptly described as beef factories where animals are scientifically fed and then marketed.

Cattle drives have been replaced by trucks, and horses now travel in style. However scientific the industry has become, its basic components remain the same.

The sweeping changes in valley history have revolved around cattle, grain, citrus, deciduous fruits, dairying, and water. Each change can be traced to a man or a group of men who had the courage and vision to try something different. History is an extension of biography, and thus the changes illustrate the contributions made by men.

Thomas Fowler was one man who may be cited as an example of the fictional cattle baron. He was a self-made millionaire, a highly respected businessman, a capable State Legislator — and he lost it all because of his stubbornness.

Fowler was born on St. Patrick's Day in County Down, Ireland, a fact he never let anyone forget. He came to America as a young lad and found work in New York, Louisiana, Texas, and Mexico. He arrived in California in 1853 with his partners, Jim Fisher and Thomas Davis. On the way to the mines they were impressed with and later named Antelope Valley, near present-day Woodlake. They reasoned that if hundreds of antelope grazed in that protected valley, stock could too. The trio mined for a while and then opened a butcher shop in Carson City. When they had saved enough money they went to Mexico, bought stock, and drove the cattle back to Antelope Valley. Jim Fisher settled near what is now Ivanhoe. Fowler and Davis continued their partnership and in 1868 registered their cattle brand, years after they had arrived in the county. We do not know how long their partnership lasted. Thomas Davis stayed in Antelope Valley, and his descendants still live in that location.

Fowler's personality had much to do with the legends that surrounded him. He was a big man, genial, boisterous, definitely opinionated, champion of the underdog, a heavy drinker, and was known to hundreds of people as "Honest Tom." He was a life-long Democrat.

In 1865 Fowler and Richard Carmen bought the property of E.C. Ferguson and Andrew Darwin, in what is now the Minkler and Reedley areas. The original owners, Ferguson and Darwin, had registered their 76 brand in 1857 in both Tulare and Fresno Counties. The brand went with the property. Fowler bought out Darwin, and in a few years his 76 brand was on an estimated 200,000 head of cattle, which grazed over 40,000 acres. It was the day of the open range, and his real estate was not contiguous. One method he used to acquire land was described by Albert Dickey.

Tom Fowler's brand — 76 — was on most of the cattle along Tule River. He had acquired considerable acreage by having his riders homestead or pre-empt land, and as they proved up on it, he took it over for practically nothing. His method of taking land was to have a man file on a string of 40 acre parcels along the outer border of the section, each man taking four forties; in that manner there were 160 acres of government land left in the center to which no one had access without crossing his holdings which was forbidden.[3]

Mr. Dickey also wrote that some of Fowler's cattle were shot when they stampeded through grain fields in the Woodville country. After that episode, farmers were not bothered by his cattle anymore.

"Honest Tom" was elected to the State Senate in 1869 and in 1871. He lost in 1874 over the bitterly battled no-fence issue. He was re-elected in 1877. Between those years he was frequently mentioned as a candidate for Governor. Many of his constituents were cattlemen who opposed construction of a valley railroad. Fowler was voluble in his opposition. However, he did not oppose the railroad per se. He opposed the federal land grants given to the railroads, and its later takeover of the government of California.

The Central Pacific Railroad built its line from Lathrop to Goshen in 1872. At that point construction was taken over by the Southern Pacific. Lathrop, Modesto, Merced, Fresno, Goshen, Tulare, Pixley, Tipton, Delano, and Sumner were all railroad-created communities. A location along the railroad, ten miles southeast of Fresno, was a logical place for Fowler to load his cattle. The site was named Fowler Switch, and he used it for the first time in the fall of 1872. It is ironic that he had little to do with Fowler and much to do with Traver, which did not bear his name.

The No-Fence Law was not put into practice in a hurry. Fowler did not start to fence his 76 Ranch until 1877. By that time he was financially committed to projects in Traver and Mineral King. His involvement in the Empire Mine in Mineral King preceded his investment in Traver, but we shall delve into Traver's history first.

The Water Witch *was used by hunters on Tulare Lake from 1878 until 1880 when it capsized near the mouth of Kings River during a storm.*

In 1882 Peter Y. Baker, a civil engineer, planned an extensive irrigation project in northern Tulare County and southern Fresno County that would turn rangeland into farmland. Irrigation water would be diverted from the Kings River. He interested a group of men who secured an option on Fowler's 76 Ranch. They then incorporated the 76 Land and Water Company. Fowler took $40,000 in stock for the land. Construction of the main canal was difficult, but on April 8, 1884, water flowed through the 76 Canal, and town lots and farmland were auctioned off. Excursion trains had brought in dozens of people, and local people were there in droves.

The new town was named Traver for Charles Traver, a member of the 76 Company. Traver rapidly became one of the major grain shipping points in the nation. Water literally turned the plains into profitable farms. Within a decade Traver was slowly becoming a ghost town. Over-irrigation had brought alkali to the surface of the ground. Devastating fires wiped out the business district several times. The construction of the Eastside Railroad in 1888 had created new towns, such as Dinuba, which competed with Traver. By the

Tulare Lake was dry after 1923 and the lake bed was farmed extensively. The lake filled again during the floods of 1937. Dredges and pumps such as these were used to drain the bed and aid in repairing levees. Taken a few miles southwest of Corcoran.

time Traver went into limbo, Fowler had lost his fortune in Mineral King.

Mineral King, in the high mountains east of Visalia, is newsworthy again today because Disney Enterprises is seeking to develop it as a winter sports and recreation center. A century ago it was also in the headlines as another Comstock. James Crabtree of Porterville discovered the mining field there in 1873. He was a spiritualist and said that his celestial guide, an Indian maiden, had guided him to the canyon. He named his mine "The White Chief." Times were hard in the 1870's, and news of the strike aroused considerable excitement in Porterville, then Visalia, and then in the rest of the state. Trails from Porterville and Visalia were worn down by men and by pack animals loaded with equipment. There were several marketable metals, but silver was the lodestone. Visalia merchants benefitted from the strikes, just as they had when mines were booming along the White and Kern Rivers, and later in the Owens Valley.

There was both good and bad news from Mineral King. Because of its elevation, operations had to close during the winter. Snow avalanches were common. A good road was an immediate necessity to bring in supplies for the two to three thousand people who worked during good weather. The ore was rebellious ore, which meant that its components had to be recovered by smelting. That called for expensive machinery, experienced machinists, and capital outlay. In spite of the bad news, hundreds of claims were filed, companies were formed, and stock was sold. By 1878 the ore had defeated the miners. That was the year Senator Fowler bought the Empire Mine and brought Mineral King back to life.

Why an astute businessman like Fowler bought the mine is still a mystery. He knew about the ore; he knew a road was needed; and he knew about expensive machinery. There is not much doubt that he was shown a faked assay report. When he made his first trip to the mine and went down the shaft, the torch light made the stalactites shimmer like pure silver. Fowler yelled that he was looking at so much silver that he would build a mansion on Nob Hill in San Francisco, pay the national debt, and then buy Ireland. Newspapers all over the state re-echoed his boasts. Everything he did or said was magnified. Men asked, even begged, to buy into his venture.

In 1879 Fowler promoted the incorporation of the Mineral King Wagon and Toll Road, which officially opened that fall. He was so anxious to be the first one to drive into Mineral King that he unhitched his team and had workmen carry him in his buggy over the unfinished last 600 yards of the road.

Fowler poured money into equipment, the mine, and the road and got little back. His monumental egotism probably kept him from admitting his mistake. In 1880 claims totaling $114,014.94 were filed against him. He hired a business manager, and the value of his property was shown in this trust deed account:

Value of all land in Tulare, Kern, and Fresno Counties	$ 330,600
Cattle	15,000
Horses	6,000
Two stores	15,000
Empire Mill	100,000
Mine tramway	20,000
Assay office	6,000
Two blacksmith shops	4,000
95,000 shares in Empire Mine	1,375,000

The manager was to supervise the trust and pay all legal claims but was enjoined from selling the stock. He and Fowler were soon in litigation. Fowler was in a financial morass. That would probably explain his exchanging the 76 Ranch for Traver stock. He drank more than usual. He re-entered politics and was considered by his party as a candidate for Lieutenant Governor. He went to Mexico to buy cattle but came back without them. On April 15, 1884, Fowler fell as he left the train at Goshen to take the Palace Hotel hack to Visalia. The next day he was dead.

In 1868 Fowler had married Mary Farley and they lived in Visalia, where their five children were born. Two of the children, Amy and Clarence, died in 1878 and 1879 and are buried in Visalia, as is Senator Fowler. Little is known of Mary Fowler, Irma, and Emmett, the other children. One son, Leonard, was a well known attorney and at one time was Attorney General of the State of Nevada.

1. *Visalia Weekly Delta,* October 12, 1864.
2. Frank F. Latta, *Little Journeys in the San Joaquin,* Tulare, 1937.
3. Albert Dickey, *Personal Reminiscences,* Dinuba, No date, Typescript.

CHAPTER 7

VISALIA SADDLES

Because of its location, Visalia was and is the hub of a large trading area. During the days of the open range, vaqueros rode many miles to order handmade saddles from Visalia's famous saddle makers.

The Federal Census of 1860 listed the firms of Simpson Bossler and Homer Townsend as saddle makers in Visalia. Joseph Samstag was listed as a journeyman saddler. The census also revealed that the firms were doing well, for their combined capital investment was $4,000, and they employed three men at an average monthly wage of $75.00 each, or $225.00. The annual product was 300 saddles valued at $6,000, and 100 sets of harnesses valued at $3,500.

The most famous of all western working saddles is the Visalia saddle, which was the composite handiwork of several men. The original saddle is traditionally credited to Juan Martarell, who made it in his saddle shop in Hornitos. As the story went, a vaquero brought in a saddle to be repaired. Martarell overhauled the saddle instead of making repairs. The customer was delighted and spread the word that Martarell could make a saddle that was lighter, stronger, and more comfortable for both rider and horse.

Martarell moved to Visalia in 1869 and his assistants, Alsalio Herrera and Ricardo Mattley, went with him. He made the first saddles in his home, but found a building on Center Street between Encina and Locust Streets that was suitable for a shop. In his first advertisement of the Visalia Saddle, he called the product The Vaquero Saddle. It was also called The Easy Riding Saddle. However, the customers called it The Visalia Saddle, and that became the name of both the saddle and the saddle shop.

The Visalia Saddle differed from the cumbersome Spanish saddles then in use. The high horn and long stirrups were eliminated, and a skirt was added to protect the rider's legs. Most of the material for the saddle was gathered locally. The cantle was made from valley oak wood, the side pieces were willow wood, and the horn was carved from carefully culled oak crotches. Hand-made silver ornaments and designs on the leather took time and skilled craftmanship.

Juan Martarell was a Sonoran who came to California during the gold rush. He settled in Sonora, named for his province in Mexico. From there he went to Hornitos, where he learned to make saddles and harnesses. While he created the Visalia Saddle, he actually did less for its development than his contemporaries. He sold his shop in 1870 and went to work for the new owner, David E. Walker. He later worked for Fred Uhl in the Grey Horse Harness Shop.

Martarell married Maria Chacon in Visalia. His son Pete has provided some interesting recollections on his parents and their life in Visalia:

During the time he was working there (Grey Horse Harness Shop) some of his friends called on my father and invited him to a meeting for the purpose of organizing a lodge which was called Los Ocho Amigos (the Eight Friends). My father was elected secretary and instructed to write the by-laws and constitution.

My father bought a home for us consisting of a lot with two houses on the corner of School and Bridge Streets. He used the front room for his office. When a member of the Lodge came to pay his dues, my mother told me that I would carry a spitoon and put it next to his chair. This was my own idea, nobody ever taught me to do it. I was about three or four years old.

My father died when I was between seven and eight years old. He was buried by Mr. Locey who had his funeral parlor on Court Street between Main and Center Streets.

My mother, Maria Chacon, was born in San Gabriel in 1864. Her parents, Jose and Bernarda Chacon, were from Hermosio, Sonora, Mexico. My mother's father was a shoe maker. My mother told me that he would make a load of shoes and put them on pack horses and take them to San Francisco to sell them. They came to Visalia in

Alsalio Herrera, left, and Ricardo Mattley

1873 or 1874 and bought a house on North Bridge across from where the ice plant is now. On the back end of the lot he planted some cactus. We used to go there when I was a little boy and fill up on prickly pears.

At that time, coming from the north side of town, you had to cross the creek on a plank to reach Main Street. My grandfather did not know how to read. One day while crossing the creek he fell off the plank into the water. His fall resulted in rheumatism. Not being able to walk much he asked my grandmother to teach him to read. The credit for my grandfather learning to read will have to be awarded to the creek that runs through Visalia.[1]

Ricardo Mattley, also from Sonora, came to California in the early 1850's. With the exception of Martarell's first saddle tree, Mr. Mattley carved every Visalia Saddle Tree for more than 20 years. After Martarell sold his shop, Mr. Mattley made custom saddle trees for individuals and for other saddle shops.

In 1880 he married Apablasa Forquero, whose forebears had come to California from Chile in 1822. In Visalia, in 1889, Mattley's stepdaughter, Louisa Forquero, married Manuel Estrada, who also came from pioneer Spanish ancestry. For many years Mr. Estrada was employed by Miller and Lux. He passed away suddenly in 1913, leaving his widow with ten children to support. She did the thing she knew best, traditional Spanish cooking, and started the famous Estrada Spanish Kitchen in Visalia. Before her death in 1932, Mrs. Estrada and her family had established Spanish Kitchens in Fresno, Bakersfield, Colma, and Los Angeles. Ricardo Mattley passed away in 1935.

Alsalio Herrera learned the silversmith's craft from his father in Hornitos. Working stock saddles were not ornamented with silver, but vaqueros and stockmen wanted silver ornaments, bits, spurs, and conchas to add a personal touch to their equipment. Little is known about Mr. Herrera, and it is possible that he went with the shop when it was moved to San Francisco.

David E. Walker bought the Visalia Saddle Shop in 1870. His daughter wrote that her parents had arrived in Visalia about 1869, traveling by stages from San Francisco.[2] David Walker immediately began a sales promotion campaign that placed him far ahead of his era in merchandising. He printed handbills that were mailed all over the United States, Canada, and South America. Later he incorporated the handbills into well illustrated catalogues. The sales campaign paid off well.

Each saddle bore the distinctive D.E. Walker Trade Mark. Walker also increased the "sundries" to include hand-made ring bits, hand-made spurs, hand-braided rawhide reins, hand-braided riatas, caronals, conchas, quirts, tapaderos, stirrups, chaparejos, and a variety of harnesses. Mexican dollars were used for all silver work.

Walker went into several partnerships. At different times the firm was Walker and Shuhan, Walker and Wade, and Walker and Wegner. The Visalia Store was at 60 Main Street, and later at 221 California Street in San Francisco. Since the bulk of his orders came through the catalogues, the economic changes made by the railroad and the No Fence Law did not hurt his business. In the 1891 catalogue he wrote, "We have 6,000 saddles in use, and ship them to every state and territory in the Union, also to British Columbia, Australia, Hawaiian Islands, Central America, Argentine Republic, and Chile."

In 1887 David Walker sold the Visalia Shop to his nephew, Edwin Weeks, and moved his family to San Francisco, where he passed away in 1894. Weeks phased out the Visalia Shop and the firm carried on in San Francisco in order to take advantage of better shipping facilities. Through the years there were other owners, and eventually the Visalia Saddle Shop was moved to Sacramento. Presently (1976) it is located in Grass Valley, although the principal business is in accessories and not in saddles.

The Tulare County Museum has two Visalia Stock Saddles on display, as well as catalogues and many of the tools used in the original Visalia Shop.

A contemporary and equally well known saddle maker was Jesus Salazar (1838-1903). He was born in Sonora, Mexico, like so many of the Mexican people who came to California. He had learned the trade of making shoes and saddles before he arrived in 1857 to settle with his parents at Hornitos.

The family came to Visalia in 1867, and Jesus Salazar set up a repair shop on East Main Street. His daughter, Mrs. Edith Madrid, recalled that her father, Mattley, Martarell, and Herrera were all good friends from their boyhood days in Sonora, Mexico.

Mr. Salazar's business grew, so he rented the rear section of the Grey Horse Harness Shop. Later he rented the entire upper floor. Since he was primarily a worker in leather, his saddles were more elaborate. His daughter said he used no pattern, but drew designs free-hand. He made his tools from

David E. Walker

spikes, cutting off the top and etching stars, rings, checks, and other designs. The hand tooling, especially on heavy leather, created highly prized saddles. Many of the saddles were encrusted with silver. Today, Salazar Saddles are either in private collections or museums.

Jesus Salazar married Trinidad Sesna in Stockton in 1860. After her death he married Carmen Romero in Visalia. Her mother, Mrs. Edith Romero, had started a Spanish Kitchen restaurant in her home, located on what later became the site of the Santa Fe Depot at Main and Santa Fe Avenue. Visalia has a long reputation for excellent Spanish food, and Mrs. Romero's home restaurant was the first of several famous establishments. When the Santa Fe Railroad came to Visalia in 1897, she sold her property and moved her Spanish Kitchen to 417 East Main. Her friend, Mrs. Pablo, had also set up a Spanish Kitchen at what is now Court and Acequia Streets.

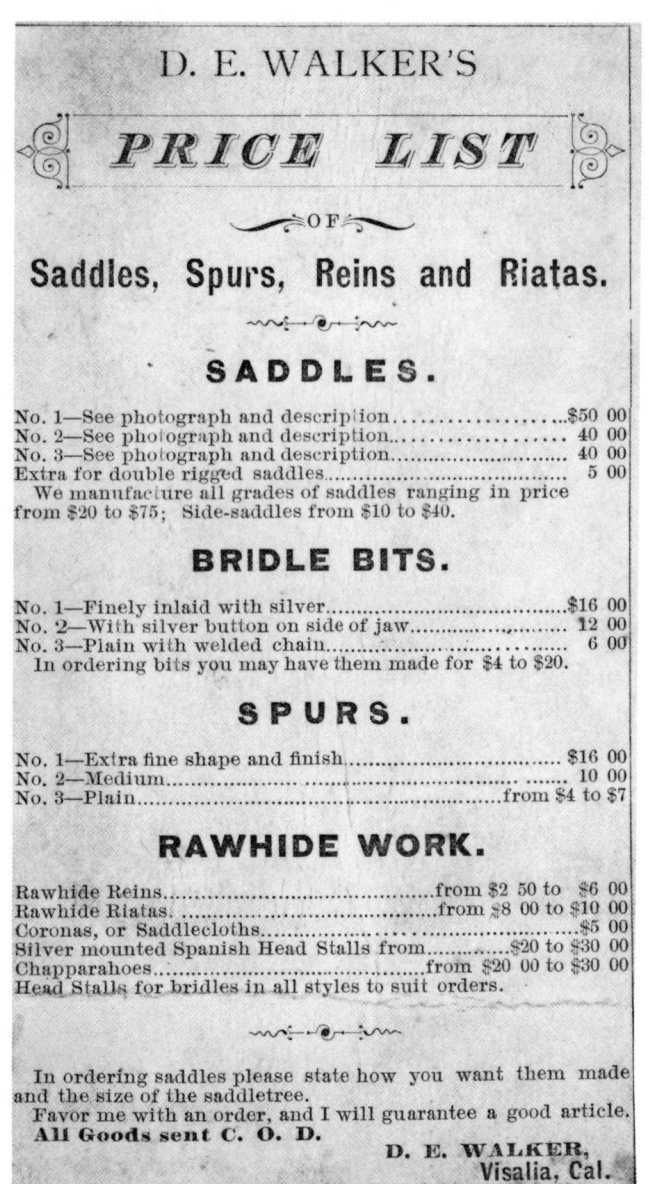
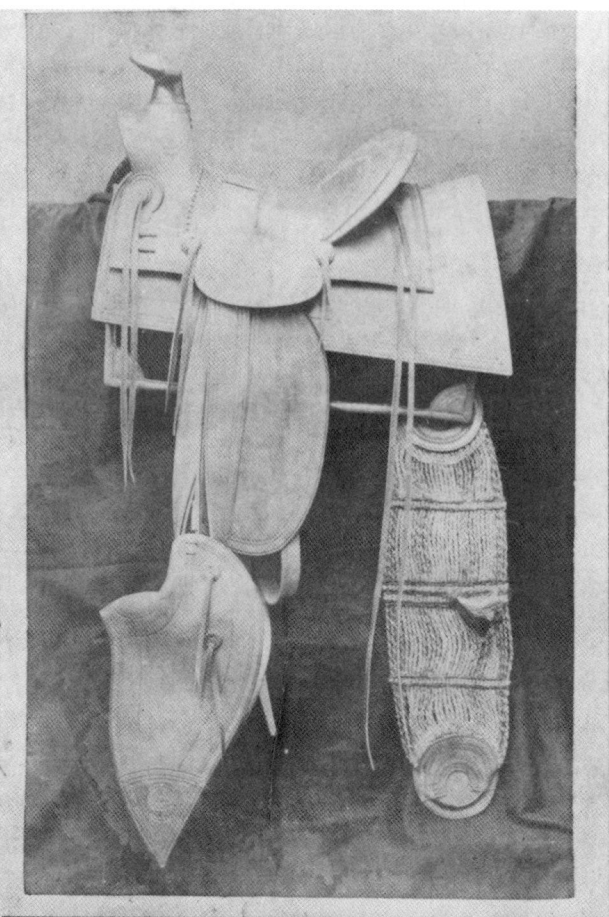

Pages from Walker's Catalogue

1. Letter from Mr. Pete Martarell to Mr. Roy Brooks of Visalia, January 25, 1960.
2. Letter from Ada Walker McCullough to author, April 18, 1948.

CHAPTER 8

ROBIN HOODS OR HOODS WHO ROBBED

Gunslingers were spawned by the Civil War. William Quantrill showed them the way. Regrettably, they will ride the range and rails forever in movies, books, and television as folk heroes. In real life they were overrated and over-publicized. Their ranks included both men and women. Many came from good families, and many were related. All of them were drifters, and most of them died young.

The citizens of Tulare County have always had respect for law and order, so it must have galled old-timers to learn that the county was used as a hiding place by notorious bad men. They all came: Murietta, Black Bart, the Mason-Henry gang, the James boys, the Dalton boys, Vasquez, Jim McKinney, and Sontag and Evans.

The James brothers invented bank holdups, train robberies, and the practice of shooting up the town to terrify the citizens. Their father, Reverend Robert James, a most respected minister, came to California during the gold rush. He died here and is buried in Marysville. The James', Youngers, Daltons, and John Ringo were all related.

Their uncle, D.W. James, was a prominent Paso Robles businessman and represented San Luis Obispo County in the State Assembly.

The James boys and their gang held up a bank in Kentucky in 1868, and another in Iowa Territory in 1873. It is not known which holdup prompted the boys to visit their uncle in California, but they came. There is rather conclusive evidence that Frank and Jesse James hid out near Cramer in southeastern Tulare County. Tradition has it that one of them was recovering from gunshot wounds. Old-time gunslingers sought anonymity, not notoriety. However, the James boys' exploits for the remainder of their lives gained them a fixed place in folk music and folklore.

The Dalton brothers were well known in Tulare County. Their father, Lewis Dalton, married Adeline Younger, daughter of Colonel Charles Younger. Like most frontiersmen, Lou Dalton worked at a number of jobs, but was best known as a buyer and seller of horses. He brought the family to California in the 1880's and settled near Fresno. Of their 15 children no one hears of Charles, Ben, Simon, Henry, or U.S. Marshal Franklin Dalton, killed in the line of duty. Neither do we hear of the girls or of Littleton, who farmed near Clovis in Fresno County. Gratton, Robert, Emmett, and William made headlines. William was probably a victim of his brothers' crimes. He married Jane Blivens, daughter of Cyrus Blivens, who farmed near Livingston in Merced County. William Dalton was a good husband and father, and a respected member of his community.

Grat, Bob, and Emmett were drifters and gamblers. When they showed up in Tulare County, they were fugitives. Their lifestyle and choice of companions were anything but exemplary. When the boys arrived, the valley people were caught up in a wave of dislike and mistrust of the Southern Pacific Railroad. The tragedy at Mussel Slough in 1880 was a constant reminder of the power that the railroad had in California. It was with mixed feelings that the people learned of the first train robbery in 1889. Their reaction was excitement and not indignation.

As the Southern Pacific train #17 pulled out of the Pixley station on February 22, 1889, two masked men climbed over the tender into the cab and ordered the engineer to stop the train two miles out of Pixley. The holdup men took the engineer and fireman as hostages to the express car. A curious passenger, Charles Gulbert, got out to see what was going on and was killed. Ed Bentley, a deputy sheriff from Modesto, realized what was happening and tried to aid the crew. He was also shot and died a few days later. The amount of money taken in the holdup was not revealed. By the time the train backed into Pixley the trail the bandits had taken toward the coast was cold. Wells Fargo Express and the railroad posted sizable rewards, and company detectives swarmed into the county.

On January 24, 1890, Train #19 was held up the same way when it was about two miles south of Goshen. Jonas Christianson, who was riding the brake beams, rolled out to see what was going on and was shot and killed. The description of the robbers fitted the two men who had held up the train outside of Pixley. One was described as about six feet tall, wearing a dark hat, brown bib overalls, and brown shoes. The other man was about five feet seven, wore a dark slouch hat and blue bib overalls. Both wore long masks with cutouts for eye-holes. Each man carried a revolver and a shotgun. It was rumored that they took $20,000 from the express car safe.

Local officers and company detectives had no definite clues to either holdup. On February 6, 1891, Train #17 was held up a couple of miles from Alila (now Earlimart). This time the bandits ran into trouble. Charles Haswell, the express man, refused to open the door and started shooting. Fireman George Radcliffe was killed in that shootout. Ironically, Haswell was tried for that murder but acquitted. For the first time, a third man was seen holding horses for the getaway. The reward money was boosted to $7,000. James Hume, Chief Detective for Wells Fargo, took over the bandit hunt. He was one of the few detectives who made a favorable impression on the citizens of Tulare and Fresno Counties.

Sheriff Kay of Tulare County and Sheriff O'Neal of Fresno County were convinced that the Daltons were involved. Circumstantial evidence was strong. The Daltons had unsavory reputations, no visible means of support, and were known to have traveled several times to Paso Robles. Grat was arrested in Fresno County and Bill in Paso Robles. Bob and Emmett hightailed it back to Oklahoma. Both sheriffs said the holdups then were solved. The Tulare County Grand Jury returned true bills against the Daltons, and trial was set for May 1891. Bill was out on bail, and later was released for lack of evidence. After deliberating 22 hours — an unusually long time — the jury convicted Grat Dalton of complicity in the Alila holdup. His lawyer filed for an appeal. The court reporter said he could not get the transcript ready for a quick appeal, so Judge Wheaton Gray set the hearing for September 21, 1891. Grat was remanded to jail, which was fortunate for him, for on September 3, 1891, the same familiar bandits held up a train pulling out of Ceres. Bill Dalton and Wiley Dean were arrested at Maggie Rucker's home near Traver. Bill was jailed in Modesto, but released for lack of evidence. He came to Visalia and was re-arrested because one of his bondsmen had defaulted. Sheriff Kay was so sure friends of the Daltons would rescue them that he had the local National Guard protect the jail.

The National Guard should have stayed longer. On September 28, 1891, Grat walked out of Tulare County's fine new escape-proof jail. Grat took two prisoners with him, W.B. Smith and John Beck. Sheriff Kay swore in a posse: George Witty, Bob Hackett, Perry Byrd, Calvin Burland and Fred Hall. They were joined by Sheriff Hensley of Fresno County and his deputy, Ed McCardle.

Grat had outside help. The reporter who wrote this account of the break was accurate, but he also wrote with tongue in cheek:

In the afternoon the prisoners are given the jail and at night they are confined to their cells. Dalton had been confined at night in an iron cell known as the tank. He had prepared a dummy on Sunday and placed it on his cot and when the jailor went on his evening tour of inspection, seeing the supposed man in bed, he concluded all was right and passed on.

Dalton is supposed to have been on top of the tank, and when nightfall lent help to his scheme, he crawled down and after liberating W.B. Smith who was convicted of burglary, and John Beck who was waiting trial for horse stealing, the trio unlocked the door, passed out, then relocked the door. Thus they left no trace and were not missed until Monday morning.

That they had an accomplice is certain, for in Bill Dalton's cell, a piece of coated wood had been inserted instead of the iron bar. A later inspection of Gratton's cell revealed that some one had provided him with a saw and he had sawed out several iron bars and replaced them with painted broomstick handles.

A team belonging to G.N. McKinley, which was tied up in front of the Methodist Church, was missing and it was supposed the prisoners took it. The team was later found in Tulare, this adds strength to the impression already existing that the fugitives are enroute to Oklahoma where the rest of the notorious gang is concealed.

Bill Dalton was still confined in his cell in the upper corridor of the jail, and kept up the spirits of the officers Monday morning by singing them songs suggestive of his brother's escape.

> They never missed my brother till he was gone
> They'll never catch him till the river runs dry.

The song was so pointed that Bill was put in a dark cell so as not to wound the feelings of the officials. The Southern Pacific Railroad Company has offered a reward of $3,000 for the return of Dalton to the Sheriff's office in Visalia.[1]

Bill Dalton was tried for complicity in the Alila holdup and murder of Haswell. It took the jury just 20 minutes to find him not guilty. As friends and relatives were congratulating him, he was re-arrested on a warrant from San Luis Obispo.

Sheriff Kay continued the hunt for Grat, Smith and Beck. It must have irked him to read in newspapers such witticisms as "Well, just who did rob the train?" or "The little wire fence placed around the jail is put there to keep Grat Dalton from getting back in again." Sheriff Kay was a good law officer. He trailed John Beck to the State of Washington, and he agreed to talk. Kay then trailed and captured W.B. Smith. What they had to say was mortifying to all valley lawmen. Grat Dalton had never left the valley. He and Wiley Dean had a well-stocked hideout in the mountains east of Centerville, in Fresno County. Sheriffs Kay and Hensley swore in a posse and staked out the camp. Dean was captured in a shootout, but Grat Dalton escaped.

By that time it was obvious that someone else had robbed the trains. If Grat had not escaped jail, he would have been acquitted. Instead he caught up with Bob and Emmett. The three were in the gang which tried to hold up two banks at Coffeeville, Kansas, on October 4, 1892. In that memorable gun battle, Grat, Bob, and three others were killed and Emmett was severely wounded.

Bill Dalton led an upright life after his release from jail, but he was jinxed by his past. He and his family were visiting in Ardmore, Oklahoma, in 1893, and he was shot by a posse who thought he was involved in a bank robbery. Later on, Emmett said Bill was not involved. Mrs. Dalton brought his body home, and Bill Dalton is buried in the old Turlock Cemetery.

Emmett miraculously survived the 23 slugs from the Coffeeville fight. His life sentence was commuted after 15 years, and he came back to southern California. He passed away in 1937 and is buried next to Bob in Coffeeville.

On August 3, 1892, the familiar bandits held up a train pulling out of Collis. They are supposed to have looted the safe of $15,000. Their names were Evans and Sontag, and they are among the valley's most famous outlaws.

Christopher Evans was a well liked and respected resident of Tulare County. At one time he said he was born in Vermont, and that his family moved to Canada. In the Great Register of Tulare County 1880, he stated that he was born in Canada and was naturalized in Oregon in 1877. He served in the Civil War and came to Visalia in 1871. Three years later he married Mary (Molly) Byrd, a member of a pioneer family. Their home in Visalia was in the 500 block of North West Street, near the home of Molly's mother. Chris was essentially an outdoors man. Like many men of that time, he worked at many jobs and moved several times. At one time or another he worked in lumber mills east of Visalia, mined, drove team, farmed, worked at loading platforms along the Southern Pacific Railroad, and was part owner of a livery stable at Modesto. Chris and Molly were to have seven children. He was a devoted husband and father, and just about as unlikely a bandit as anyone could imagine.

John and George Sontag came from Minnesota. They had taken their stepfather's name; their real name was Connant. They were not unknown to law officers in Minnesota. John came to California and worked as a brakeman for the Southern Pacific. In 1878 his foot was crushed in an accident, and he spent many weeks in the hospital. He asked for lighter work, but was told he would have to take his old job or quit entirely. The incident made him bitter toward the railroad for what he felt was unjust treatment.

Chris Evans spent some months working at the Pixley warehouse. He had plenty of time to study train schedules, and there he met John Sontag. Their first three holdups were about a year apart, which gave the men plenty of time to plan and also go about their regular work.

The bandits followed an almost exact method in the first three holdups. When the train was several miles from the station, two masked men crawled over the tender into the cab. After the train ground to a stop, the engineer and fireman had to go to the express car where the bandits threatened to shoot them if the expressman did not throw out the valuable freight. The bandits made their hostages puff cigars. That weird request was explained later on. It was a signal to the man or men holding the getaway horses.

Rewards posted by the railroad and express companies had run into a considerable sum by 1891. By the time the blood hunt was over, railroad detectives, express company detectives, U.S. Marshals, and Pinkerton men, as well as lawmen from two counties, were after the bandits. Two Apache trackers, Pelon and Jerico, were brought in to trail the bandits. Big city newspapers sent in top reporters. For four years Evans and Sontag were probably never more than 50 miles from Visalia. They were in the Evans house many times, and once spent a holiday season with Chris' family. It is almost unbelievable that they were not betrayed,

Chris Evans (From *Evans and Sontag,* Hu Maxwell, 1893)

especially with a small fortune in reward money as a lure.

After the holdup at Pixley, Evans and Sontag went to Modesto and bought a livery stable for $5,000. Chris moved his family to Modesto. In January 1891 the stable burned, 20 horses were killed and the stable boy died from burns. A month later the train was robbed at Alila.

It would be interesting to know what excuse Chris Evans used when he left Visalia in June 1891. He showed up in Mankato, Minnesota to visit George Sontag using the alias Charles Naughton instead of his own name. In a few days John Sontag arrived. On July 2, 1891 a train was held up at Kasota, Minnesota. The method and the description of the bandits was most familiar. Chris and John came back to Modesto and moved the Evans family back to Visalia. Either they needed money or they felt they were immune from detection, for they held up and robbed Train #19 a few miles from Ceres on September 3, 1891.

On November 12, 1891 a train out of Western Union Junction, Minnesota was held up. The description of the men tallied. The Sontags were definitely involved, but Chris would not admit complicity later on. It is certain that the next holdup was planned in Mankato. As Train #17 pulled out of Collis (Kerman) on the night of August 3, 1892, two masked men held up the crew and proceeded as usual. This time the expressman refused to open the door, and the bandits dynamited the car. Estimates of the loot varied. Unfortunately for the bandits, much of the gold coin was Peruvian money.

Wells Fargo agents had been following George Sontag, and John and Chris were under suspicion. This bulletin was sent out by the American Express Company:

WANTED FOR TRAIN ROBBERY
AT COLLIS, CALIFORNIA — AUGUST 3, 1892

JOHN SONTAG (alias John Connant) native of Mankato, Minnesota; age 33 years; height 5 feet eleven; weight 165 pounds; even cut features; fair complexioned; prominent cheek bones; rather good looking; hair dark and moustache medium and dark; lame in left ankle; when last seen wore dark felt hat, dark coat and vest, cut away style, dark pants, light colored shirt.

CHRISTOPHER EVANS (alias Charles Naughton) native of Canada, of Welsh and Irish descent; aged 45; height 5 feet eight or ten inches; weight about 160 pounds; sandy complexion; sandy or light hair, beard and moustache rather dark and sandy; blue eyes; large bony hands; has a spring in both knees when walking; walks rather fast; when talking grins and smiles; moves his head sideways from shoulder to shoulder; has a slouching appearance; when talking any length of time has a slight Irish accent and droops or squints his left eye; has shrill speaking voice. When last seen wore dark grey, square checked sack suit. Has a wife and family at Visalia, California.[2]

George Sontag drank too much and talked too much. He was followed from Mankato to Fresno in July, 1892, and after the Collis holdup was trailed from Fresno to Visalia. Detective Will Smith and Deputy Sheriff George Witty arrested him in a Visalia saloon for complicity in the Collis robbery. They hired a dray to drive to the Evans house, where George said he had stored his trunk. At the time local officers had not been informed that either John Sontag or Chris Evans were under suspicion. In retrospect, there was little cooperation between outside agencies and local officials. It is also hindsight to say that the local sheriffs could have picked up the bandits when they stopped blaming the Daltons.

As Smith and Witty approached the Evans house, they saw John Sontag go in the back door so they decided to talk to him about his brother. Eva

Evans, who was then engaged to John, answered the door. She said neither her father nor her brother were at home. Will Smith, an excitable, pompous, publicity seeker, ran to one side of the room, pulled aside a curtain and found John, who started shooting. So did Evans, who later said Smith had cursed Eva. Later Eva said she had not known her father or John were in the house. Evans apparently aimed at Smith, but in the small room his shot wounded Witty. Smith ran out of the house. He bragged later that he vaulted the fence, but a witness testified that the terrified Smith ran so hard that he smashed the picket fence. He jumped into the dray and left the wounded deputy. To his credit, however, he notified Sheriff Kay.

Sontag and Evans escaped in a buggy. They had no time to take supplies, so officers staked out the area and waited for them to return at night. They came back so quietly that only Oscar Beaver heard them. Along with other men, he had offered to help and had been deputized. Beaver was lying in high grass. He called out, asking for identification. His answer was bullets. In a running gun battle, Beaver was mortally wounded.

Chris and John were trailed into the swamps east of Visalia and then into the mountains, where the trail was lost. Chris had lived in Redwood Canyon, worked in the lumber mills, and mined in the area. He was familiar with trails, springs, and places to seek cover. He had friends and relatives in the mountains who willingly and unwillingly provided food and shelter. As the search went into weeks and then months, law officers were harshly criticized in city newspapers. Valley newspapers were more fair because local reporters knew the difficulties under which the lawmen worked. After Evans was captured he said he could have shot local officers many times as they passed him in the brush. He remarked to one startled officer, "I could have slapped you with my hat, you were that close to me." Evans' friends and relatives were naturally apprehensive, but as time went on they suffered more from the antics of blood money hunters who were after the reward money.

Tulare County officers were still smarting from Grat Dalton's escape from the new County Jail, so George Sontag was carefully guarded. Nevertheless, someone smuggled in a sharp tool of some sort, and George started to cut a hole in the cell ceiling which was discovered before he finished it.

Mrs. Evans and the children were harrassed by out-of-town detectives. One evening a contingent went to the barn and began to dig. They said they found two sacks of Peruvian coins as well as the

Encounter at the Evans home. (From *Evans and Sontag,* Hu Maxwell, 1893)

material from which the robbers' masks had been made. The outside officers were so thoroughly disliked that many Visalians were convinced they had planted both the money and material. That tenet was defendable. It would not seem likely that Evans and Sontag, who had eluded officers since 1889, would come back to Visalia and bury such items in the Evans' barn.

When George Sontag was questioned, he talked and talked. He blamed Chris and John. He said he confessed because his aged mother, who came to help him, was not treated well by Mrs. Evans. George was tried and convicted of complicity in the Collis holdup and received a life sentence, to be served at Folsom Prison.

The evidence that convicted him showed how carefully the holdups were planned. George was probably in California in 1889, but would only admit to a visit in 1890. He testified that he first met Chris Evans as Charles Naughton in Mankato, Minnesota, in 1891. Evans posed as a fruit buyer. Special agents who trailed George said he left Mankato July 7, 1892 for Fresno. He registered at a Fresno hotel on July 14th. Three days later he went to Visalia to look up his luggage, stored at the Evans house. He returned the next day, getting off the train at Mendota instead of Fresno. Two days later he took a southbound train, got off at Reedley, and took a stage for Dunlap. There he met Chris. On August 1st they left the mountains. Chris walked and George rode horseback to Visalia to meet John Sontag. John Sontag rented a rig at Bequette's Stable on August 2nd, making sure the hosteler knew that he was going to the mountains to pick up Chris Evans. Instead he picked up George at the Evans house and drove to Fresno. The three men stayed in George's hotel room that night. The next day they robbed the train at Collis.

Mr. Hickey, a special agent, picked up their trail at Collis. He found that two men had walked through a plowed field to a two-horse wagon hidden behind a schoolhouse. He then traced the wagon into Fresno, and learned that John Sontag had rented the wagon and taken it out the night of the holdup. The prosecution showed that the team could have been driven from the holdup into Fresno in 30 minutes. John and Chris Evans drove the Bequette team back to Visalia at daybreak. George came to Visalia on the train, went to a saloon, talked about the holdup, and showed items that he said he had picked up at the scene. The evidence that convicted George Sontag implicated Chris and John. They were known to be in the mountains east of Visalia. In September they showed up at the ranch of S.L.N. Ellis, who knew them well. They stayed for supper and demanded a team. The Ellis family had been reluctant hosts, and sent word to Sheriff Kay as soon as the men left.

On September 14, 1892, a posse accompanied by the two Apache trackers surprised Evans and Sontag at Young's cabin located on Sampson's Flat in the foothills. Actually the posse was more surprised than the bandits, and it is a wonder that more men were not shot. When the posse rode toward the cabin, two men ran out shooting. Victor Wilson, a Wells Fargo agent from Arizona, and Deputy Sheriff Andrew McGinnis from Modesto were killed, and Deputy Al Witty from Modesto was wounded. The bandits escaped. The shootout created a lot of excitement, especially in San Francisco. Two of the many reporters who came to Tulare County, Ambrose Bierce and Joaquin Miller, were famous. Miller announced in his reports that he had trailed and interviewed Evans and Sontag, but local men said he wrote the interview in the safety of a Visalia saloon.

After the Sampson Flat shooting the reward money reached $10,000, which was a fortune at the time. The mountains were criss-crossed by real and would-be detectives. People who lived on ranches were almost afraid to do their chores or ride after cattle because of the trigger-happy sleuths.

As a matter of record, it was found later that Chris and John had been in Visalia several times so Chris could see his family. Sometimes they stayed several days. In April 1893 they were recognized but eluded the officers. A few days later they held up the Badger stage. When they were convinced that Detective Will Smith was not a passenger they told the driver and passengers to go on. They even visited Sequoia Mill, ate dinner with the crew, and watched them work.

On June 15, 1893, their luck ran out at Stone Corral (near Orosi). John Sontag wanted to go to Mexico, but Evans felt he was safer in the mountains and did not want to leave his family. They split what money they had and started down the mountains. They were seen on the way, and word was sent to the officers. U.S. Marshal George Gard was in Visalia, and quickly organized a posse. The posse staked out a cabin at Stone Corral. Toward dusk Evans and Sontag crept out of their hiding place to get to the cabin. The posse started shooting, and the bandits ran toward a haystack. Chris was hit, but the shooting went on for about an hour. Later Chris told what had happened. Though he had been hit, he managed to keep on shooting. John was mortally wounded and begged Chris to shoot him and get away. When darkness came, Chris made John as comfortable as possible and then slipped away. Fred Jackson, a posse member, was wounded and, as he was carried to a wagon, John fired a final shot in an effort to kill himself. He was found semi-conscious at daybreak. He was taken to the Tulare County Jail and received medical attention, but for his own safety was taken to Fresno, where he died on July 6, 1893 at the age of 33.

George Sontag was in the Folsom Hospital. In a complicated plot, hatched in Visalia, guns were smuggled to him. He tried to shoot his way out of prison, but he was shot and his companions were killed. George Sontag was to be a cripple for the rest of his life.

After Chris Evans left Stone Corral he went up Wilcox Canyon to the Elijah Perkins ranch. (The Perkins family was related to Molly Evans.) Evans washed his wounds at the pump and entered the house so quietly that he was not discovered until someone saw the bloodied pump. Chris was a pitiful sight. His left arm was shattered, he had a deep head wound, and one eye was almost gone. He was weak from loss of blood, and thin from lack of food. He was still defiant, but the family talked him into surrendering. He agreed only after exacting a promise that Molly would get the reward money. The disposition of that money is another story, but Molly Evans never saw any of it. The officers did not take Evans to Visalia until evening in order to avoid the crowds that had milled around John Sontag. After medical treatment, Chris Evans was also taken to the Fresno County Jail.

Concurrently, Eva Evans and her mother were starring in a San Francisco theater in "The Great Collis Train Robbery," a corny, hastily written melodrama. The women had little talent but drew big crowds for the newspapers had a field day with the Southern Pacific Bandits.

Evans and Sontag had operated from 1889 until 1893. They held up five trains in California and two in Minnesota. Seven men were killed and eight were wounded. The total amount taken was never disclosed, but it probably was much less than the sensational publicity said it was. Unfortunately, the imprisonment of George, the death of John, and the capture of Chris Evans did not finish the story.

Doctors had amputated Evans' arm and he had lost an eye, but he recovered enough to be arraigned. At the time it was customary for meals to be brought into the Fresno Jail. Prisoners were allowed to eat in the corridor facing their cells. On December 28, 1893, Mrs. Evans was visiting Chris and was still there at 5:30 when Ed Morrell brought in the meal. Ed Morrell was a waiter whose real name was Ed Martin. He had a prison record and had made a hero out of Chris Evans. Along with the food he had brought two pistols. When the jailer opened the door to let Morrell out, he was taken hostage by Ed and Chris.

The events that followed were unbelievable. Mrs. Evans was on the floor in a dead faint. The jailers were yelling. Ed and Chris, walking down the street outside the jail, met S.H. Cole, one-time mayor of Fresno, and used him as a second hostage. Apparently Ed Morrell had made no plans for a getaway. The men saw a rig down the street, and as they started for it, they met City Marshal J.D. Morgan, who fired at them. He missed, but Chris wounded him. A newsboy was delivering papers from a cart, and the desperados grabbed the horse and cart and headed for Centerville. The horse and cart were abandoned at Sanger. Mrs. Evans was arrested but later released, since she had no knowledge of the bizarre breakout.

No one saw the escapees from December until February, although it was known that they were back in Evans' familiar territory and were getting supplies. Eva later said she delivered many of the things they needed. On February 8th two detectives, walking a trail near Badger, saw Chris, but he got away. The next day their abandoned camp was found near Badger. It was easy to trail them in the snow. When officers surrounded the second camp they heard men talking, but an elaborate alarm system gave them time to fade into the brush. Chris

At Stone Corral - the last battle. (From *Evans and Sontag,* Hu Maxwell, 1893)

left so suddenly that his artificial arm was still in the brush tent.

Later in the month, Sheriff Kay received a tip that Chris and Ed were in the Evans home in Visalia. Mrs. Evans and Eva were acting in San Francisco, and a Mr. and Mrs. J.V. Brighton were taking care of the younger children. Many people later believed that the Brightons were also being paid by one of the investigating agencies, and that the anonymous tip came from them.

U.S. Marshal Gard was notified, and all of the streets around the Evans house were blocked by deputies. In spite of previous shootings a crowd began to gather. The people were not in an ugly mood; they sensed that time had run out for Chris Evans. Sheriff Kay wrote a note to Chris Evans. Joe Evans, the youngest child, brought an answer to Sheriff Kay.

Chris had written: "Sheriff Kay; Dear Sir, Come into the house, I want to talk to you. I will not harm you. My little boy will come back with you."

Sheriff Kay sent Joe Evans back with his reply. "Mr. Evans, you have a chance to surrender. Surrender now and you will not be hurt. If you give up to me, I will protect you and the law will take its

John Sontag at Stone Corral. Members of the four-man posse were Sheriff Hi Rapelji (second from left), U.S. Marshal George Gard (third from right), Detective Tom Burns (fourth from right), and Deputy Sheriff George Witty (fourth from left). The other men are local citizens or reporters.

course. I will disperse this mob if you say, and meet you."

Joe Evans came back with the last note. "Sheriff Kay, Dear Sir, Send the crowd away and bring Hall [a deputy] with you to the gate and we will talk. I will not harm you. You are the Sheriff of this County and I am willing to make terms with you but with no one else. I will step out on the porch when you come to the gate. Yours, Chris Evans."

Kay got rid of the crowd and went to the gate. Chris and Ed Morrell came out and the men shook hands. Evans kissed each of his children. Once again, for their safety, both men were taken to the Fresno County Jail.

Evans was tried for the murders of Wilson and McGinnis and received a life sentence. Morrell was tried for robbery, and he too received a life sentence. He was released after 19 years and spent the rest of his life lecturing on the topic "Crime Does Not Pay." He also wrote a book, *The 25th Man*. George Sontag was later released and spent his time warning the younger generation that the way of the transgressor is hard.

The Evans family moved to Oregon. Chris was paroled in 1915 and lived with his family in Oregon until his death in 1918.

Evans was not tried for train robbery, and so the true story of the holdups was not revealed under oath. Other people had to be involved. Strong but circumstantial evidence leads to speculation how the loose ends of the holdups may be resolved. First, eliminate the railroad as a cause. Although Sontag did not feel he had received just compensation for his accident, the bandits had no more reason to hate the railroad than other people who did not turn into criminals. Chris and John were more often cold, hungry, and hunted than harbored and fed by sympathizers. One nagging question that will always go unanswered is, "With a price on their heads, why didn't someone turn them in?"

There is more than idle speculation to link Chris Evans with the Daltons. When Emmett thought he was dying at Coffeeville, he said Grat and Bill Dalton were involved in the Alila holdup. After he recovered, he denied it. It was significant that the railroad and the express companies did not list Alila in the reward posters for Evans and Sontag. Contemporaries believed it was Chris Evans who helped Grat Dalton break jail.

A strong link in the circumstantial evidence concerned Chris Evans' twin brother Tom. He may be the secret Chris did not want to reveal. Tom Evans and his family stayed at the Redwood Canyon Ranch with Chris and Molly from 1873 to 1875. He worked at the mills, mined, and hunted. In 1875 Tom supposedly took his family back to Canada. In the stories that came out of Coffeeville immediately after the shootout, Tom Evans was listed as one of the dead holdup men. Emmett Dalton said the man was Tom Evans. Then he was identified as Bill Powers, about whom nothing was known. *The Visalia Delta* used the name Tom Evans. Who would have identified *that* Tom Evans as the family man who lived in Redwood Canyon? If Tom Evans rode with the Daltons, and there is suspicion that he did, it might account for their presence in Tulare County. It may be only coincidence but Chris Evans, the James brothers, the Dalton brothers and Tom Evans all came to the area within a short time span. The timing also suggests that these men did not rob trains to right wrongs.

People in the county must have been pleased to have an end to the publicity involving the famous bandits. However, they had not seen the last train holdup.

In March 1896 Sheriff A.P. Merritt received a tip that the northbound Southern Pacific train would be robbed somewhere between Tulare and Goshen. He swore in a posse and sent them out of town, one by one to avoid any slipup. Deputies Earl Daggestt and G.V. Reed decided to take the southbound train from Goshen to Tulare just in case directions were wrong. They got on the coal car, just behind the locomotive. It was cold, and they had barely made themselves comfortable when a masked man crawled up from the tender and started shooting. Both deputies were wounded but managed to blast the bandit off the train. The posse later found the body of a man identified as Dan McCall near the tracks. The robbery had been planned by amateurs in Si Loverin's saloon in Visalia. That saloon was a sore spot to Visalians because of the nightly fights and other sordid activities there. The men who planned the robbery were McCall, Loverin, Charles Ardell, a man named Britt, and the bartender known as the Missouri Kid. They planned to flag down the train with a lantern wrapped in red cloth and then rob the expressman. At the last minute only McCall and Britt showed up, and Britt did not get on the train. At the trial Ardell was acquitted. By that time Britt had disappeared and McCall was dead. The Missouri Kid was not charged with the holdup. In a sensational aftermath, Loverin was convicted of complicity by furnishing the guns and the red cloth. He spent years in San Quentin, and when released came back to Visalia, where he died in 1937.

The last train holdup netted its perpetrators $80,000. It was both bizarre and unbelievable. A group of men were sitting in Harry Burke's saloon in Traver when one said, "If I was going to rob a train this is what I would do." A few days later the Southern Pacific train from Goshen was held up in the way he had described. Two men stopped the train at Cross Creek, four miles south of Traver. The crew was forced to uncouple some cars and move them across the bridge. Accomplices were waiting by the baggage car. The expressman refused to open the door, so the robbers dynamited the express car. The expressman convinced them that the safe had a time lock, so that was dynamited too. The express car was completely wrecked. Baggage, mail, and silver money were scattered along the right-of-way. A rancher who lived nearby rode over to see what was going on. He recognized some fellow citizens and a few days later accused one of them. After he was threatened, however, he decided not to talk. It was said that for a few days after the robbery there were more twenty-dollar gold pieces in circulation in Traver than ever before or since. A few men were suddenly able to pay their mortgages. Traver stores did a bustling business. The robbers could have been identified the morning after, but no one offered to name them, and the mystery was never solved.

The early train robbers were by-products of the Civil War. Their exploits had a certain picaresque quality. Some people regarded them as Robin Hoods, but actually, in today's slang, they were hoods who robbed. The folklore that grew up around them passed lightly over the fact that they shot to kill.

There were other men and women whose crimes produced newspaper coverage instead of folklore. Law-abiding Tulare County played unwilling host to many of those dubious outlaws. Three typical bad men were Tiburcio Vasquez, Jim McCrory, and Jim McKinney.

Tiburcio Vasquez' forebears came to California with Captain Juan de Anza. They were respected residents of Monterey, where Tiburcio was born in 1839. He was the family "black sheep" and grew up interested in females, fandangos, and fighting. He began his criminal career at the age of 14, and from 1852 until he was hanged in 1875, he terrorized California with a series of brutal murders, raids, and robberies. He made many unannounced visits to Tulare County. He was easily identified because he rode a white stallion. His hideout was Spanish Camp in Yokohl Valley, and he spent many an evening in Visalia's rowdy red light district.

One of his most publicized raids was made in Kingston, then in Tulare County.

Kingston was a busy trading village which had grown up around Whitmore's Ferry on the Kings River. Just at dusk on Christmas Eve, 1873, Vasquez and his gang galloped over the bridge, shooting and yelling. They robbed 35 men and looted the hotel and the three general stores, taking about $2,500 in cash as well as anything of value carried by their victims. The surprise attack was not all one-sided as we see it through the eyes of one of the victims. Not everyone was in the hotel or stores. Vasquez gave the signal to leave before the whole town was aroused.

In the meantime the Negro who had escaped from Reichart's Hotel had given the alarm and three young men, Pres Bozeman Jr., Bob Scronce, and John Sutherland armed themselves and took up a position near the bank of the river. As all men carried revolvers in those days, it was not difficult to become ready for a fray in short order...the three young men near the river opened fire upon the Mexicans, which was returned by those outside, and also by the guard left on the west side of the river. In the hurry to leave Sweet's store, the bandits overlooked some gold watches in the safe.

The next morning a party was organized and started in pursuit of the Mexicans. They went to a town called Liberty inhabited by Mexicans, who lived mainly in dugouts, five or six miles west of Kingston. They made a search of the place but found no one there. They found blood on the bridge across Kings River, and later it was reported from other sources that Chavez, who ranked next to Vasquez, had been shot in the thigh. In the dark I was unable to tell how many men Vasquez had with him, but it was thought there must have been fifteen to twenty in the party, as they had the town well guarded.[3]

Vasquez eluded the officers, but his career was drawing to a close. He was captured in Los Angeles, tried, and hanged at San Jose on March 18, 1875.

Tulare County has had only two known lynchings. The first was a multiple lynching of Indians who murdered Mrs. Jessie Bonsall and her two babies near Plano in 1870.

The second lynching took place in Visalia on Christmas Eve, 1872. It was sordidly spectacular and was directed as much toward the bawdy red light district as toward its victim.

Shooting scrapes and fist-fights were not unknown in the "good old days." Living conditions were short of conveniences, men wore knives or revolvers, liquor was plentiful, and tempers often flared over trivial affairs. The tenderloin only intensified those factors. At one time the editor of the *Visalia Delta* was so annoyed that he wrote, "If you have to shoot somebody, do it at home. I am tired of walking down the street sideways."[4]

James McCrory came to Tulare County from Mariposa County before 1867, but the first record of his appearance in Visalia was in that year, when he leased the El Dorado Saloon. He was also deputized as a constable for the Township of Visalia. It was in that capacity that he aided Constable John Williams when the two shot John Schipe, the claimant of a fabulously rich gold mine. The secret of the mine died with Schipe, but prospectors are still hunting its location a century after the shooting.

McCrory, unlike many bartenders, was a heavy drinker. He was an inveterate gambler and had a violent temper. In 1870 he wounded a fellow player in a crap game. A few months later he went to the Fashion Saloon and killed Manuel Barcla in a drunken rage. He was jailed, but then some of his friends smuggled in a dozen hacksaws. A short time before, several prisoners had carved their way out of the old jail with jackknives, so it was to Jim's credit that he did not use the hacksaws. He was tried and sentenced to prison for 15 years. His lawyer appealed, and McCrory was set free on a legal technicality. He left for Arizona, where he killed another man.

Visalia did not see him again until December 24, 1872, when he got off the Goshen Stage stone sober. He went to the El Dorado Saloon and borrowed money from his friend, George Allen. He came back in the evening fighting drunk. The bartender refused to serve him. Jim pulled out his pistol, intending to shoot the bartender, but killed George Allen instead.

The community had had murders before, but this time the citizens must have been fed up with the denizens of the saloons and the tenderloin. McCrory was taken to jail, and the Constable deputized 15 men to guard him. They were no match for the crowd that gathered, armed with guns, knives, ropes, crowbars and a long iron pipe. The door was battered down and McCrory was dragged out and hung over the Court Street Bridge railing. One reporter penned a vivid account which stated that the mob was composed of "our most influential businessmen." That was most unlikely, for that same evening Visalians were dedicating their new $30,000 schoolhouse with a community dinner and entertainment by the children. The perpetrators were probably inhabitants of the "other side of the tracks" who had been ushering in the holiday season in the saloons.

The lynching had an interesting aftermath. The spectators sobered up enough to take up a collection in order to provide McCrory with a decent burial. The editor of the *Delta* commented, "We are opposed to mob law, but the case we have chronicled, was assuredly the quickest, cheapest, and the best way of accomplishing the desired end."[5] Very quietly, Tulare County's one and only vigilante committee was organized.

After the San Francisco Vigilante Committee disbanded, meetings had been held around the state to discuss formation of local vigilante groups. Men in Tulare County believed that duly elected officers should and could keep law and order. So did men in Mariposa County. One of the men who had signed such a statement in Mariposa was James McCrory.

On January 1, 1873, Simon Sweet, Wiley Coughran, John F. Smith, Alfred Balaam, Francis Balaam, and Edwin Balaam, all substantial and respected men, organized The Committee on Public Safety. Handbills carried this message:

We bind ourselves together and agree to aid each other in the maintenance of public peace and order, and in the full and just execution of the law, upon every violation thereof, without fear or favor, and we further hereby covenant and agree with each other, that we will personally and together exert ourselves in every proper way to the end that no criminal in Tulare County shall hereafter escape the punishment due his crime. And in furtherance of the same, we agree to meet together at Visalia at 7 o'clock P.M. on January 8th, 1873 to perfect an organization of vigilance, and to elect officers for such an organization, and to establish regulations thereof.

James McKinney was born in 1861 in Illinois to respectable, hard-working parents. There were four boys in the family — Jim, Matt, Ed, and Jake. The aftermath of the Civil War made it necessary for men like Andrew McKinney to move about in order to find work to support a family. In 1878 the family moved to Leadville, a place not famed for the sanctimonious conduct of its citizens. A couple of years later the family moved to Farmersville, California, and Andrew went to work at the W.G. Pennebaker ranch.

There is no doubt that Jim had been in trouble in Leadville. He wore expensive, fancy guns. His favorite was a bone-handled six-shooter. More than once he said men were looking for him. He spent much time practicing with the guns and was rated an expert shot.

The younger boys went to Union and then Locust Grove Schools. It was at the latter school that Jim knifed an opponent during a fight. The episode caused more excitement than the school program which the McKinneys were attending.

Like Chris Evans, Jim McKinney's appearance was deceiving. He was of medium height, had blue

Jim McKinney, standing, and Julian Scott. This picture was taken about 1888 before Jim started his criminal career. Scott was not involved with McKinney's crimes.

eyes and dark hair. Like Chris, he had a host of friends. However, when he was drinking, his mild-mannered, friendly disposition changed to a mean, coarse, cruel personality.

In 1886 the McKinney family moved to Porterville. By that time Jim was a drifter who worked as little as possible. His habitat was the tenderloin districts in Porterville, Visalia, Traver, and especially Bakersfield. Booze, gambling, pimping, and soliciting kept those districts going. In Merced, Jim met Al Hulse and Robert McFarlane, who were his companions until he was killed.

In 1889 McKinney was arrested for assault with a deadly weapon after a shooting spree in Porterville. McFarlane was already in the County Jail when Jim was booked. Friends helped them escape. They were trailed to Merced, where they had taken an eastbound train. Nothing more was heard of the pair until 1890, when Tulare County Sheriff Daniel Overall received a tip that Jim was in Cheyenne, Wyoming. He was arrested there, extradited to Tulare County and tried. He was sentenced to San

Quentin for seven years. Upon his release he drifted through his former haunts. He had little visible means of support, but it was during that time that he and his brother Ed were hired as shotgun men. Irrigation was rapidly making it possible to make a living from small farms. Most of the small farmers were stockholders in irrigation ditch companies. There was no trouble until dry years; then farmers tore down headgates and smashed diversion dams. The Pioneer Ditch Company of Porterville, along with other companies, hired shotgun men to patrol the irrigation ditches.

In December 1900 Jim and his friend Thomas (Long Red) Sears were on a prolonged drinking spree in Bakersfield. One evening they started an argument and fired at each other. The fight adjourned to an alley, and Sears got down on his knees, opened his coat and invited Jim to shoot him. Jim drilled him through the heart. There was no gun near Sears' body when police arrived, but McKinney pleaded self-defense. He was acquitted because the witnesses were as drunk as the participants, and contradicted each other in their testimony.

Jim had a lady friend in Porterville, and he began to spend more time there. People were fed up with notorious bandits, red light districts, and saloon rows. Reform movements sprang up to rid communities of such sordid spots. When Porterville incorporated in 1902, the officials started to clean up the town. Men Like McKinney quickly developed a strong dislike for Marshal John Howell and his deputy, John Willis.

On the night of July 27, 1902, Jim McKinney gave the newspapers of the state plenty of copy. He and his friend Scotty Caldwerwood were refreshing themselves at the Mint Saloon, where Jim worked off and on. Jim livened up the proceedings by firing a couple of bullets. Then he went outside, where he did more shooting. Scotty joined him, and they went on to the chophouse where Scotty worked. Jim decided to give an exhibition of trick shots. He shot the blades from a fan, the bottles on the bar, and through the window into the card room. He explained to bystanders that he was only trying to shoot the spots off the cards the men held. Scotty tried to help, but couldn't get his revolver out of its holster. Jim was having a good time, shooting and yelling that the drunker he got the better he could shoot. His audience did not stay around to find out.

Marshal Willis, Constable W.T. Tompkins, and William Lyon, a railroad employee, arrived. Jim started running, reloading his pistol as he fled. Marshal Willis shot him in the leg, but was himself badly wounded. McKinney eluded the men and made it home. He took a rifle and a shotgun and went back. Two friends, William Linn and Clint Kelly, were on the way to Jim's house to try to calm him down. When he saw them he killed Linn but missed Kelly. People were out on the streets, trying to find out what was going on. In the confusion, McKinney ran to the Arlington Stable and forced the hostelers at gunpoint to harness a team. Once in the buggy, he raced down Main Street, shooting all the way. He wounded George Barron and W.B. West. He drove on to the home of Dave Mosier and said, "Dave, I've got into a hell of a mess. They came after me; I whipped them all. I killed three or four of them. I've hurt one or two pretty bad. They have not treated me right." He asked Mosier for money, and gave him a key to a saloon safe where he had $100. He was in pain from the shot in his leg. As he left he told Mosier, "I'll die game. Tracy won't be in it with me." (Tracy was an outlaw later shot in Spokane.)

On the way out of Porterville he met Dr. J.L. Hardeman, who had been called to treat the wounded men. At gunpoint he made the doctor dress his leg wound. All the time he was ranting about his bad treatment in Porterville. Trying a bit of psychology, the doctor said, "Jim, how is your mother?" Jim was devoted to his mother and immediately quieted down. He let the doctor go if he promised to tell Mrs. McKinney what had happened.

Jim left the buggy at Lemon Cove. According to reports, he was seen in many parts of the state. Local officers believed he was still in Tulare County, and they were right. Like Chris Evans, he had many friends who willingly and unwillingly helped him. He had worked his way to White River and hid in the Mitchell barn to recuperate from his leg injury. Friends and relatives sent food and supplies to him through a friendly stage driver. After he was well enough to travel, friends helped him over the mountains and into Arizona. A sizeable price was offered for his capture. He drifted down into Mexico, and then went to Cedar, Arizona, and worked in that mining camp. It was near Cedar that he ambushed Charles Blakely and Roy Winchester and callously murdered them. A posse started trailing him across the desert, and were not far behind Jim when he was killed in Bakersfield.

On April 19, 1903, Bakersfield officers received a tip that McKinney was hiding in a Chinese joss house. The information came from Al Hulse, who had talked too much in a saloon. Officers gathered from Bakersfield, Tulare, and Kern Counties, surrounded the joss house and, in typical western

THE PORTERVILLE ENTERPRISE—PIONEER PAPER, ESTABLISHED 1888–

A CANDIDATE FOR GALLOWS

"Jim" McKinney Runs Amuck, Shoots Five Men and Decamps.

W. G. LYNN, ONE OF HIS VICTIMS, DIES.

Now at Large—Posses in Pursuit—Still Thought to be in Tulare County—Latest Developments.

Befuddled with liquor, aggravated by the thought that sooner or later law and order, which had already caught in its meshes others of his ilk, since the town of Porterville had become incorporated, would soon have him in its grasp, incensed against the officers who had performed their duty, and knowing that he would have to give up his evil ways or leave for some other town more congenial to his acts, the "brute" which had been smoldering in ex-convict "Jim" McKinney broke out in all its hideousness Sunday morning last.

Knowing the character of this outlaw, it was not the unexpected that happened, but that his acts should result as they did is a calamity that the community deeply deplores, and has made our officers even firmer determined to clear the town of any and all that are not law-abiding citizens, and who in any way shirk an honest way of gaining a livelihood.

A WASTED LIFE.

In November, 1—, James McKinney had trouble with — James Carter, a then partner in the — business ? Frank Jersey, in their saloon on Main street. He drew his gun on him, pulled the trigger three times, the gun fortunately snapping. Constable Mike Rady was on hand and arrested him. He was charged with simple assault. Whilst awaiting his examination he mixed up in another row in the same saloon with Lee Wren, hitting him over the head with his gun, knocking him insensible. He was charged with assault with a deadly weapon. He made good his escape from the Visalia jail on November 26, 1889, with one Bob McFarland, but was captured two months later at Rawlins, Wyoming. He was tried and convicted and given five years for breaking jail, two years for the assault on Lee Wren and fined for attempting to shoot Tap Carter. His behavior during the incarceration at San Quentin being good, after serving about five years he was released and returned to Porterville. He seemed to have repented of his evil ways, but never did any actual labor outside of guarding the dam of the Pioneer Water Company during the low water season, to prevent other ditch companies from appropriating the water the company was entitled to. Knowing the character of the man, he was not interfered with, and the purpose of the company was a success. At Bakersfield on December 14, 1900, he shot and killed, in the rear of a saloon, his gambling partner, Thomas Sears. He put in a plea of self defense and was acquitted. He then went to Randsburg, and returned to Porterville about a year ago, when he consorted with a woman of the right arm and lodging in a coffee-pot in the chop-house. A second shot from McKinney's revolver catches Tompkins in the arm. McKinney's revolver then snaps and he commences to run. "We've got him now," says Willis. "Come on, boys," and starts in pursuit. Up to this time Howell and Lyons had emptied their revolvers; Tompkins had shot one, shot and Willis three. Tompkins follows up, shooting two shots as McKinney ran across Main street. Willis comes up with McKinney at the corner of the Palace Hotel and fires his last two shots. Now, at this point it is thought McKinney was wounded. Willis is then right on McKinney. He lifts his cane bringing it down with all force on McKinney's shoulder. McKinney had meantime reloaded and throwing his gun over his shoulder, fires, the ball striking Willis in the mouth, and he drops just outside the kitchen door of Kincaid's residence. Tompkins — his remaining two shots at th— —ive, who dis— appears round Sec— — How— — ell and Lyons h— g— — Tompki— and w— tr— — to Wil— n to the doc— medical assistance and then go in search of further ammunition.

LYNN RECEIVES HIS FATAL WOUND.

We now follow McKinney, who makes for the home of Vera Mason, his paramour. Here the woman offers to dress his wound, but he pushes her aside roughly, and she, according to her testimony, became scared at his actions and left immediately for Nettie Smith's, opposite. McKinney was then seen by Kit Tatman, who was at the Smith house, to be moving hurriedly about the house, and it is supposed that here he armed himself with a rifle and shot-gun and ammunition. He was in the house but a few minutes, came across the block and hurriedly comes up Oak street. Lynn and Clint Kelly are coming leisurely down. At Clarke's McKinney stops, fires, and Lynn lies mortally wounded on the opposite corner. He levels his gun at Kelly. "In Christ's sake, don't shoot me; I'm your friend," says Kelly. "The s—— b——s have crippled me; anybody that gets in my way I'll shoot them," was the reply. He then passed by Kelly, going north, turning by Dr. Hardeman's office along the alley, when he came upon Geo Hanes. "Where are you going?" he said. "To see who it was that was shot," replied Hanes, and passed on.

GETS A TEAM.

The next we hear of McKinney is at the Arlington stables. At the point of his gun he wakes up Frank C. Butler and Thos. King, and tells them to be quick about it and get him a team. The —ain. It's all off with me, and I don't —— ——. Don't forget to tell old ——— (meaning Isham), I am his —— —ll him how this happened, and —— may see him again.' I gave him — money I had in the house, $61.50. —— money was found in the safe, as ——, the next day."

This was the last seen of McKinney in Porterville. He drove out of town past the school house headed for Lindsay. He then followed the County road past Lindsay to where the road forks off for Exeter and Visalia, some shells being found near the half-way house, which he is supposed to have dropped. He continued north eight miles to the Cottage postoffice, crossing the Kaweah river at that point, turning east through Antelope valley through Naranjo, and is supposed to have turned his horses loose two miles north of Lemon Cove. He was seen taking a drink near the Iron bridge and limping badly. He took dinner at the home of Dee McKee, a relative of his, and spent the afternoon there, leaving in an easterly direction towards dusk, and it is now thought he is hidden in the Kaweah swamps.

LYNN'S DEATH AND STATEMENT.

William G. Lynn, who was shot on the corner of Second and Oak streets, died from the effects of his wounds at 10 o'clock Sunday evening. He was operated on by Drs. Hardeman and Barber, who found eighteen buck-shot wounds in his body from the chest to the knees and a bullet wound in the fleshy part of the arm. The wounds that caused death were the two shots that entered the abdomen, having pierced the bowels. The doctors washed out the bowels and sewed up the wounds but some of the contents of the bowels escaped into the abdominal cavity and peritonitis set in, causing death. Lynn lived twelve hours after the operation, being ———scious about three hours —— —— ——. Lynn swore to a —— —illful murder of his brother.

Deputy District Attorney Murry, who immediately came over to Porterville on hearing the news, took the following statement from Lynn before he lapsed into unconsciousness:

"I was gambling in the back room of Zalud's. Scottie and Jim was in the chop-house shooting. He shot through the window a couple of times first, and it broke the game up. I came right up to Scottie's and Jim just stood in the door and here comes the officers, or three of them. They hollered to him to stop, and he started to walk up the street. They hollered to him to stop and he just whirled and commenced shooting. He shot the first shot; shot me through the arm. He shot two at Willis, or one at Willis; passed me though. I stood there quite a little while. Then he started and come off down town, and Clint Kelly I says to him let's go down and see. I thought maybe he got shot. He was standing right by Clarke's, right by them trees. I was across the street over there right by the fence. Jim never said a word; just turned loose and shot me. Then by that he was going to kill Clint. I thought he was mistaken in the man, you know. No grievance at me whatever. He just shot. Didn't make no difference who it was."

Question. "Did you have any trouble with him?"
Answer. "No."
Q. "No trouble between you at all?"
A. "No trouble whatever."
Q. "Never held any grudge against

Jim McKinney's exploits were chronicled by several Valley newspapers. This account, only a part of which is shown, appeared in The Porterville Enterprise *on August 1, 1902.*

style, shot it out with McKinney. Jim killed City Marshal Jeff Packard and Kern County Deputy Sheriff Will Tibbets before he was killed by Will's brother, Bert Tibbets. Hulse escaped but was later captured, tried and acquitted.

The McKinney family claimed the body for burial in Porterville. Mrs. McKinney asked one of the valley's most respected clergymen, Reverend John Milligan, to conduct the service. His comment concerning the request is worth repeating, for it eloquently reveals the selfless service given by pioneer clergymen to families in time of need.

The service was conducted in the home, as was customary.

I was in the room for a brief time before the service and while there I noticed a large, powerfully built man come in. With just a word of greeting to me he passed by the side of the improvised bier and drew the sheet down from the face of the dead man and stood there for some time in silence, looking at the dead face.

Then I heard him say softly, Jim, oh, Jim, you were a thoroughbred. I did not know the man, only that he was one of Jim's pals. His words were a pal's eulogy spoken in accordance of his conception of a thoroughbred. I did not find much in the words of his lament to help me in the part I was expected to perform on the morrow. It was a difficult place to fill.

It was not my mission to either eulogise or berate or condemn Jim McKinney. In the trail that led to his ending of life's career, there was blood from six killings credited to him. It was my business to help a bereaved mother and his brothers in what to them was a time of even greater sorrow than in an ordinary death, and to render the service in such a manner that some hints from the words spoken might convey the idea that, "The way of the Transgressor is hard."

I was criticised by some for conducting a funeral for such a man as Jim McKinney. I told one of my critics that the service was for the friends who mourned the tragedy of both his life and death; that the broken hearted mother needed our help the more, the sadder the case might be.[6]

1. *Visalia Times,* September 28, 1891.
2. Wells Fargo "Wanted" Posters.
3. Kathleen Small, *History of Tulare County,* page 379, quoting from newspaper interview with George Butz.
4. Ibid.
5. *Visalia Delta,* January 4, 1873.
6. *The Farm Tribune,* Porterville, Progress Edition, November 3, 1949.

CHAPTER 9

EXPERIMENTERS AND INNOVATORS

Farmers must be able to do many things. They are machinists, agronomists, businessmen, and patient experimenters who must gamble on climate, soil, variable weather, and market fluctuation. They must have the courage to try new crops and new ideas. Pioneer farmers were blessed with the same trait as all pioneers: an insatiable curiosity to see "what was on the other side of the mountain."

Cereal grain farming followed the open range. It is not surprising that many pieces of farm machinery were invented in the valley. Neither is it surprising that many new varieties of fruits and vegetables were originated in the valley.

Who were these experimenters and innovators? To be fair, one would have to name many people. However, a few stand tall among the rest. A resume of their achievements encompasses the work of many men. Their stories will also record the development of agriculture in the valley.

Bonanza grain farming was made possible by machinery. The single share walking plow was woefully inadequate on the flat valley floor. There were few trees and almost no rocks to impede plowing. Soil was light and pliable. Hog wallows were the only major obstacle. Large sections of the plains were covered by mounds whose origin was the subject of a wide range of speculation, from gas pressure under the soil to burrows made by giant prehistoric gophers.

Out of the need for improved plows came the Stockton Gang Plow. That machine had four plow shares mounted on a heavy wheeled frame high enough to clear stubble. The Stockton Gang Plow was supposedly devised in 1891 by Wesley Underwood of Manteca. Several men made improvements, and it was eventually manufactured in a Stockton foundry. Farmers who bought the Stockton Gang Plow not only finished their own plowing faster, but could hire out to plow neighboring fields. It must have been a delight to see plows and teams lined up plowing the rich soil in machine-like precision. Many farmers were still harrowing with brush pulled by teams. Faster plowing called for improved harrows and seeders.

The next demand was for improved harvesting equipment. Farmers planted before the winter rains. Large-scale grain farming was necessary because part of the land had to lie fallow in summer. The grain did not have to be gathered into shocks since it ripened in the field. In the 1880's and 1890's, when grain farming reached its peak, harvesters were pushed or pulled by 36 or more horses and mules. A header wagon was driven beside the harvester. Crews of ten or more men operated the harvester and header. Grain was threshed in a portable thresher that had its own crew. That unit had a steam engine, separator, derrick wagon, water wagon, and cook house. The unit moved to meet the needs of the harvester crew.

The first steam thresher was brought into Tulare County in 1870 by William Beinhorn and William Mehrton, who planted 4,000 acres near present day Exeter. As planting increased, men began to tinker with farm machinery. For example, William Mehrten made a hog wallow leveler.

William Mehrten of Lewis Creek has a hog wallow leveler of his own invention working on his ranch. The machine consists of two scantlings 24 feet in length, bolted together with 10 foot scantlings on which are fastened iron plates with the lower edge sharpened. The ground to be leveled is first plowed and then this long sled is dragged over it, which drags the loose earth on the knolls down into the hollows. Mr. Mehrton had quite a number of acres of land over which it was difficult to run a header on account of the hog wallows, and he devised this cheap method of leveling it. Twelve to sixteen head of horses are used in dragging the leveler which accomplishes the work in a satisfactory manner.[1]

The impact of better farm machinery and the

The Fresno Scraper.

utility of the biggest machine of all, the railroad, are apparent in these figures from Tulare County.

	1867	1882	1887
acres cultivated	6,310	115,240	1,172,141
acres of wheat alone	3,236	76,430	349,452[2]

During that period two of the most useful of all farm machines were created by valley farmers. They were the Fresno Scraper and the Berry Steam Harvester. Both were the handiwork of George Stockton Berry (1847-1917).

John Berry brought his family to California in 1857. They farmed around Lodi and Placerville, and moved to Grangeville in 1874. Two of the sons, George and William, bought several thousand acres near present-day Lindsay and planted grain.

The old slip scraper was an essential tool for use on farms, for building roads, and for digging out irrigation ditches and canals. The first ones were useful but primitive. A section was cut from a tree, leaving a limb projecting at a right angle in the rear. The man who drove the team stood on the limb until enough dirt was piled up in front of the log. Then he stepped off the limb and the log rolled over the dirt. The next improvement was a slip scraper made with a metal bottom, wooden end pieces, and handles. The driver had to bend over to hold the handles. Abijah McCall and Frank Dusy of Fresno made improvements on the scraper and sold some patent rights. History does not record that transaction accurately. However, the improvements made by Stockton Berry and James Porteous are well known.

In the early 1880's Stockton Berry had a contract to build part of the Herndon Ditch in Fresno County. The slip scrapers did not move dirt fast enough for Mr. Berry to finish the job on time. He stopped work and had the men cut an oak tree and saw out a six-foot section for a scraper. He cut a deep groove along one length of the log, and had a matching length of boiler plate cut in Stockton. He hauled it to the ditch and heated it red hot. Men grasped the boiler plate with long tongs and stood it on edge in the groove. Sledge hammers were used to hammer the plate over the log. Runners were bolted to the log, and a long lever to dump the load was bolted into place.

James Porteous, who owned the Fresno Agricultural & Implement Works, became interested in the scraper and urged Mr. Berry to take out a patent. An interesting facet of most of the early innovators is that they were more interested in expediting work than obtaining patents. Stockton Berry was not interested in manufacturing. Mr. Porteous made further refinements on the scraper, which he patented, and the scraper became the principal item of manufacture in his plant. In 1902 more than 500 of the Fresno Scrapers were sold to railroad contractors.[3]

Large-scale grain farmers had been trying to solve, or at least mitigate, two problems. One was to save horses and mules that died each summer from overwork and heat. The other was to speed up harvesting. The Berry Brothers were using a stationary

John Martin using Stockton Gang Plow to break the sod on his ranch west of Ducor.

Mitchell & Fisher steam engine to power their thresher. They decided to build a machine around it. Stockton Berry probably knew something about a combine harvester. The story of its invention involves Andrew Y. Moore, another pioneer of the county.

Hiram Moore of Climax Prairie, Michigan, invented the first combine in the 1830's. It was operated by a neighbor, Andrew Y. Moore (no relation). In 1843 A.Y. Moore had a combine built for himself, which he operated every year until 1853, when he shipped it to California. In 1854 the combine was used to harvest about 600 acres of grain at Mission San Jose. The crew did not know how to oil the machine, and the next year it burned in the field. However, its efficiency had been demonstrated, and soon several firms were building combines. Andrew Y. Moore moved his family to Tulare in 1877 and lived there until his death in 1888. His son, Colonel Orlando Moore, is also buried in the Tulare Cemetery. An American flag always flies over his grave, but that is another story.

Stockton Berry drew plans for his new machine. Much of the preliminary work was done in the Visalia Iron & Agricultural Works. Fortunately for posterity, Visalia editors were interested and followed the progress of the machine.

Mr. Berry has an old stationary engine, and the idea occurred to him that it could be made into a traction engine and be utilized to haul a combined harvester. Feeling convinced that this was possible he made arrangements with the iron works of this city to make the necessary additions to the old machine. Mr. Chris Bergstrom, proprietor of the iron works, sent a draftsman to Mr. Berry's place, and elaborate drawings were made of the engine and in this way the expense of

George Stockton Berry (1847-1917)

transporting it to Visalia was avoided. The plans drawn at the ranch have formed the basis of all the work in the machine shop, and in a few days the machinery will be complete.[4]

Later, in July 1886, the newspapers reported that the combined thresher, header, and locomotive was working satisfactorily.

The Berry Steam Harvester was an adaptable machine. The engine was mounted between the header and separator when it was used as a tractor. Drive wheels were mounted in front of the boiler, and a tiller wheel steered the front wheels.

The ingenious feature of the harvester was the fuel. Stockton Berry used the cheapest and handiest fuel possible — straw. Straw had been a drug on the marketplace for years. Tons of it went to waste each year when it was either burned or plowed under.

Berry Steam Harvester.

Schemes that ranged from using it as fertilizer to using it in textiles had been proposed.

In the Berry Steam Harvester the straw from the separator was pushed back onto a rack, and the fireman pitched it into the firebox. Everything involved in harvest was tinder dry. Anyone who has ever lived in a grain area knows the terror of seeing a column of light smoke during harvest time. Men dropped whatever they were doing and helped fight fire with wet sacks, shovels, and firebreaks. The Berry Harvester increased fire hazards, and several times the crew had to jump off the harvester to put out fires.

It took a crew of 11 men to operate the smoke-belching steam monster. Included were the engineer, two firemen, two water bucks, a sack sewer, sack tender, separator tender, header tender, steersman, and grain hauler. The summer heat, augmented by the firebox, led crews to call the Berry Steam Harvester a "plenty hot invention."

Berry's Steam Harvester was an object of both curiosity and interest. Farmers came from all parts of the state to watch it in action. The first season, the crew harvested an average of 50 acres a day, and when Berry's crop was harvested, the crew harvested 2,600 acres owned by Elias Jacob. An excellent first-hand account comes from the recollections of Mrs. Arthur Hutchinson, whose husband's company started Lindsay, a name derived from Mrs. Hutchinson's family.

These brothers were known as the Berry brothers, as they did everything together. They were first rate mechanics as well as farmers and had built a steam engine on wheels, which dragged behind it 40 plows, behind each plow a seeder, and behind that 40 harrows. It was a sight to see. Once it started, a double crew kept it going night and day. The huge headlight marching across the arid plains at night was a sight never to be forgotten. They did 75 acres in 24 hours. In harvest times, in place of the plows, a threshing machine was placed on, and that was another sight, the beautiful grain being cut and lifted automatically into the machine on one side, the chaff flying off on another, and on opposite sides from a platform, a man forked with lightning speed, fastening grain sacks on a spout to catch the threshed grain. While one sack was filling he rapidly sewed the previously filled sack and tumbled it off the platform. Those bags were gathered up by the teamsters operating a chain of three huge wagons fastened together and pulled by 16 horses. The bags of grain were then driven to some warehouse where the grain was stored until sold.[5]

Mrs. Hutchinson wrote about a dual use for the machine. Berry first used it as a harvester but realized quickly that it was more useful as a tractor. As a harvester it actually ran backward, and as a tractor it moved forward. Several large-scale grain farmers ordered the steam harvesters from the Benicia Iron Works at a cost of $7,000 plus freight. There was so much interest in the machine that Stockton Berry broke its operation into cost factors in a letter to the *Visalia Times* on November 11, 1886.

I am now plowing with my engine. I unhinged the separator and header and hooked on twenty, ten inch plows. It walks off with them without any trouble. I have been running ten days and have averaged thirty-five acres a day. The land where I am running now is red, clayey land and is very knolly. The unevenness of the land does not seem to have an effect on the running of the machine, whatever. The plows do better work then could possibly be done with them were they drawn by horses, for they are all fastened together so that they have to keep the furrow, which is not the case when horses are used.

I am burning straw which I gather from the field where the harvester left it. It takes five men to operate the machine and plow at the same time at the following daily cost.

engineer	$2.00
a man to guide	1.00
a man to fire	1.00
a man to haul water	1.00
a man to gather straw	1.00
4 horses for team	2.00
oil	.75
board for men	2.50

This makes a total daily cost of $11.25. This makes my plowing cost me aside from plow shares and interest on the capital investment, 32 cents an acre. I save by this method $15.00 a day on the feed of stock required to do the work, and besides that, the stock must be fed, work or no work. The engine, on the other hand, eats nothing of value.

Please call the attention of inquiring minds to this fact. There is a stage running to my place, thrice a week from Visalia and persons wanting to see my method of plowing will be welcome.[6]

The only serious mechanical problem during the 1886 season was with the buff clutch differential which wore out because of constant turning. Berry devised a heavier gear which operated in a box filled with oil. He had patented the mechanism which transmitted power from the engine to the power wheels. He did not patent the differential, which is essentially the same as that used in modern vehicles.

In 1888 Stockton Berry was elected to the California State Assembly, and two years later to the State Senate representing Tulare, Kings, Kern, and Inyo Counties. He sold his patent to Daniel

Lubking Harvester - taken in 1904 on the Lubking Ranch south of Ducor.

Best of San Leandro. By 1889 Best had a steam harvester on the market. He added a small engine which operated the sickle and separator separately. Two years later he had a steam harvester with sickles that varied from 14 to 20 feet. Best advertised that his machine could cut 60 to 70 acres each day.

Meantime, Benjamin Holt of Stockton had invented a track lay. By that time Best's machines were using gas instead of steam power. In 1908 Daniel Best sold some of his patents to the Holt Brothers, but his son continued the business as C.L. Best Gas Tractor Company. In 1925 that company merged with the Holt Brothers as Caterpillar Tractor Company.

Berry's Steam Harvester was not only the forerunner of self-propelled farm machinery. It was the forerunner of tractors and of tanks used in modern warfare.

Stockton Berry served in the Senate until 1894. He continued to farm with his brother, but lived on the coast, where he passed away in 1917.

The first issue of the *Tulare County Record & Fresno Examiner,* the San Joaquin Valley's oldest newspaper, editorialized:

Every kind of grain flourishes here with the greatest luxuriance, every kind of fruit grows with tropical splendor, the soil is particuarly adapted to the cultivation of the vine, its broad plains covered with rich grasses render the advantage of stock raising the equal if not superior to any in the state.[7]

The flowering editorial vision of more than a century ago is now a reality. Tulare County has consistently ranked among the four richest agricultural counties in the nation. Cereal grain has contributed heavily to agricultural income.

Wheat has always been an important crop in California. It helped make Alta California self-sufficient. Russian colonists came down from Fort Ross to trade manufactured goods for wheat. In the gold rush era, ships' holds were filled with wheat both for ballast and to sell in home ports.

The first settlers in Tulare County planted small fields of wheat, corn, oats, and barley. The first manufactured item in the county was flour and corn meal ground at the Matthews' Grist Mill in Visalia. Originally the owners charged 75 cents per hundredweight or 1/5 of the finished product. The 1860 Federal Census showed that the Matthews' Mill used 20,000 bushels of grain a year at $24,000. The mill produced 4,000 barrels of flour. It had one run of millstones powered by water and employed two men at $180 per month. The Federal Census also revealed that 40,268 bushels of wheat and 6,355 bushels of corn were raised in Tulare County. By the mid-1880's, California was the largest producer of grain in the nation, and most of its grain was grown in the lower San Joaquin Valley.

William Scruggs hauling wheat to the Terra Bella warehouse in 1909.

John J. Cairns (1844-1926)

The first large-scale planting of grain was put in by Samuel Carothers in 1871 near Fountain Springs. The crop averaged ten sacks to the acre, but since the sacks had to be hauled to Stockton, the experiment was not financially successful. Two years later William Mehrten and William Beinhorn planted several thousand acres in the Lewis Creek country near present-day Lindsay. A few years later Warren Hastings planted a large acreage near Terra Bella. By the mid-1880's the day of bonanza wheat growers had arrived. The combined planting of the Roth Brothers, John Tuohy, John and Lewis Keeley, Elias Jacob, George and William Berry, John Cairns, and the Mehrton Brothers stretched from Farmersville to the southern county line and from the foothills to Tulare Lake. By 1884 Tulare Lake had dried sufficiently for large scale grain farming.

If one person were to be singled out to demonstrate the courage and imagination it took to engage in large-scale farming during that period, it would have to be John J. Cairns. Cairns was born in Scotland. As a young man he went to Australia and then to New Zealand, where he went into the sheep business. In 1871 he sailed to California and soon bought a flock of sheep which ranged over the plains of the San Joaquin Valley. During the terrible dry cycle of the 1870's he took his sheep to northern California in search of forage. When the valley plains once more produced sufficient forage, he came back with his flocks.

Mr. Cairns was a big man, well over six feet tall. He never lost his Scottish burr. He was kind, hardworking, and considerate of the men who worked for him. Because he worked as hard as or harder than the hired men, they soon learned that he did not tolerate shirkers. A man who worked for him for several years said, "He could almost burn the hide off of the man who was trying to take advantage of him."[8]

In 1881 Mr. Cairns rented the John W. Jones ranch (9½ sections) west of Porterville. For the next few years the family lived there, and that ranch was the headquarters for his expanding operation. He bought several thousand acres south of Ducor on the White River, and in 1886 he bought more land west of Lindsay, now known as Cairns Corners. The latter ranch became the family home and the site of his experiment in deep well pumping as well as his experimental planting of olives and oranges.

In 1884 he planted 6,000 acres of grain on the Poplar ranch and harvested a good crop. 1885 was not a good year, but in 1886 he planted 12,000 acres, and in 1891 he planted 18,000 acres of wheat and barley. Two years later he put in 20,000 acres. Prices were good and the yield was above average, so in 1894 he planted 23,000 acres. That was the year that the large-scale farmers went broke.

Just listing the number of acres planted does not really indicate the capital investment or the scope of work and planning involved in such large-scale farming.

The crews got up before dawn to feed, water, and harness the teams. Then they ate their own substantial breakfast, provided by the farmer. Machinery had to be checked before they went into the field. Water wagons and cook wagons were placed as near as possible to the field in which the men worked. The crews stopped in mid-morning for a light meal. At noon the men had a substantial meal, and the animals were watered and rested. In mid-afternoon the men had another light snack. Food provided for the crews was part of their pay, which usually was set at $1.00 per day plus board. The men continued to work until it was almost too dark to see. Once more the animals were taken care of before the men had their supper.

Harvesting was done under the blistering sun, with little or no protection for either men or animals. Dust, whirlwinds, chaff, and heat enveloped the crews, but they worked as a team in order to keep the harvesting operations running smoothly. In 1886, when Mr. Cairns planted 12,000 acres, his crews started plowing on September 4th and finished on March 14th. The harvester crews used five headers and a thrasher unit with five header wagons. It took 80 men to keep those units going during the three-month harvest period.

Mr. Cairns was a progressive farmer, always looking for better machinery and improved methods of planting and harvesting. He bought the first two Berry Harvesters manufactured in Benicia at a total cost of $14,000 plus freight. The machines were shipped to Pixley and then driven under their own power to the Poplar ranch. Cairns used the harvesters for the first time in 1888, when the crop averaged 22 sacks to the acre. In 1891 it took 65 men driving 320 mules and horses to prepare the land. In that harvest season he used one horse combine, two Berry Harvesters and 15 header wagons.

The sack sewer was the key man on a harvest team. He had to be incredibly quick to fit a sack around the grain spout, pull it off filled, pull another sack around the spout, and sew up the filled sack with heavy twine and push it off the machine. Wagons followed the harvesters and picked up the sacks, which were hauled to a depot or a warehouse. Before the Eastside Railroad came in 1888, the nearest depots and warehouses were Alila, Pixley, Tipton, Delano, Tulare, Cross Creek, and Traver. Usually grain buyers visited the farms and made their offers before the harvest ended. Some men stored wheat and barley and gambled on a higher price later. It was indeed a gamble for the simple reason that large-scale farmers operated on credit, faith, and borrowed money.

The roads to the depots were not very good. Teamsters drove across the plains trying to avoid the chuckholes and deep ruts characteristic of the roads. The dust was so thick that sometimes the driver could not see the lead mules. Whirlwinds were another problem. When the teams reached the depot they had to wait in line — for hours if they were lucky, for days if they were not. When the warehouse was filled, the sacks were piled along the right-of-way.

The teamsters were like the old-time stage drivers, a breed of men unto themselves. Hard work, heat, dirt, and delays did little to soothe their tempers. Cards, whiskey, and women in the larger communities like Traver caused brawls and sometimes gun fights. A good teamster knew his animals by name and knew the capability of each one. A jerk-line teamster was skilled, and his driving showed it. However, it was better to watch the teamsters than hear them, for most drove team with a stream of cuss words indigenous to that era. It was said that a first-rate teamster could drive from the Tule River to the railroad and never repeat a cuss word.

Mr. Cairns employed 80 to 100 men. Some worked all year round. In addition to the crews there were cooks (usually Chinese), a bookkeeper, a time-keeper, blacksmiths and their helpers, and roustabouts.

Most of the large-scale farmers kept herds of goats, hogs, and sheep as well as milk cows. These animals fed on stubble, scraps from the kitchen, and skimmed milk, and in return provided food and an income from wool. Elias Jacob, who had extensive land holdings, probably had as much income from farm animals as from farming. In 1887 he listed 15,000 sheep, 1,500 Angora goats, and 1,200 hogs on his Lucerne Valley ranch, which is now in Kings County.

Labor and wages became a problem for the first time in 1886. The farmers met and set up a pay scale.

header wagon driver	$1.50 a day
loaders	2.00 a day
header operator	2.50 a day
pull back man	3.50 a day
straw back man	2.00 a day
water buck	2.00 a day
sack sewer	2.50 a day
hoe down	2.00 a day
derrick tender	2.00 a day
cooks	$45 a month

The inventory of machinery necessary to keep large-scale operations going was fantastic. At one time Mr. Cairns listed the machinery used at his Poplar ranch as 26 gang plows, 56 harrows, 10 disc plows, 9 scrapers, 4 seeders, a seed cleaner, a barley mill, 41 wagons, 24 wagon beds, 12 header beds, 60 sets of harness, 8 feed racks, 4 mowers, 2 horse rakes, 8 wagon nets, 3 derrick forks, 4 cookhouses, and 3 water tanks. This list did not include the harvesters, threshing machine units, and combines.

1894 had looked like a good year, but a late frost damaged the grain and heads of wheat, and the barley did not mature. The failure could not have come at a worse time because the whole nation was in a severe depression. Mr. Cairns' loss ran into six figures. In order to meet his obligations he lost

Artesian well at Artesia, now in Kings County.

most of his machinery as well as thousands of acres of land.

1894 marked the zenith of bonanza grain farming. Large-scale farmers did not quit, but they cut down the number of acres planted. Other crops were competing with grain. Citrus and other fruits, olives, alfalfa and dairy products were beginning to pay well. These could be produced on small farms. Land which once sold at prices ranging from $1.25 to $5.00 or $10.00 an acre began to sell at from $50 to several hundred dollars an acre. The only large acreages which were not affected by the changeover were in the southern and western sections of Tulare County. Sheepmen and cattlemen who pastured their animals in that section turned to large-scale grain farming, and much of the grain is still produced there. In other sections wheat, barley, oats, corn, and grain sorghum fit well into a rotation pattern with alfalfa and cotton.

John Cairns bought his Lindsay ranch about the same time Captain Arthur Hutchinson and his wife's family, the Pattons, bought the Hayes Ranch, the Jacob Ranch, and the Lemon Cove Ranch to sub-divide. The Berry Brothers had rented the 2,000-acre Jacob Ranch for some years. In 1888 George Frost had planted the first large grove of oranges near Porterville, and Hutchinson saw possibilities for citrus groves through the newly-formed Lindsay Land Company. All the company needed for proper development of that plan was water. Captain Hutchinson planned to divert water from the Kaweah River. John Cairns had an idea that not only changed the company's plan but also changed the agricultural development of the San Joaquin Valley.

Mr. Cairns recouped his fortune in citrus and olives, but that story must wait. Like all innovators, Cairns was observant, and he saw that sheepmen dug shallow wells for their animals if they were not near running water. Mr. Cairns noticed that these shallow wells did not dry up as they had done in New Zealand. He concluded that under the dry plains there was a water table. Many of his contemporaries found that idea amusing. Ironic as it may be, the stockmen believed that nothing would grow on the plains. They derisively called farmers sandlappers and sky farmers, overlooking the lush feed that grew each year on the same plains.

Mr. Cairns and his neighbors, Julius Orton, Captain Hutchinson, the Berry brothers, and John Tuohy, had been experimenting with oranges and olives. Sky farming was all right for grain, but these men realized that citrus and olives could not be raised profitably without a dependable source of water.

First substation at Lindsay, built in 1899 to supply the first large-scale irrigation pumping project in the U.S.

In 1890 Mr. Cairns went to San Francisco and bought a 10-horsepower Byron Jackson centrifugal pump. He had a 20-foot pit dug on the Lindsay ranch and lined it with brick. His original plan called for a well to be dug in each corner. Power for the pump came from a steam threshing engine. The first well exceeded all expectations, for a veritable stream flowed from the 14-inch casing. Most accounts now agree that this experiment was not only the first powered pumping of irrigation water in the valley, but also in the state. There are varying reports of the depth of the well, but all agree it was not deep. The *Visalia Delta* of June 4, 1891 said that the pump was down 19 feet, and the well from there was 30 feet deep.

Thus Mr. Cairns proved the existence of a water table and changed the economy of the entire area.

Captain Hutchinson scrapped his plan to divert water from the Kaweah River. In 1892 he dug a well west of the Fremont Trail and piped the water to his home. More wells were bored, and water ditches distributed water to groves. The Lindsay Land Company incorporated the Lindsay Water Company in 1893. Land sold at $70.00 an acre, and a share in the water company cost $2.00 an irrigated acre.

In 1894 Basil Prior planted a citrus grove and was hired as superintendent of the Lindsay Water Company. He recalled that the trees were hand-watered before irrigation water became available. He also recalled an amusing sidelight on irrigation practices. The ditch tenders had to wait their turn

Captain A.J. Hutchinson's home. The citrus trees around it were planted in May, 1891.

for water, so they would take off their shoes and socks, put their feet in the ditch, and catch some sleep until the cold water woke them up.

Even more wells were bored when electricity generated by the Mt. Whitney Power and Electric Company became available. The first cut-in on power was made from the Lindsay Sub-Station June 26, 1899. The first subscriber was the Postlethwaite Ranch, and then Captain Hutchinson. The rate was a flat $50.00 per horsepower per year. As an inducement, the power company allowed the subscriber to use electricity for house lights when his motor pump was not operating.

Who could forsee the consequences of powered pumping? Within 25 years over-pumping of the underground water and a series of dry years had lowered the water table to the point where it had a saline content that actually killed small trees.

To provide water for the overplanted and overpumped areas, Captain Hutchinson's plan to take water from the Kaweah River was revived. The Lindsay-Strathmore Irrigation District began to sink wells on the property known as Rancho de Kaweah, which also revived the age-old struggle between riparian water rights and the right of appropriation. As a result, the Tulare Irrigation District *et al* filed suit against the Lindsay-Strathmore Irrigation District in 1916. Seven judges heard the case over a period of 20 years. Whatever the outcome, the people on one side or the other would be ruined financially. The bitter litigation was finally compromised in 1936, when the Central Valley Project became a reality.

For about two decades after Mr. Cairns' well produced a reliable source of water, farmers planted olives, deciduous fruits, and citrus. Mr. Cairns was one of the first to experiment with olives.

The origin of the olive is lost in time. For centuries it has been the symbol of peace. Olives flourished in the warmer climates of the Old World and readily adapted in the New World. Father Serra brought either seeds or cuttings with him in 1769 and planted olives at Mission San Diego. Olives followed the missions, and today they are inextricably part of mission history.

The first olive tree of record in Tulare County was one grown by Wiley Watson in his Visalia garden. The cutting was given to him in 1857 by that peregrinating pioneer, Dr. Samuel George. Wiley Watson transplanted the tree several times, and cuttings were planted in various gardens in the county.

The first mission olives were planted in the Lindsay area in 1892 by Stockton Berry and John Cairns. They and a neighbor, Julius Orton, planted oranges and grapes at the same time. Mr. Cairns planted his olives in three rows around the Lindsay ranch, where they acted as a windbreak as well as producing trees. The border type of planting he used set a pattern for future use on orange, grape, and even grain farms.

The first commercial grove of olives (60 acres) was put in at the Bonnie Brae Ranch north of Exeter in 1897. The olive is an extremely hardy tree, and many of the trees planted in the 1890's are still producing.

The market for citrus and deciduous fruits at that time was expanding. There was little market for olives, since most of them were still home-cured. In 1898 Mrs. Freda Ehmann of Orville, known as the mother of the California olive industry, pickled olives in barrels and sold them to grocers in the larger communities. The next step, which came slowly, was learning how to process olives in cans which could be shipped to markets. When that became practical, the price for olives rose dramatically. In 1908 Mr. Cairns sold 65 tons of olives from the three rows of trees for $55.00 a ton.

Julius Orton (1825-1912) and Mrs. Orton (nee Lucretia Kirby). He came to California in 1849 and to the Tule River country in 1858.

Three years later processors from other sections of California were offering as much as $140.00 a ton, and growers could not meet the demand. In order to be assured of a stable supply, buyers began to offer growers three- to five-year contracts. By 1913 prime mission and manzanillo olives brought $300.00 a ton. The high prices for olives and citrus led to overplanting and overproduction. The *Lindsay Gazette* noted in 1915 that half the 1914 olive pack was not sold, and that olive oil is "even worse."

Today, more than one-half, approximately, of the olives in California are grown in Tulare County. The acreage is small compared to that of Spain, but the ripe olive industry is unique to California, and it processes 100% of our nation's supply. Tulare County also processes some olive oil as well as Spanish and Sicilian style olives. The Lindsay Ripe Olive Company, a grower-owned co-operative, is the world's largest olive processing plant. There are also independent processing plants in the county.

The first olive processing plant was actually in Terra Bella and not in Lindsay. In 1907 A. Adams, who owned the Sunland Processing Company in Southern California, built an olive plant in Terra Bella. Most of the olives must have been shipped in, for the first large olive grove was not planted near Terra Bella until 1911. That same year (1911), STOMA, the Southern Tulare Olive Marketing Association, was formed in Terra Bella.

Lindsay growers took note of that marketing association, and the Lindsay Ripe Olive Company was formed in 1916 with a plant north of the waterworks and adjacent to the railroad. The plant could handle 125 tons of olives a day. The company reorganized in 1921 as a growers' stockholders' company. The *Lindsay Gazette* of November 24, 1922 featured the plant with some interesting facts. The capacity of the plant had tripled. Ninety grower members owned 1,000 acres of olives, and the annual payroll was $35,000 to $45,000. Two years later the Lindsay plant was the largest processing plant in California. Today it is the largest canner of ripe olives in the world.

In the 1960's the Feather River Olive Growers merged with the Lindsay Ripe Olive Company, and then the company bought the Lindsay plant of V.R. Smith. In 1966 the Lindsay Ripe Olive Company merged with the Orinda Company of Corning to form the Consolidated Olive Growers. In 1973 the grower members voted to change back to Lindsay Olive Growers.

Tulare County's place as the processor of the nation's ripe olives is also due to another top canning company. Early California Foods started in Visalia in 1964 when three olive companies — Pacific Olive Company of Visalia, Glick Olive Company of Corning, and Sunland Olive Company of Terra Bella — merged. The Pacific Olive Plant in Visalia, located on East Tulare Avenue, was established in 1940 in the old Visalia Cannery buildings. Since then it has been entirely modernized. Unlike the Lindsay co-op, Early California Foods is a publicly owned corporation. The bulk of its production is olives, but the plant also cans cherries, potatoes, pickles, salad dressings, and mayonnaise and various bar mixes.

It has been less than a century since Tulare County farmers first planted olives and processed them in barrels for home use, but today the industry provides a multi-million dollar return on its worldwide sale.

It has been less than a century, too, since citrus fruits were regarded as luxury foods, and the men who experimented with commercial groves then were daring innovators.

All citrus varieties are natives of the sub-tropical and tropical areas of Asia and the Malay Peninsula, where they were cultivated for centuries. The first variety to become known in Europe was the citron, mentioned as early as 300 B.C. Sweet oranges originated in China, and travelers brought some to Europe in the 15th Century. Columbus brought citrus seeds to the New World, and missionaries

First commercial orange grove, located now at 271 East Gibbon Street in Porterville and owned by Mr. and Mrs. Rodney Homer.

planted citrus at all missions. In Alta California, citrus did exceptionally well in southern California. The Tehachapi Mountains were believed to be the dividing line for the planting of commercial citrus groves.

Today Tulare County is California's Number One county for citrus acreage and production. Nearly 90,000 acres are now planted to citrus. Navel oranges make up 65% of the acreage. Valencia oranges constitute 28%. Lemons follow with 5%, and the remaining 2% is made up of grapefruit, tangerines, and citrus hybrids. In 1986 citrus sales totaled $287,857,000.

These facts are even more impressive when we find that commercial groves were first planted in the county in the late 1880's. It is an interesting sidelight in this "era of women" to find that three ladies had much to do with starting the citrus industry in California and in Tulare County.

In 1873 Mrs. Luther Tibbets of Riverside received two seedling orange trees from friends in Washington, D.C. They were Bahia Navels, named for their place of origin in Brazil. She renamed them Washington Navels. One tree matured and was the sire of California's navel orange industry.

Valencia oranges came from the Azores. In 1876 A.B. Chapman and George Smith received from England some unlabeled seedlings for their nursery. Chapman planted them at San Gabriel and named them Rivers for a noted English nurseryman, Tom Rivers. Later on the trees were correctly identified as *Naranjo de tarde Valencia*.

The part that Mrs. Huffum White and Mrs. Deming Gibbons played in starting citrus planting is now Tulare County history. Both lived in the Tule River country. Mrs. White lived in Frazier Valley, and Mrs. Gibbons lived in Plano. In 1862 or 1863 both ladies and their children were visiting friends in Visalia. The exact year was not recorded, as neither woman realized she would make history. Mrs. White and the children were invited to a picnic at Camp Babbitt. Citrus was a luxury item during pioneer days, so the children were delighted when Captain Moses A. McLaughlin gave them a few oranges. Mrs. White saved the seeds and planted them at the ranch in Frazier Valley. One tree lived and in seven years bore ten oranges. She sold the oranges for $1.00 apiece and donated the money to her church. That parent tree produced fruit until 1905. Seeds from the oranges which it produced were planted in family orchards all over the county.

Mrs. Gibbons' children also received a few oranges at Camp Babbitt, and she planted their seeds at the ranch in Plano. Mr. Gibbons saved seed from the trees which grew, planted, and replanted until he had a grove of 74 trees. In 1885 his oranges won first prize at the Los Angeles County Fair, much to the surprise of Southern California growers.

Actually, there was a citrus planting earlier than the ones at the White and Gibbons ranches. In 1856 Sardis Wilcox, who lived east of Porterville, planted 600 grape cuttings and 600 orange seedling trees. The grapes survived, but the oranges did not.

Because citrus of any variety was scarce, there are many references to oranges, lemons, and limes in old letters and newspapers. As an example, in December 1870 the editor of the *Visalia Delta*

Mrs. Huffum White (1830-1906, nee Jerusha Anthony Brown) planted orange trees at her home in Frazier Valley in 1862-63.

thanked Mrs. Peter Goodhue and her daughter for bringing him a few oranges from a tree growing in their yard. He added that after sampling one he was convinced that even tropical fruit would do well in Tulare County. In 1870 S.Z. Curtis, who ranched near Twin Buttes, reported that he had 18 Seville orange trees in his home orchard. J.W.C. Pogue grew both oranges and lemons on his ranch in what is now Lemon Cove. Lemons had been considered too tropical to grow in the county until he experimented with them in the early 1870's.

In 1876 Zachariah Miller, who ranched in the Venice Hill area east of Visalia, brought in the first full box of oranges for the Christmas trade. Two years later Alfred Everton planted a grove of 200 trees in Three Rivers, and Bahwell's Gardens in Visalia advertised 179 seedling oranges for sale.

Commercial planting has followed a pattern in the county. It began around Porterville and spread to Strathmore, Lindsay, Orosi and Dinuba. About 1910 a reverse geographical pattern emerged, and planting went south to Deer Creek, Terra Bella, Ducor, and Richgrove.

Albert Henry planted the first commercial grove in Porterville in 1879. More important was the fact that he introduced budded trees into the county. He had bought 160 acres in the low foothills bisected by the Pioneer Ditch, and his location also set a planting pattern, for it was believed foothills were freer from frost. Mr. Henry's trees came from Riverside, and he returned there to study citrus culture and to learn how to bud trees. He and his brother, Oliver Henry, and their nephew, Willshier Henry, started a nursery in Porterville. In 1886 Albert Henry's grove consisted of 40 seedlings, 40 Mediterranean Sweet Oranges, 20 St. Michaeles Oranges, and 1 Malta Blood Orange.[9]

George Frost, a well known Riverside nurseryman, was anxious to find a new market for citrus stock. He heard of the successful planting at Porterville and made an inspection trip in 1888. He decided that he had found not only a new market, but a place offering ideal growing conditions. Oranges ripened earlier than they did in Southern California, so they could be shipped for the Thanksgiving market. There was little frost, ditch water was available, and there was neither scale nor smut. Transportation was available over the new Eastside Railroad. Mr. Frost made a deal with the Pioneer Land Company for 100 acres of land north of Porterville, along with water rights from the Pioneer Ditch. He agreed to plant and care for orange trees for two years. Then he had an option to buy the land at $100.00 an acre, or the Pioneer Land Company agreed to pay him for the trees and his labor. The trees thrived, and the rest of that experiment is history. Mr. Frost exhibited both citrus and nursery stock at fairs, especially mid-winter fairs in San Francisco, where he won many first place premium awards.

The success of the Henry and Frost experiments with citrus certainly influenced Captain Hutchinson, John Cairns, Stockton Berry and Julius Orton. It was also George Frost who interested A.C. and R.C. Merryman in the possibilities of growing citrus in the county. They came in 1896 and planted the Bonnie Brae and Merryman groves northeast of Exeter on the slopes of Badger Hill and the area now known as Merryman. The first citrus was packed in a barn on the Bonnie Brae ranch, and the first packing house in Exeter was built by Bonnie Brae in 1901.

The hub of the early citrus industry was in Porterville, Lindsay, and the J.W.C. Pogue ranch. Reverend John A. Milligan, who was a pioneer in the Porterville area, compiled a partial list of early citrus ranchers. These men raised oranges and, in some cases, lemons.

Worth District:
A. H. Adams, Fred Bailey, J. Orr, D. Pratt, Mr. Campbell.
South Tule:
Witt brothers, James Wardlaw, C. Reese, Will Putnam, Sterling Schmittou, Peter Ting.
Zante:
Pioneer Land Company, Lumley brothers, Henry Pe-

The Porterville Citrus Fair was held in December 1892 under the auspices of the Porterville Horticulture Society. The exhibit was then sent to the San Francisco Mechanics Fair where it took first prize.

terson, Joseph Weisenberger, T. Bearess, C. Buswell, C. H. Flanders.

Pleasant Valley:

W. E. Sprott, Joseph Carter, M. Davidson, Dr. Hardeman, Dr. Brumfield, J. H. Williams, H. F. Brey, Schultz & Willson, A. A. Abbey, Henry brothers, Emil Newman, E. O. Giddings, J. S. Lewis, Mark Burgess.[10]

In 1890 Captain Hutchinson bought 200 navel orange trees from a Riverside nursery. His foreman, August Millinghausen, recalled that the trees came in June and "there being no other way of irrigating, I placed a 300-gallon tank on a wagon, filled it with water from the domestic well, attached a hose and irrigated the trees as we planted them. After the trees were irrigated for the first time, I made basins around every tree to hold the water and filled the basins with mulch. I watered the trees in that fashion for the rest of 1890 and all of 1891. After that additional wells were provided and the water was supplied by pumps.[11]

Although young trees in Tulare County were not afflicted with scale or smut, there were grasshoppers. Mrs. Hutchinson left a graphic account of that menace. She was in Southern California when her husband telegraphed and asked her to buy bolts of mosquito netting.

He put this over the trees with the result that the grasshoppers ate the mosquito netting. Poor dismayed Arthur scoured the country and bought droves of ducks to eat the grasshoppers. This worked fine for a few days until the ducks were satisfied and full of hoppers and could hardly quack. He got rid of these and scoured the country again for turkeys buying them wherever he could find them. The turkeys thought they had got to the land of plenty, and they did noble duty for several days. Then they wouldn't even notice a hopper. It meant everything to save the trees, so at last he did the only thing that worked. He and the men who worked on the place rode horses up and down those few rows of trees, and hit each tree with a barley sack. They did this day after day until grasshopper season was over.[12]

John Cairns recalled that he tied a heavy barley sack over his citrus to protect them from grasshoppers. As irrigation increased, infestation of grasshoppers decreased, since the grasshoppers incubate in dry ground.

Mr. Millinghausen recalled that by 1894 there were enough oranges on the trees to send samples to Goldberg-Bowen in San Francisco for the Christmas trade. The idea paid off, for the next year the firm sent a buyer to Lindsay. The Lindsay Land Company and John Cairns sold them a carload of navels at $6.50 F.O.B. Lindsay.

John Cairns planted 160 acres of oranges at the Lindsay ranch, but he did not plant all of them at once. He was also experimenting with olives and Thompson seedless grapes. A Cairns memorandum states that he planted 32 acres of navels in 1893. Newspaper advertisements during that period indicate that most of the seedlings came from River-

John Wirt bringing oranges to Exeter in 1900.

side or Redlands and sold at $25.00 a hundred "and downward re quality and variety."

The first full carload of oranges (navels) from Tulare County was shipped from Porterville in 1893. The carload was consigned to a San Francisco commission house. No one could overlook it. The freight car was decorated with flags, and on each side was a car-length banner proclaiming: "PORTERVILLE ORANGES. FIRST CARLOAD WASHINGTON NAVEL ORANGES FROM THE CENTRAL CALIFORNIA CITRUS BELT. BEST ORANGES IN THE WORLD."

These oranges were packed in a shed on Mill Street in Porterville. However, John Cairns had the first "real" packing house in the county. In an interview he said:

The first car of oranges packed and shipped from Lindsay was in 1896. [They] were packed and graded at my home ranch and hauled and shipped in car lots to Francisco and consigned to a commission house in San Francisco. The oranges were shipped and packed by Mr. and Mrs. Sam Baggs. The year after this there was a packing shed where the old Plate house now is. The year following that we packed in the grain warehouse. We formed a corporation and built a packing house. The corporation was called the Lindsay Orange and Lemon Growers Association. This was the first growers' association in Lindsay. (1905)[13]

In the early days, packing was done by "eye" for size and color, but Mr. Cairns, always willing to experiment, bought a hand sizer. The growers were at the mercy of the commission merchants until fruit exchanges or associations were formed to regulate the sale of citrus.

The Hutchinson family moved to the Bay Area, and in 1908 the Cairns family moved to Los Angeles and later to Berkeley. The oldest son, Walter, took over active management of the Lindsay ranch, but John Cairns came back during the packing season to help. He and his wife made many trips to continue in community affairs in Lindsay. Like that of his fellow pioneer experimenters, John Cairns' ingenuity changed the course of agri-business.

Lemons, limes,* grapefruit, tangerines, and mandarins grow well in Tulare County, but for many years they remained in the "let's wait and see" stage commercially. Lemons were a prized fruit during pioneer days. Their history also goes back to Columbus, who introduced them to Haiti in 1493. Missionaries brought lemons and limes to California, and they grew well in southern mission gardens. The popular Lisbon lemon was imported from Portugal and planted at Riverside about 1874. The equally popular Eureka lemon originated from a seedling planted in Los Angeles in 1872.

*Bearss Limes are a variety originated by J.B. Bearss of Porterville, 1895

Hauling boxes of oranges to the Porterville packing house, 1920.

Inside a citrus packing house. Taken in 1918 at Terra Bella.

The lemon industry in the county was started by James W.C. Pogue, who gave Lemon Cove its name and lived to see his vision of citrus groves in the land he pioneered become a reality. He came west in 1857 in a wagon train led by Reverend Jonathan Blair. Two years later he married Reverend Blair's daughter, Nancy Melvina Blair. In 1862 J.W.C. Pogue brought his family from Santa Rosa to Tulare County. They lived for a time near Venice Hill, and later near Bravo Lake. The flood of 1868 washed them out, so he bought land on Dry Creek, across from what is now Lemon Cove. In 1877 Mr. Pogue began an experiment with oranges and lemons in his family orchard. He planted a mixed lot of 20 trees and was especially pleased with the lemons. Malaria drove the family to higher ground, and they settled at what is now Lemon Cove in 1879. The present Woman's Club House in Lemon Cove was built in 1879 as a home and hotel for the Pogue family. That was the era of the Mineral King mining boom, and the Pogue home made a good stopover for travelers.

Of vital import to the fledgling citrus industry was the fact that Mr. Pogue moved his orange and lemon trees from Dry Creek in 200-pound balls of dirt. Twenty survived, and he planted ten more — four Washington navels, two Valencias, two Lisbon lemons, and two lime trees. They all grew in the new location, but the lemons exceeded everyone's expectations. It was evident that Mr. Pogue had an ideal place for lemons. In 1885 he exhibited lemons at the Los Angeles Fair and won first premium. In 1894 he subdivided his property, part of which he put into town lots and named Lemon Cove.

Within a few years, Lemon Cove was indeed the center of lemon culture. Local businessmen as well as Eastern capitalists formed companies and planted lemons in that area. The growers organized in the late 1890's to improve the handling and marketing of lemons. In 1905 the Mt. Whitney Power and Electric Company started supplying power to run pumps, and the next year the Visalia Electric Railroad began passenger and freight service for that section of the county.

The Porterville and Springville areas also produced lemons. Mr. Gibbons sent a box of lemons to the Los Angeles Fair in 1887. In 1901 the Porterville Citrus Association bought land at Olive and E Streets and built two packing sheds — one for lemons and one for oranges. The Earl Fruit Company bought most of the lemons produced in the county. In 1900 that company shipped the first full carload of lemons to New York. The freight car carried fruit from Porterville and Springville and sold for $1,100.

The heavy freeze of 1913 hurt all varieties of citrus, but the lemon trees were almost wiped out. Most of the surviving trees were pulled or budded to oranges. The 5% of citrus represented by lemons is still centered around the areas where Mr. Pogue began his experiment a century ago.

The Spaniards laid the foundation for almost

every aspect of California's vast agri-business empire, but other ethnic groups also made great contributions. The Russians grew hardy fruits and vegetables at Fort Ross; the French, Italians, Japanese, Chinese, and especially the Armenians brought the fruits and vegetables indigenous to their homelands. Americans who came from the "states" brought seeds, cuttings, and slips from favorite flowers, fruits, and vines. Family gardens and orchards provided a large share of the pioneer family's food. The same family gardens and orchards made it possible for curious and patient experimenters to develop better varieties of fruit and vegetables.

Today Tulare County is one of the most diversified fruit-growing areas in the world. Sub-tropical fruits such as citrus and avocados grow just as well as temperate zone fruits such as peaches and apples. Deciduous fruits are sold fresh, dried, processed and frozen.

The Luther Burbank of Tulare County was Isaac H. Thomas (1838-1923), who gained statewide recognition as a horticulturist. He and his brother, Joseph H. Thomas (1816-1902), came to California in the 1850's. Joseph came to Visalia in 1856 and the next year bought the Smith and Hatch Lumber Mill in the mountains east of Visalia. He changed the mill's operation from water to steam power. This necessitated bringing in all of the machinery by mule. In the first issue of the *Tulare County Record & Fresno Examiner* (June 25, 1859), he advertised for teamsters. He also urged people to come to his mill, where he would sell lumber at a discount. He later sold the mill and built a larger one about a mile away. He built a fairly good road at his own expense, and was doing well until the flood of 1862 washed his mill and 40 big pine trees off the flat. Isaac had been associated with his brother in running the second mill. After the flood they had to find other ways to make a living. Joseph opened a blacksmith shop in Visalia and in 1857 built the first brick house in town on the northeast corner of Court and Acequia Streets.

Isaac Thomas bought land east of Visalia. He had had some experience as a nurseryman, and he began to scientifically select and plant fruit trees. The best market at the time was for dried fruit. He planted trees whose fruit could be dried, such as apples, plums, peaches, prunes, pears, and apricots. By selecting and culling, he produced several new varieties and also introduced standard stock. Many of the varieties produced or originated by Mr. Thomas have been phased out in favor of fruit developed to serve the multiple uses of canning, drying, freezing, and now the world-wide shipping of fresh fruit.

When railroad transportation became available in the 1870's, Isaac Thomas began experimenting with boxing and shipping fresh fruit to market. It was a costly experience. In 1884 he set up the first commercial drying and packing shed in the county, at the corner of Main and Court Streets in Visalia. At the same time, he turned his farm into a stone fruit nursery. The next two decades might be called the era of citrus and deciduous fruit in the county. Citrus was confined to the low foothills, which provided thermal drainage, but deciduous fruits grew anywhere. Real estate developers bought large tracts of land, and subdivided them into small plots with water rights.

Men, women, and children found plenty of work in the summer, picking, cutting, pitting, and drying fruit in the sun. Large farms such as Paige & Morton, Tagus, Redbanks, and Mineral King had their own packing sheds. Packing sheds were also built in most communities to take care of the small farms' output. Good "cutters" could earn as much as $2.50 a day.

The first annual Fair of the Tulare Valley Agricultural Association was held in Visalia in 1887. The 15th District included both Tulare and Kern Counties. There had been smaller fairs, but this time fruit displays made up a large share of the exhibit space. Joseph Spier & Son and Isaac Thomas exhibited dried fruits. James Martin from Porterville showed oranges. A.J. Weston and the Blossom Orchard of Three Rivers exhibited apples. Wiley Watson showed pickled olives and Joseph Thomas exhibited canned fruit. There were tall jars of brandied fruits, and the new Visalia Cannery had a commercial exhibit. The man behind the Fair was Isaac Thomas, who was rapidly becoming a one-person Chamber of Commerce for all of Tulare County agriculture.

In 1888 Thomas was responsible for a magnificent exhibit of stone fruits at the Mechanics Institute in San Francisco. The exhibit won first prize and much favorable newspaper coverage. From that time on, Mr. Thomas kept an exhibit of stone fruits at the State Board of Trade Rooms in San Francisco at his own expense. He also sent exhibits to fairs in all sections of the nation.

One facet of his role of encouraging people to plant fruit trees earned him the nickname of "the widows' friend." He had advertised that he would give trees for a family orchard to any widow in

Isaac Thomas (1838-1923) celebrated his 80th birthday with several friends in 1918. Left to right, front row, are: Rufus Gilmer (age 93), Mr. McClosky (93), Isaac Thomas (80), Tod Robinson (84), Henry P. Perkins (79). Center Row: Milt English (67), Henry Keener (75), Erasmus Warner (76), John Knox (81). Top Row: William Wright (62), Paschal Bequette (71), Mark Thomas (50).

Tulare or Fresno County if she had land where the trees could be planted. The response was enthusiastic, and he estimated that before it was all over he had given away about $700.00 worth of fruit trees. Just for fun, because he did not expect an answer, he advertised that he would give free trees to old maids over the age of 55. To his surprise, he received several requests!

Although income from dried fruit provided a stable source of revenue for the farmers, Mr. Thomas constantly sought to develop a market for fresh fruit. He shipped small lots of fresh figs, plums, and peaches to Texas, Arizona, and Kansas. The market was unpredictable, but by 1900 he was shipping out more than half a ton of fresh fruit during the fruit season.

Other deciduous fruit growers were willing to take a chance on unstable markets. The first full carload of green fruit was shipped from the Giant Oak Ranch near Farmersville in 1894. E.F. Pinkham supervised the loading of 600 crates of Clyman plums, 400 crates of Alexander peaches, and 200 crates of apricots.

1894 was a year of labor unrest, including racial problems. Many growers sold the fruit on the tree to Chinese buyers who brought in their own crews to pick the crop. Work was scarce in the hard times of the early 1890's. Large advertisements in the Visalia newspapers called for anti-Chinese meetings "to consider the matter of employing Chinese in orchards." A week later the editor commented that three attempts had been made to hold anti-Chinese meetings which developed into a ridiculous farce.

The Santa Clara Valley had been a production center for deciduous fruits and grapes. When men like Isaac Thomas demonstrated the productivity of Tulare County's soil and climate, experienced horticulturists came to see and then to buy land. Among the earliest were Charles and George Flemming, who bought near Farmersville, as did J.K. Armsby. John Briggs came in 1887 and farmed near Farmersville. He was the brother of horticulturists Joseph and George Briggs of San Jose and Marysville. Frank Briggs and Martin Rouse located east of Visalia. They sent a mixed lot of crates of plums and peaches to San Francisco in 1888. The boxes were loaded on the Visalia-Goshen Railroad in Visalia, hauled to Goshen Junction and then reloaded on the Southern Pacific. The railroads did not guarantee rapid transit for any freight, and many a citrus and fresh fruit grower worked all year only to end up with a freight bill for fruit spoiled before it reached market.

Neal McCullom's ranch is now part of the community of Orosi. Eben F. Pinkham and Frank B. McKevitt developed the Pennebaker ranch southeast of Visalia into the famous Giant Oak

Paige and Morton Ranch near Tulare had the first cannery in Tulare County in 1886. (From an old lithograph)

Ranch. They also planted the California Prune Orchard. The Mineral King Fruit Ranch south of what is now Cutler Park was developed by Richard Chatten. One of the largest ranches in the state was the Paige and Morton Ranch near Tulare, where 1,900 of its 3,000 acres were planted to deciduous fruit. The first cannery in Tulare County was started on that ranch in 1886. Apricots, nectarines, peaches, and tomatoes were canned in glass jars. The ranch also had a cutting and drying shed, and hired between 200 and 300 people in fruit season.

Two well known nurserymen from San Jose, Thomas and Morphew Jacob, bought land east of Visalia and established a nursery and an experiment station and planted an orchard. They were the first to grow prunes on a commercial scale. The trees bore in four years, and the fruit sold for $55.00 a ton. For the next decade the best income crop of all deciduous fruit was prunes, especially French prunes. Thomas Jacob also introduced varieties of walnuts, peaches, and plums to the county. Mr. Jacob was a member of the first Board of Forestry, which developed Mooney Grove Park, and it was largely through his efforts that the county obtained the famous statues, "The End of the Trail" and "The Pioneer."

Hulett C. Merritt laid the foundation for the world-famous Tagus Ranch north of Tulare when he bought 3,000 acres in 1903. The ranch expanded to 7,000 acres, producing diversified crops. It became well known to travelers on Highway 99 by way of its billboards which proclaimed the ranch the world's largest producer of peaches.

Isaac Thomas' work was recognized officially when he was appointed to the State Board of Horticulture in 1884. In 1904 he was hired as horticulturist for Redbanks, one of the county's large diversified ranches. The ranch is located on the slope of Colvin Mountain near Ivanhoe. Thermal drainage makes it possible for that ranch to produce some of the first peaches to ripen in the state.

The leading deciduous fruits often had interesting historical sidelights. Apricots grew well in the county and were popular both for canning and drying. One of the most popular varieties was the Tilton, which was developed from a seedling on the ranch of J.E. Tilton near Hanford.

Peaches have always ranked first in popularity. They are classified as clingstone or freestone, but a multitude of varieties have been developed. Canners prefer clings, and California produces a large share of the nation's cling peaches, which are now handled through the California Canning Peach Association. The Persian Cling originated near Visalia. One of the first varieties to ripen was Briggs Red May, developed from a seedling found in 1870 on the Feather River Ranch of John Briggs.

Prunes did exceptionally well around Farmersville, Tulare, and Visalia. By definition a prune is a variety of plum which can be dried whole without pit fermentation. Among the scions that

Fruit drying at Mineral King Ranch south of Cutler Park.

the Pellier Brothers brought to San Jose in 1856 was one from the d'Agen district of France. It was grafted to a wild plum rootstock and produced the famous French prune, which grew in all the valleys of California. It was overplanted here as elsewhere, and by 1900 many trees were pulled and replaced by peaches. There are still enough prune orchards in Tulare County today to place the crop in the multi-million dollar category.

Most early settlers had fig trees around the house. Figs grow quickly from cuttings, and thousands of cuttings were taken from mission trees. The oldest fig trees in Tulare County were planted at the first Tule River Indian Reservation in 1856. John W. Williams brought the cuttings from Southern California. The trees lived on for years after the Reservation was moved to its present location east of Porterville.

One of the attractions for planting citrus and deciduous fruit in Tulare County was the absence of scale, smut, and harmful insect pests. Growers who came from Southern California knew that this might not always be the case. The State Legislature had made provision for the appointment of County Boards of Horticulture as well as local inspectors in order to detect or prevent the importation of diseased trees and plants. Tulare County Supervisors appointed the first Horticultural Commission in 1884. The members were I.M. Wright, Frank Briggs, and E. Sanbourn. They were paid for the time spent on a job, not to exceed $500.00 a year for each member. In 1892 N.W. Motherall was appointed County Entomologist, and the Supervisors appropriated $75.00 so he could buy a magnifying glass to identify insects. The glass cost slightly more than $75.00, and the District Attorney was authorized to bring action against Mr. Motherall.

The outcome was not recorded, but Mr. Motherall stayed in office.

In spite of constant inspection at receiving stations, the deadly San Jose scale gradually appeared. In the Horticultural Commission's report of 1890 we find a realistic statement as well as a prediction that has come true.

Insect pests for some cause not clearly defined, have disappeared almost entirely in the western part of the County (now Kings County, which separated from Tulare County in 1893). The lime, sulphur, and salt compound has been used unsparingly against the San Jose Scale, and orchards not sprayed are as clean as those that were. The season and parasites likely have done most of the good work. All along Tule River and around Porterville, the San Jose Scale is still doing its deadly work. All the apples and pears are spotted with scale. Little has been done to destroy the insect. The wooly aphis and coddling moth are both very troublesome in this district. Around Visalia insect pests are kept in check, and the fruit is clean. The same may be said for Tulare.

It is difficult to predict the future of this County. Unless some calamity befalls our fruit and raisin industry within the next five years, this will be the fruit and raisin industry of the State.

There were other problems besides scale. Planting had been done with contagious furor, with little concern for soils, proper cultivation, or care of the trees. The major flood of 1906 washed away topsoil, and since the water remained in many places for days, budded rootstock rotted. There were labor troubles. The severe drop in the water table affected the growers who depended upon pumped wells. In spite of these problems, the fruit industry flourished and provided work for hundreds of people.

Entire families worked in the fields, canneries, and packing sheds. After the fruit was picked,

*Thomas Jacob (1852-1930)
His experiments with deciduous fruits and walnuts helped develop these important crops in Tulare County. As a member of the original Board of Forestry, Mr. Jacob was instrumental in developing Mooney Grove and in securing the well-known statues, "The Pioneer" and "The End of the Trail."*

women and children cut and pitted peaches and apricots and put them on trays for sun drying. Huge trays of prunes were dipped before the fruit was sun-dried. Grapes were dried between the rows of vines, but care was taken to place muscats so they would dry in clusters. Men and the larger boys turned and stacked trays, carried boxes of fresh fruit to the cutters, and emptied dried fruit into lug boxes. The hours were long and the pay varied from $1.50 to $2.50 a day, but if the family worked, the income was good. Many growers preferred to pay by the box or by the hour as an incentive for good, fast workers. There was a camaraderie that helped pass the time. If you wanted to find people during fruit season, you went to packing sheds or canneries.

Refrigerated freight cars and marketing associations stabilized the fresh fruit market. Canneries were established in all of the larger communities. There was more call for semi-skilled labor. People earned more if they could grade and pack fresh fruit quickly. Women who could peel quality fruit neatly and quickly earned more. Men were needed to make boxes, stack cans, and load freight cars. Machinery and conveyor belts began to eliminate the old care-free days and replace them with speed, noise, and precision.

The seasonal work in California created the so-called fruit tramps who were an important segment of the working force in agriculture. Fruit tramps were not migrant workers. They were hard-working people who earned good money by being willing to put up with the inconveniences of moving up and down the state. Since most were family groups, children suffered the most because of frequent changes of schools, or no school at all. Usually fruit tramps started in the Imperial Valley, and gradually worked their way into the San Joaquin Valley to pick plums, peaches, prunes, apricots, and other varieties of fruit. If they wanted to stay, they picked walnuts and oranges. If not, they went on to Santa Clara, San Jose, Napa, and on into Oregon for the pear and apple harvest. Winter found them back in the Imperial Valley. Farmers and packing shed operators counted on these people, and usually the same families came back to the same farms every year.

The day of the fruit tramp began to wane when stricter child labor laws took effect and authorities began to pay stricter attention to school attendance. World War II brought new wages and working hours. Labor unions forced better working conditions. The eight-hour day, with rest periods for women, made it necessary to work in shifts. Modern methods of cold storage, as well as pro-rated markets, prolonged the fruit season and provided more work. It was advantageous for these nomadic families to settle down, and the day of the fruit tramp became a part of farming history.

1. *Tulare County Times,* February 9, 1888.
2. Federal Census Figures, also County Records.
3. J.M. Guinn, *History of the San Joaquin Valley,* Chicago, 1905. Biography of James Porteous.
4. *Visalia Times,* July 3, 1886.
5. Mrs. Sadie Lindsay Patton Hutchinson, *Recollections of Early Days in Lindsay,* Edited by Harold G. Schutt, *Lindsay Gazette,* August 7 to November 6, 1974.
6. *Visalia Times,* November 11, 1886.
7. *Tulare County Record & Fresno Examiner,* June 25, 1859, Visalia.
8. *Terra Bella News,* August 3, 1934, Article by James M. Wood.
9. *Resources of San Joaquin Valley,* June 1886.
10. *Porterville Farm Tribune,* November 8, 1956.
11. Interview with Sylvia Wylde, possible in 1940's.
12. Mrs. Sadie Lindsay Patton Hutchinson, ibid.
13. Ina Stiner, *Porterville Recorder,* October 25, 1949.

CHAPTER 10

THE LAND OF MILK AND MONEY

The dairy industry is the fastest-growing business in Tulare County and now ranks third in farm income. Favorable climate, available land at reasonable prices, a large feed supply, available labor, and local processing plants have all contributed to this rapid growth.

Like the fruit industry, the dairy industry owes its start to courageous men in the county in 1860. Perhaps even before 1860, for Elisha Packwood pastured his herd of milch cows in the Tule River country in 1853.

The first record of a dairy is found in the *Visalia Weekly Delta* on February 18, 1860.

It is a fact that we now have a milk wagon running through the streets of Visalia. Mr. Elijah Smith will deliver milk to the citizens of the town every morning and evening. This astonishing enterprise in a cow county should be encouraged.

The comment was justified. Farm families kept a few cows to provide milk, butter, and cheese, and some people living in town also kept a cow. Housewives traded butter and eggs for staples at the grocery store. Ladies who made good butter received top trade value. Merchants also had to take inferior butter, and it was a trade secret that poorly made butter was sold cheaply to a few discreet customers who found it a good substitute for axle grease.

Elijah Smith sold both milk and butter to individuals and stores, and he did well. One of his pleased patrons was the editor of the *Delta* who every so often ran a comment such as this:

PURE MILK: Don't fail to notice our old friend, Elijah Smith's card. No cow ever returned home at sun down to leave her lacteal supply for the little ones more regularly than our friend's visits to us, or brought a purer beverage. GIVE HIM A CALL.[1]

As other communities were started, similar milk routes were set up. Many were sideline sources of income. Whatever the size of the "herd," milking and processing the milk was a never-ending job. Cows were milked by hand at daybreak. The milk was taken to the kitchen or the milk house and poured into large, heavy pans so the cream would rise. After the cream was skimmed off, the skimmed milk was fed to calves, hogs, and chickens. Butter was churned in a hand churn. A by-product of the churning was buttermilk, a nutritious and especially welcome drink in hot weather. If the farmer had a milk route for cream, butter, and whole milk, he had to sterilize his bottles, gallon, and even ten-gallon milk cans. In the evening the same tedious process was repeated. Pasteurization and homogenization were unheard of safeguards. So was refrigeration.

The early methods of cooling were crude but somehow effective. However, they were a far cry from our modern methods of refrigeration. Ice from the mountain lakes was available in the summertime, but it was a luxury item usually bought by restaurants and saloons. Many people had meathouses whose double walls were insulated with sawdust. Almost everyone had a cooler — upright shelves somewhat like a book case. The shelves were screened on the back and sides and had a screen door in front. The top boards carried a sheet metal pan filled with water. Burlap sacks or wide strips of flannel hung from the water pan down the back and side of the cooler. The dripping water from these outside coolers, aided by breezes, kept food remarkably cool. However, these methods were not completely effective, for ptomaine poisoning was common, and summer complaint among infants was not only common but, in many cases, fatal.

In the 1890's ice was brought in by railroad freight. During the railroad strike of 1894, that source was cut off. A few enterprising men went to Mineral King and cut ice from inside the old Empire Mine and sold it in Visalia. The first ice plant

The Visalia Creamery, built in 1910, on Oak Street is now remodeled for the Railroad Shops. The creamery workers and delivery men are not identified.

in the valley was started in Visalia in 1897. It was the Visalia Manufacturing Company on East Main Street, and David Wishon was the first manager.

Home ice boxes were a welcome innovation. Most held at least 50 pounds of ice, and the ice man came twice a week to fill the box. His visit was a high spot for the children, for he could be counted upon to slip them chips of ice to suck. Another nostalgic memory from the day of the ice box was the drip pan under the box. It had to be emptied each day, and there must be some old-timer left who can remember jumping out of bed to do that chore before a mop-up job was necessary.

The dairy business began to expand in the 1880's and 1890's when land use patterns changed. That was the period when land companies subdivided tracts into small holdings with water rights. The small farms were planted to citrus, deciduous fruits, and that backbone of the dairy business, alfalfa.

James Evans, who lived south of Visalia, planted the first alfalfa in the county in 1860. His small field produced a good crop. Not until the drought of 1864 did the stockmen realize how dependent they were upon rainfall for range feed. Then a few farmers began to experiment with alfalfa. It grew well in the Mussel Slough country and around the Tule River. In the latter area John Walker planted four acres and harvested 2,000 pounds of seed, which he sold for $175. His neighbor, J.D. Owen, also planted alfalfa and sold the seed for $350.[2]

The introduction of alfalfa into California is an interesting bit of agricultural history. The plant originated in southwest Asia. In Arabia it was given its name, which simply means "best forage." The Persians took the plant along when they invaded Greece. The Roman armies took it to the countries which they conquered, and the Spaniards brought it to the New World. In France and Italy the plant was called lucerne, from a valley in northern Italy. It is still known by that name in the eastern United States.

Dr. E.J. Wickson dated the arrival of alfalfa into California as 1851, when W.E. Cameron planted a field near Marysville. He enlarged the planting until he had 270 acres in alfalfa in 1858.[3]

Alfalfa and small dairies thrived together in Tulare County. One acre of alfalfa maintained two cows. The crop was cut several times a year, and since it is a legume, alfalfa was rotated with other crops to avoid soil depletion. In 1986 alfalfa hay returned an income of $63,150.00 to county farmers. Much of the crop is sold directly to local dairies or feed lots.

As small dairies multiplied, the farmers realized they had to find a wider market for their milk. In 1886 a dairy union was organized in Tulare County, and its members visited Hanford, which had a cheese factory. The men organized a joint stock company with shares set at $50.00 each. W.H. Blain was elected President and Reverend Samuel T. Gilliam, Secretary.

In 1889 a versatile pioneer, Daniel K. Zumwalt, built the first commercial creamery on his ranch midway between Tulare and Visalia. That same year the joint stock company built the Visalia Creamery two miles west of Visalia on the Visalia-Goshen Railroad. Both plants were equipped to make butter and cheese. Butter was made into two-pound rolls and the cheese into 25- to 30-pound rounds. The Visalia plant handled 5,000 pounds of milk a day, collected from 18 farms. Zumwalt's plant did a similar business. They paid 90 cents per 100 pounds of milk, which at the time tested 8 ½ pounds to a gallon.[4]

In a few years both plants were having financial difficulties, for several reasons. Citrus and deciduous fruits were THE crops and the profits from the fruit were so good that some dairy farmers went into that phase of farming. Los Angeles was, and still is, the market for the milk products from this area. Freight rates and poor delivery drastically cut into the creameries' profit. The business recession of 1893-4 was followed by a paralyzing nationwide railroad strike. Since there was no ice to refrigerate butter, the local creameries had to make cheese. The Zumwalt plant lost 20,000 pounds of milk before it could be converted into cheese.

The Visalia Creamery did not pay its stockholders until the butter and cheese were sold, so the farmers had to bear the loss of many pounds of milk. Both plants closed. Isaac H. Thomas, representing a majority of the stockholders, bought the Visalia Creamery at auction for $1,760, and for a few months it was back in operation. In 1898 Wooster Cartmill of Tulare re-opened both creameries as skimming stations, but closed them when he started his own skimming station in Tulare in 1900.

Although Daniel K. Zumwalt operated the first commercial creamery, the industry actually owes its beginning to the Cartmill family, who came to Tulare in 1861.

Dr. William Cartmill was to recall that he started his dairy with 25 cows, $100.00, and misfortune. He was born in Ohio in 1822 and graduated from medical school before starting overland for California in 1849. Like so many argonauts, he did not find his fortune in mining. He went into partnership in a general store in Lower Rancheria, and that venture was profitable. Whe he had saved enough money he went home and married Sophia Barnes. They sailed for California, and when the Cartmills arrived in Lower Rancheria they found the partner had sold the store and decamped with the money. Dr. Cartmill worked in the mines and

Dr. W.F. Cartmill (1822-1906)

also practiced medicine. He began to buy heifers from the best stock driven across the plains. In 1861 he came into the county looking for suitable rangeland for his herd of some 100 cows. His son, Wooster Cartmill, who was born in Lower Rancheria in 1857, wrote his recollections of family events. A few excerpts will vividly recount their pioneer life in Tulare County. A complete account may be found in *Los Tulares #89,* March 1971.

Father returned to Amador County and in September (1861) started to Tulare County. The outfit consisted of two wagons, prairie schooners, drawn by four oxen, driven by a man by the name of Conner. Mother, myself and sister Flora were loaded into the wagon and father and another man whose name I have forgotten drove the cattle....

On October 26, 1861 we drove onto the old Cartmill Ranch (Note: Dr. Cartmill had bought a claim from Joe Gashwiler, an old acquaintance from Missouri). There was a small shack made of oak shakes split from the timber all around at that time, there was no floor and only one window, consisting of four small panes of glass.

I think it was the second night on the place, someone or something stampeded all of our cattle and although father was out after them in a few minutes, most of them were gone and although he followed them for several days he found only a part of them, losing about sixty head, that he had spent all the money that he had to buy. That left Father again with nothing. He saved or rather found 25 head of the good heifers. He told me that he had exactly $100.00 to start in business again. By dint of hard work and the assistance of a Mr. Collins, a merchant in Visalia, he managed to exist until spring when

Ranch and residence of W. F. Cartmill, six miles northwest of Tulare. (From an old lithograph)

many of the heifers came in as milk cows. He and mother ran a dairy for several years, selling the butter and eggs to a man who took them over the mountains on pack animals, to a mining camp called White Pine.[5] They got fifty cents per pound at the ranch. It was packed in rolls covered with cheese cloth and packed in strong brine. Sometimes we would have several hundred pounds when the man came after it. Father and mother must have worked very hard without any recreation or rest, as I know of nothing more confining and laborious than running a dairy, up at 4 o'clock and work until after dark. I soon learned to milk one old white faced cow that I can well remember. It was always my job to get in the wood and kindling every night. For a long time mother cooked in the fireplace. Some time during the second year they got a stove...Shortly after we located, father bought some hogs, which he fattened with acorns gathered from the oak timber and some wheat which he bought from a neighbor living west of the ranch about two or three miles on Packwood Creek. As soon as they were fat, father killed them and made sausage and bacon, separating off part of the house for a smokehouse.

W.B. Cartmill described the flood of 1862. His parents worked all night to keep water out of the house, but finally they had to leave. The family spent two weeks with the Frank Thomas family, their neighbors to the west. When they came back the smoked meat and staple supplies of flour and sugar were ruined.

The flood of 1862 was shortly followed by the drouth of 1864 and so dry was it that year that my father has told me no green grass was visible on the plains, and I can remember seeing the cattle just reeling across the plains from sheer exhaustion, and one was never out of sight of dead animals....During that summer Father moved us down to the lake — and I can remember father saying that if it had not been for the salt grass, all the stock would have perished. That fall father bought a few tons of hay from a neighbor at $40.00 a ton just to keep his saddle horse and a milk cow alive.

Wooster Cartmill took over active management of the ranch in 1894. He continued the dairy but planted grapes, prunes, peaches, and 160 acres of alfalfa. When he started his skimming station in Tulare in 1900, he also laid the foundation for Tulare's present major industry. He advertised that his skimming station would separate cream from milk, return the skimmed milk, and pay the highest price for butter fat.

In 1903 the Tulare Co-operative Creamery was incorporated and Wooster Cartmill was selected manager. He organized a fleet of wagons to gather milk at contributing farms. Today people would be aghast at the sight of large milk cans beside the road, bereft of refrigeration, waiting to be picked up by the creamery milk wagon.

In the early years of this century dairymen and all farm folk were hailing a new machine, the milk separator. With a separator farmers could separate the cream immediately and thus eliminate some of the heavy work. The creameries also inaugurated payment every month, and this stable income induced people to go into the dairy business which began to cluster around Tulare, Tule River, and Visalia. Dairymen also came to realize that the day of the "low producer and high kicker" was over. They began to replace scrub stock with Holsteins, Jerseys and other breed that produced milk with a higher butterfat content.

In 1915 the Tulare Co-operative Creamery was sold. Mr. Cartmill continued ranching, and also served as Tulare Postmaster for a term. He served his community in many civic and social enterprises as this excerpt from his obituary on January 29, 1938 points out:

W.B. Cartmill led an active and eventful life, and has been a force for great good in the community. Had he done nothing aside from taking the important and far-reaching step that led to the establishment of the creamery business in Tulare, he would forever be entitled to the gratitude and praise of the residents of this locality.

Daniel Kindle Zumwalt (1845-1904) built the area's first commercial creamery. Born in Illinois, he came to California with his family in 1854. His father, Jacob Zumwalt, farmed near Sacramento until he moved to Visalia in 1872. Daniel Zumwalt graduated from College of the Pacific. He taught school for a time, then read law and was admitted to the bar. He came to Tulare County in 1869 and bought land midway between Tulare and Visalia (now south of Liberty School). He did start the first commercial creamery, but his other community contributions overshadow that achievement. He combined the practice of law with real estate. For over 20 years he was land agent and attorney for the Southern Pacific Railroad for the counties of Tulare, Kern, Fresno, and what is now Kings County. He was one of the incorporators and also served as treasurer of the 76 Land & Water Company. He also helped incorporate several irrigation associations. Mr. Zumwalt was very active in the Methodist Church and various lodges and civic groups. His most outstanding contribution to history, however, may be the preservation of the Giant Forest, and his participation in this event has been discovered only recently.

Conservationists had led a long fight to preserve the giant redwood trees in the high Sierra Mountains. Congress finally passed a bill on September 25, 1890 which created Sequoia National Park. Much to local surprise, a second bill was introduced by Congressman Vandever on October 1, 1890, and it too passed. This legislation not only doubled the size of the Park, but included the magnificent stand of trees known as Giant Forest. Recent research has revealed that D.K. Zumwalt was the guest of Congressman Vandever at the time and induced him to enter the legislation which preserved Giant Forest from the lumberman's saw and axe.

Another early dairy center was the Tule River area from Tipton to Porterville. The first record of a commercial enterprise is in 1889, when John D. Owen built a cheese-making plant which turned out 130 pounds a day at his Woodville ranch. The milk came from his own herd of 25 cows and from the small herds of seven or eight neighbors.

In 1895 the Woodville Creamery was built. The stockholders were John Ball, Samuel Vincent, Joe Vossler, Martin Click, J.B. Monroe, J.H. Grimsley,

Daniel K. Zumwalt (1845-1904)

Marcus DeWitt, and A.O. Thompson. Thompson, an experienced buttermaker, was hired as manager and buttermaker. Milk for the creamery was furnished by the stockholders and the Blair, Stewart, Udell, Pratt, Rising, and La Marsna families. The creamery's next buttermaker was William W. Futrell, who had learned the trade from Thompson. The Woodville Creamery had financial problems and in 1899 sold to David Udell and James Miner, who moved the building and equipment to the Miner Ranch. Miner later bought out Udell's interest. Mr. Miner had arrived in the Rockyford District in 1869 and, with J.R. Hubbs, built the Hubbs-Miner Irrigation Ditch, diverting water from the Tule River. Miner operated the creamery until 1904, when competition from Tulare Creameries and the nearby Sunflower Creamery forced him to close.

In point of time the next creamery was the Tipton Creamery, built in 1895. It was moved at least four times and went through two disastrous fires. Like other early creameries, the Tipton plant could not depend on a stable market outlet. In 1919 it was sold to the Alfred Ice Cream Company of Los Angeles. Nine years later several ice cream companies, including Alfred, were bought by California Dairies Incorporated. The Paige Dairyman's Association closed at about the same time, and the dairymen who had taken milk there then took it to Tipton. Concurrently, dairymen found they could get a better price for "Los Angeles inspected sweet cream." **To qualify it was necessary to have dairies** and creameries under Los Angeles Health Department Inspection, and an inspector was assigned to Tipton. The Company operated its own fleet of four Reo trucks which made daily pickups at the farms.

Manuel C. Borba's dairy near Tipton. Mr. Borba was one of Tulare County's first dairymen.

Newman Dairy near Tulare, 1905.

The Porterville Co-operative Creamery. J.D. Beckwith had a dairy near Tipton. The other men bringing cans of cream are not identified.

Dairy of C.T. Brown and Son, Porterville, 1905.

Dairymen's Co-operative Creamery, Tulare.

In 1929 the Company began to develop a herd of purebred cattle. The main purpose was to make purebred sires available to local dairymen to raise the quality of their producing animals. Over the years 1,000 bulls were placed in local dairy herds. The herd project was continued until 1954, when the herd and the ranch were sold.

Another related project was raising heifers on a ranch near Porterville. Yearling heifers were transferred from the Arden Certified Herd in El Monte to Porterville and put in permanent pasture. They were sent back to El Monte as springers. This project was carried on for about 17 years.

The Arden Company owned another ranch a mile east and south of Tipton where hogs were raised. The animals were fed whey from cottage cheese then manufactured at Tipton. The program started in 1929 and was phased out in 1940.

Over the years the Tipton creamery has had many changes in size, equipment and corporate names. For many years now it has been Arden Farms, which operates the creamery as well as dairies and related farm projects.

The Sunflower Creamery in Porterville is really the story of the Ridgeway family, for it was indeed a family-run business. In 1900 the Ridgeway brothers and their families came to the County, bought land near Poplar and stocked it with Holstein dairy cattle. Both brothers, Christopher and Edward, had had previous experience in operating a dairy. In January 1902 they opened the Sunflower Creamery with an output of a ton of butter a day. Their older sons helped: Oscar was the buttermaker, Ernest was the bookkeeper, Fred helped with the management, and Leslie and Walter drove two of the three wagons that collected milk and cream. Like most dairymen, the Ridgeways had a herd of hogs which were fed skimmed milk.

When the Sunflower Creamery started, it competed against the Miner Creamery, the Tipton Creamery, Cartmill's Skimming Station and the Good Luck Creamery operated by J.H. Frew in Tulare. In 1903 the Tulare Co-operative Creamery was incorporated, and in 1904 the Porterville Co-operative Creamery was organized. All of these businesses competed for milk from small dairies.

In 1912 the Ridgeways sold the Sunflower Creamery to J.F. Raitt of Santa Ana, who ran it for two years. C.C. Ridgeway was asked to manage the Porterville Co-op, which closed a couple of years later. Fred Ridgeway bought the equipment and re-opened the Sunflower, but then had to close it in 1916. Dairymen continued to deliver milk to their customers for some time. Eventually it became more convenient for most customers to buy their milk at grocery stores, and the dairies closed.

In 1903 the economy of Tulare got a second boost when the Tulare Co-operative Creamery was organized. (The first boost had been the easing of the financial burden of the Tulare Irrigation District.) The directors of the creamery were S.B. Anderson, William Swall, P.E. Reinhart, M.G. Cottle, and Charles Meadors. They selected W.B. Cartmill to manage the plant. He signed up dairymen and sent out a fleet of wagons to pick up cream at the dairies. The Co-op was soon manufacturing 7,000 to 9,000 pounds of butterfat per day.

In a few months Tulare had another creamery. That was the Good Luck Creamery run by J.H. Frew. Competition among the creameries in the county was beneficial, for it not only encouraged more farmers to go into the dairy business but also encouraged them to replace their "high kickers and low producers" with good dairy stock. Dairymen also became cognizant of their market. Better prices would only come from better products. The Tulare County Board of Supervisors was asked to appoint a dairy inspector to enforce sanitary standards and did so in 1908.

The next year, dairymen received low prices for

their butterfat. What they needed was a real cooperative organization.

Joe La Marche, president of the National Bank of Tulare, offered to put up $10,000 to finance a cooperative if 100 dairymen would either pay $100.00 for a share of stock or sign a note for $100.00. W.J. Higdon and J.F. Murphy visited every dairyman in the area and secured the necessary money.

The Dairyman's Co-operative Creamery was incorporated November 6, 1909. The Directors were F.C. Hayes, W.E. Green, C.A. Sayre, L.W. Bardsley, and W.J. Higdon. James P. Murphy was hired to manage the co-operative. Profits went back to the participating dairymen. Under that system, the price of butterfat rose, and competing creameries either had to pay the same prices or go out of business. Officials of the DCC soon realized that selling was as important as producing, so they started their own sales outlet in Los Angeles in 1911 using the Challenge trademark. For some time, sales averaged about 100 pounds of butter a day. In 1915 the Danish Creamery of Fresno, with 2,000 members, joined the Challenge Cream and Butter Association, and as its sales increased, other valley associations joined the Challenge Co-operative.

The DCC began experimenting with by-products. Semi-solid was sold for hog and poultry feed, casein was used in the manufacture of celluloid, and cottage cheese found a ready market. In the past few years powdered milk and yogurt have been added to the by-products. Today, the name Challenge is known wherever dairy products are sold.

The DCC sells to private distributors all over the state, but principally in Los Angeles and San Francisco. The Association provides Tulare's largest single source of income.

A privately owned creamery, Nielson's of Tulare, came much later than the establishments we have discussed, but it became one of the valley's large retail and wholesale plants. George Neilson came to the United States from Denmark in 1904 and worked in Wisconsin before he came to California. He worked in several creameries and then started the Danish Creamery in Bakersfield. He sold to the Peacock Ice Cream Company and moved to Tulare in 1922, where he bought a dairy farm in conjunction with the Peacock Company. In 1935 he opened a restaurant in Tulare, which still operates under that name. Later on his son-in-law, Clare Hoffman, took over operation of the business and developed the dairy farm into several farms milking several thousand head of cows.

Two of Visalia's major industries deal in milk products. They are Knudsen's Products and the Real Fresh Milk Company.

Knudsen's is the world's largest manufacturer of cottage cheese. The company came to Visalia in 1921 and leased the old creamery building on Oak Street. The present plant, on Goshen Avenue, opened in 1927 with ten employees. The plant has been enlarged several times, and is a self-contained complex with its own shops and equipment. In 1972 Stauffer Chemical Company built an adjoining plant to use the by-product whey derived from the manufacture of cottage cheese. This protein product is used for both human and animal consumption and is exported all over the world.

One of the dreams of the dairy industry was to find a process by which milk could be canned without condensing, evaporating, or powdering, and still keep its flavor and quality. That dream became a reality in the 1940's through the experiments of Roy Graves, who made major contributions to the dairy industry.

Mr. Graves began his experiments at Oregon State College. From 1918 to 1947 he was head of the Division of Dairy Breeding of the United States Department of Agriculture. Mr. Graves, in cooperation with the DeLaval Separator Company, made several improvements in milking machines. The experiments turned his attention to canning fresh milk. In essence his experiments involved drawing milk into a vacuum tank, where it would be pasteurized and sterilized without exposure to the air.

The experiment was worked out with John Stambaugh on his dairy farm in Indiana. The first plant, under the name Med-o-Milk, was opened in the State of Washington.

Mr. Graves' sons opened the Real Fresh Milk Company in Visalia in 1952, and until his death in 1976, Roy Graves acted as a consultant.

The products of Real Fresh Milk are sold all over the world, and the company is the major supplier for the Armed Forces. Besides sterile, fresh canned milk, the company produces whipping cream, sour cream, half and half, baby formula, whipped toppings, eggnog, chocolate drinks, milk shakes, pudding sauces, cheese spreads, fruit cups, and exotic fruit drinks.

1. *Visalia Weekly Delta,* February 22, 1865.
2. *Visalia Weekly Delta,* October 28, 1886.
3. *Alfalfa In America,* Joseph E. Wing, Sanders Publishing Co., Chicago, 1916, page 65.
4. *Visalia Weekly Delta,* May 26, 1894.
5. Probably Lone Pine.

CHAPTER 11

FLEECY FIBERS

The sheep industry, like the cattle industry, began in the missions. Hundreds of thousands of sheep were raised for meat and for wool which was woven into coarse blankets and serapes. Little effort was made to improve either the breeds or the quality of their wool. Sheepshearing kept mission Indians busy, and it was one of the few trades the Indians learned that was useful to them after the missions were secularized. After that traumatic event, herds of cattle and sheep were dispersed or destroyed, and by 1848 only 17,000 sheep were listed in the livestock census for California.

The gold rush opened up an almost unbelievable market for fresh meat. The miners preferred mutton and pork when they were available, and fat mutton sold for as much as $12 on the hoof. Enterprising men were soon driving sheep into California from the South and Midwest. William Hollister not only brought in the first large flock of sheep, but also brought to the state a new breed, the Spanish Merino. At the peak of his operation, Hollister ran 80,000 head of sheep. In 1853 Solomon Jewett, another pioneer of the industry, brought sheep into what is now Kern County. Even Kit Carson drove a flock of sheep into California.

The economic importance of sheep may be inferred from the census figures. In 1860 there were 2,768,187 sheep with a wool clip of 2,000,000 pounds. Prices also reflected the market. In 1852, for instance, 40,000 sheep were driven into the state and sold for $16 a head. In 1856 200,000 sheep were driven in, and the price dropped to $3.50 a head. Just when the market was saturated, the price of wool went up and the sheepmen were saved from bankruptcy. The sharp increase in the price of wool was a side effect of the Civil War. Cotton was not obtainable in the north, so wool was substituted. In order to produce a better quality wool, Cotswolds, Merinos, and Leicesters were imported into California.

The sheep industry centered in southern California and the central valley, with its accessible mountain pastures. It depended upon large uninhabited areas, free government land in the mountains, and cheap feed. Farmers, many of whom had flocks of sheep and goats, let the animals feed on the stubble left after the grain was harvested. Usually there was plenty of feed in the valley until early summer, then herders started the slow drive into the mountains.

Unlike cowboys, sheepherders lived lonely lives. Their companions were the faithful intelligent dogs who took more care of the herds than the herders. Many well-educated men sought the contemplative life of a herder. Most sheepherders in the valley were immigrants from southern Europe, especially from the Pyrenees, where the sheep industry had flourished for hundreds of years. The Basques made valuable contributions to California's history, but since they spoke little English, they left few memoirs.

Sheepmen and cattlemen were in conflict throughout western history. A basic reason was feed and water. When a flock of sheep passed over a feeding ground, there was nothing left but bare, churned dirt. Cattlemen complained that the hooves of sheep exuded a disagreeable odor and cattle would not feed on the same pasture. John Muir learned to hate sheep, for they denuded mountain pastures and ruined water sheds. He called them "hoofed locusts."

Herders had a custom which infuriated conservationists. They built a ring of bonfires for night corrals and to foil predators. Sometimes the fires got away and burned considerable acreage. It was also common practice for the last cattlemen leaving the mountains to set fire to underbrush to improve feed for the next season. Few would ever admit to that practice.

The sheep industry was economically important in Tulare County from 1860 until the turn of the century. Since personal recollections are meager, the scope of the industry will be gleaned from a few interviews and newspaper items arranged chronologically.

The first mention of large flocks of sheep came in 1859 when Huffum White and his stepsons, Clinton and William Brown, took some 6,000 sheep into the north Tule River Basin. The family continued to take sheep into the mountains for years, using either the Jordan Trail or the old Dennison Trail. Their sheep pastured from Camp Nelson to Sheep Mountain.

In January 1860 the river boat *The Visalia* made its initial run between Stockton and Fresno City (near present-day Tranquility) on the San Joaquin River. Another boat, *The Harriet*, was also making the trip. These boats carried 25 tons and drew 12 inches of water. Their return cargo was wool from the southern valley.

Much baled wool was hauled to coastal ports by wagons. For instance, as early as 1860 Edward P. Hart, who lived near Farmersville, hauled wool to San Francisco. That year the census showed a wool clip of 16,900 pounds taken in Tulare County.

Sheepmen wanted a shorter road to coastal markets, and in 1861 road viewers went to San Simeon Bay to determine a wagon road route to the nearest point on the coast. The road was finished within a year through the joint efforts of Tulare and San Luis Obispo Counties. The principal freight carried over the road was baled wool.

High prices collapsed after the Civil War, but there was a resurgence during the early 1870's. At that time an estimated 200,000 head of sheep summered in the upper Tule River. *The Visalia Delta* of June 3, 1875 stated that, according to Samuel Coburn, 50,000 sheep had already been driven across the north fork of the Tule River into the mountains. John Tuohy ran some 6,000 sheep on his Lewis Creek ranch and summered them in the upper Tule River country. So did John and Newton Crabtree, John Hossack, and the Brown Brothers.

The sheep industry was almost wiped out in the dry years of 1877-1879, but it revived in the early 1880's. This was the era of bonanza wheat planting, which left plenty of feed after harvest. It also coincided with the arrival of homesteaders into the southern end of the county around White River, Deer Creek, and Rag Gulch. Among the early settlers were Henry and Adolph Zimmerman, William L. Smith, Henry Lubking, Harry Quinn, the Spangler Brothers, Archibald Leitch, Perry Phillips, Matt Flynn, Peter Norton, Luke Howeth, James Funston, Alex Sarthou, Ed Halbert, B.G. Labachotte, John and Tom McIntyre, John and Lorenzo Menne, Frank Salsa, Gabriel Sinarle, Peter Thompson, Joe Bartoldus, Sam Carothers, and Alex Kramer.

In an interview Santos Baca said he had come through the county in 1884 with sheepshearers from Riverside and they sheared 25,000 sheep in Bakersfield, 60,000 at Granite Springs, 80,000 in Delano, 6,000 for Harry Quinn, and 6,000 for Dan Abbot.[1]

The Eastside Railroad, built in 1888, was a boon to all livestock men. In July 1889 sheepmen from all parts of the southern valley met in Porterville to plan for a wool warehouse in that town. The money was subscribed, and the warehouse was used for the next ten years. The west side of the county, soon to become Kings County, became the center of the sheep industry as the southern part of Tulare County was given over increasingly to expanding grain farms. In 1891, for example, Lemoore shipped 463,940 pounds of wool.

Few realized it, but when Sequoia National Park was created in 1890, the era of summer pastures was over. It was estimated that there were approximately half a million sheep in the mountains. Cattle, horses, and even hogs also fed from mountain pastures. Sheep were barred from the Park, but enforcement was difficult; it was hard to police such a huge area. When herders were arrested, the owner of the sheep paid the fine and sent the herder into another section of the Park. When Park Rangers took over from the U.S. Army, regular patrols were set up and sheepmen obeyed regulations.

The decline of the sheep industry was due to many factors, one of which was the inability to summer in the national parks and forests. Many sheepmen sold out and went into the cattle business, and many others became grain farmers. Free pasturage in the valley disappeared when the railroad began to charge for "sheep feed" on what had previously been free land. At the present time a few flocks come into the county to feed, but most sheep are raised on farms for meat. The wool market is dominated by Australia and New Zealand, and synthetic fibers offer competition on the world wool market.

Our story heretofore has used such courageous men as Thomas Fowler, John Cairns, I. H. Thomas, Dr. Cartmill and Daniel Zumwalt to illustrate the personal side of various vast economic enterprises. To that list is added the name of Harry

Quinn, who was recognized as one of the West's outstanding sheepmen.

Quinn was born in Ireland. When he was 16, he went to Australia and found work on a large sheep ranch. After eight years he came to California and was hired by Archibald Leitch, whose 7,000 sheep ranged from Stockton to Kern County. Harry Quinn worked hard, saved his wages, and bought a half interest from Mr. Leitch. That same year, 1872, he came to Tulare County. In time, the firm of Leitch and Quinn owned 10,000 acres in Kern and Tulare Counties, some in the mountains. At times their flocks numbered as high as 28,000 animals. In 1886 Harry Quinn went to North Carolina to marry Miss Katie Robertson, his partner's niece. The home place for the Quinn family was always the land he homesteaded on Rag Gulch, but when the children were old enough to go to school, they lived during the school term on a 320-acre ranch west of Porterville.

After Mr. Leitch died, parts of the Rag Gulch property were sold to the Reid Development Company and the Richgrove Land Company, thus marking the start of Richgrove and the Reid ranches.

In 1963 the surviving Quinn children were asked to write their recollections of life on a sheep ranch. It was written by Mildred Quinn Richardson and read by Mary Quinn Falconer. Those helping in its preparation were John R. Quinn, Thomas Quinn, Archie Quinn, and Cletus Quinn. The eldest child,

Harry Quinn (1843-1932)

Margaret (Mrs. Nelson L. Smith), passed away in 1942. This paper is one of the few — it may be the only one — to recall life on a sheep ranch. A few excerpts will tell the story.[2]

In 1877 tragedy struck in the form of a succession of dry years. My father took 18,000 sheep to Nevada in search of feed. An early blizzard overtook them and only 2,200 sheep survived to make the return trip to California.

Early in his sheep raising career my father imported from the University of Vermont his foundation stock of

Bill of sale for 1660 sheep, a horse, bridle and saddle, and the claim on the pasture for $4551.00. It is dated November 16, 1867, at Knight's Ferry.

Above: Clinton Brown (left), Demming Gibbons and an unidentified man herding sheep near Springville in 1885. Below: C.T. Brown's sheep camp on the way to the mountains above Springville in 1889. Mr. Brown is on the right.

blooded French Merino Sheep, noted for their hardiness, size, fine flesh and abundant wool. Through the years they proved difficult to shear because of the deep wrinkles around the neck and shoulders, so by selective cross-breeding he, with other forward-looking men of the times, developed the Ramboulet strain which retained the good qualities of the Merino, but had fewer wrinkles. A large source of income was from the sale of fine bucks for breeding purposes — selling about four or five hundred a year. The market covered all the western states as far south as Texas, South America, and even to South Africa. Bucks sold in small lots might bring $50 to $60 while those sold by the carload or more brought much less. Other sources of income were the sale of fine ewes, two clips of wool a year, mutton sheep (culls), the pelts of sheep slaughtered on the ranch and tallow. This tallow was sent to Stockton in large quantities to be returned as a carload of soap. Well do I remember the big yellow bars of "Stocktonia soap."

At strategic spots on the ranch were placed sheep camps, each of which was the base for one herder and his band of sheep. At intervals, perhaps once a week in winter, twice a week in cool weather, and every day during the hot summer, the herders drove their band into the home place for water. As the bands converged each man awaited his turn at bringing his sheep over the hill and down to drink their fill at the long low troughs extending out hundreds of feet from the large tanks.

As each band was watered it left the trough and was herded to a spot on the hillside. There it settled down to rest til late afternoon when it was again brought in to drink before starting its leisurely way back to camp, feeding along the way.

Our sheep camps were provisioned weekly from the storeroom at the ranch house. A wagon was loaded with beans, bacon, coffee, tea, flour, kerosene and water. Each herder was given his share, and he made his own delicious bread in a dutch oven over an open fire.

Many of our supplies were brought in by the carload, beans, flour, rice, barrels of pickles, cases of dried fruit, huge boxes of tea and coffee, potatoes, and the ever-present canned tomatoes. Even books were bought by the box for Dad, having had little formal education, was determined that his family should know the classics and World History.

In the early days our shearing was done by itinerant workers who, when that season of the year came around, appeared as if by magic from nowhere. There were Irish, Basque, Italian, Spanish, Portuguese who came in singly on foot or by riding the brakes. In later years all our shearing was done by Indians from the Reservation. Their Chief was usually Jose Vera, a most respected citizen of the community. They made their own camp close by the well and did their own cooking but were provided with at least one sheep a day or as many as necessary to give them an abundance of fresh meat.

Our shearing shed was a long structure, open except for a roof. Underneath was a series of small corrals separated by a low panel wall and leading into individual holding pens. A shearer occupied each of the spaces and sheared his sheep on the wooden floor. As each sheep was sheared the bundle of wool was deposited on a table extending the length of the shed. As each man finished a sheep, he called out his number which was echoed by the timekeeper and marked down on the tally sheet.

After being tied into a bundle, the fleece was tossed to a man standing in the mouth of a huge sack suspended on a rack. He tramped the wool down tightly, the full sack weighing between three and four hundred pounds. Other sheepmen brought their sheep to Rag Gulch to be sheared, the shearing season lasting several weeks. It took about three weeks to shear our own. Also other shearing pens or stations were dotted around the county at convenient places. The people in the Woodville area gathered at the Gilligan Ranch to shear and dip their sheep; those around Porterville at Chico Flats (on the new site of Bartlett Park). The town of Delano started as a sheep-shearing station, and all along the west side Miller and Lux had stations, at Firebaugh and on up the Valley. At one time Lemoore was the largest wool shipping center in the state.

Payday for the shearers was one that stands out in my memory. The Boss sat at the head of the dining room table, flanked on one side by the Chief and on the other by the man who kept the tally. The money was poured out in dishpans, the gold and silver coins segregated. As each shearer came in, he gave his number and was paid off.

The Carothers family, sheep shearers and bags of wool on the Carothers Ranch east of Terra Bella, 1890.

In 1898, when sheep were banned from the mountains, many of the large operators went out of business. This act of the government was felt to be a great injustice and led to bitter feelings between the sheep and cattlemen. It would be inappropriate to go into the sheep and cattle feuds. No matter how interesting, mention of names might start other wars. However, I can't resist telling a few of Dad's experiences during his long career. At one time he lost 1,800 sheep when a cattleman ran them over a cliff and they perished. Once one of our Basque herders was so intimidated that he abandoned his band of sheep and fled. For four days our faithful dog, Pastora, took the band to water and each night herded them back to the corral. In the vicinity of Stone Corral, Dad was met by an armed delegation from Visalia. On going out to meet them Dad said to his young helper, "If they kill me take care of the sheep." The argument was apparently settled peaceably but when Dad went back to the band, the young Irishman had departed.

Less is known of the disputes among the sheepmen themselves. Those tell-tale tags of wool on the latter day barbed wire fences were mute evidence that someone's sheep had either gone on to greener pastures or come in to feast on another man's feed. Friendships ceased when it became a matter of feed.

Around 1911 Mr. Quinn and his sons sold most of the sheep and went into the cattle business. Again the herd was all registered stock. Mr. Quinn was nationally recognized, for he had served on many state and national committees of wool associations.

One chapter of Quinn's life reveals more than any other the character of the man. He was an officer of the First National Bank of Delano when it had to close in 1926. Many people lost their savings in that disaster. In settling up the affairs of the bank, Mr. Quinn paid some $100,000 out of his own funds. Every depositor got his money back.

Mr. Quinn died in 1932 and Mrs. Quinn in 1934. Their hospitality and faith in their fellow man had remained unbounded through adversity and good fortune.

1. Miss Ina Stiner, *History of Porterville,* Typescript, page 19.
2. *Los Tulares* #59 and #60, December 1963 and March 1964.

CHAPTER 12

COTTON

Cotton originated in antiquity. It has been found in ruins that date back to 3,000 B.C. The ancient city of Dacca, India produced exquisite cotton fabrics. When Columbus reached the New World, he found natives growing cotton. He took samples back to Spain as one proof that he had found India. Later explorers found cotton cultivated in many parts of Central and South America. The first known planting in North America was in 1556, when Spaniards brought cotton to Florida.

England, the center of the world textile industry, imported cotton from Egypt and India, but the textile industry was basically dependent upon wool and flax until the Industrial Revolution. Hargreaves' spinning jenny, Arkwrights' spinning frame, Crompton's spinning mule, and Cartwright's power loom made the production of cotton cloth economically feasible.

The machine which made the biggest difference was Eli Whitney's cotton gin, invented in 1793. The economic changes in the United States were rapid, and the social changes resulted in the War Between the States.

Since many of the pioneers came from the Southern states, it is not surprising that cotton culture came early to the southern valley. In 1862 Harvey S. Skiles planted cotton on Kern Island. The view of the farmers from the South was well expressed in the *Transactions of the State Agricultural Society* in 1872:

...so far as our soil and climate and cost of land were concerned, the facts were so plain to them no labored argument was necessary on the subject. They were convinced, and did not hesitate to assert their opinion, that California was naturally a cotton-raising state. Indeed, if California had not been admitted to the Union as a free state, there can be no doubt that long ere now we would have had large numbers of cotton plantations, worked by slaves brought here from the Southern States by men who were able to discover the superior advantages of our soil and climate for cotton culture. The only question that remained in their minds was whether its culture would be profitable, considering the condition of our labor supply and the rate of wages.[1]

The first commercial planting of cotton goes back to Solomon and Philo Jewett, a father and son team, who can be listed among the county's experimenters and innovators.

Solomon Jewett was born in Vermont. He served in the Vermont State Legislature, represented the state at the World's Fair in London in 1851, and was a prominent contributor to agricultural journals. His band of sheep was pure-bred, and he constantly studied to improve the strains in order to produce better wool.

He brought his family to Kern Island in 1863. His sons, Philo and Solomon Jr., had come in 1859, but returned to Nevada to round up cattle they had left in that Territory. They returned to the Tejon area in 1860 and located the Rio Bravo Ranch, where they raised cattle and sheep. Their father joined them in that phase of agriculture near Kern Island. In 1874 the boys sold the Rio Bravo Ranch and bought 2,000 acres of land near Bakersfield for prices that ranged from 25 cents to $1.00 an acre.

Solomon and Philo Jewett began to experiment with cotton culture at Kern Island in 1865. Seed was imported from Mexico and from Tennessee. The Mexican seed was planted at the end of April, the Tennessee seed at the end of May. Sea Island seed was planted last. The Tennessee seed was most productive. The cotton was ginned at the ranch and sent to Oakland to be woven into cloth.

In recounting the experiment, Mr. Jewett stated that he paid his laborers, mostly Chinese, from $22.00 to $30.00 a month. He had recruited an experienced superintendent from the South and paid him $50.00 a month. He estimated that his experiment cost $7.00 an acre, which included clearing the land. He also estimated that the yield was about 70 pounds to the acre, unginned, although better spots yielded a bale to the acre. He had high praise for the Chinese, stating that they did their work well and were faithful to a fault.[2]

The price of cotton dropped after the end of the Civil War, but valley farmers continued to experiment with cotton. History owes much to observant newspapermen who traveled around the valley to get first-hand news.

The *Visalia Weekly Delta* noted that Mr. Rector, a local druggist, was giving away seed including Egyptian, Sea Island, Petty Gulf, and would buy back cotton for 25 cents a pound.[3]

The paper also noted, in February 1866, that a Joint Stock Cotton Association was going to be formed, largely because of the previous year's experiment by Solomon Jewett. In the summer of 1867 the reporter wrote rather prophetically:

Cotton is in full bloom. The crops planted are small but much finer than any other season. What a pity we do not have the labor and capital necessary to make this crop a success.[4]

In that same period Burchardy and Kinkead planted 100 acres of cotton on the upper Kings River. The seed was Mexican seed, and the reporter noted that the plants looked thrifty growing in the warm sandy loam.[5]

1871 was a milestone in valley cotton culture. A group of English investors planted 1,000 acres in Kern County, but production costs and a labor shortage prevented the project from making a profit. On the brighter side, the California Cotton Growers Association was organized in Bakersfield with Julius Chester as president and James D. Johnson as secretary. The organization was especially significant because most farmers waited till long after specific crops became vital parts of the valley economy to join associations.

Two years later a large acreage was planted in Fresno County. The *Tulare Times* commented rather caustically:

Are we always to be behind. The soil and climate of Tulare County are as well adapted to the cultivation and production of cotton as any in the world. Why is this industry allowed to languish when our sister counties are making such progress in its development.[6]

Apparently the editor did not know that cotton culture had arrived in Tulare County on a commercial scale.

COTTON CULTURE IN TULARE: The largest enterprise and the first of any magnitude in this county is that of Jackson & Co. about 12 miles northeast of Visalia.

One hundred and thirty acres were seeded but owing to the ground being new, and a want of seasonable plowing and through pulverization during the wet season, the ground was very lumpy and unfit for the reception of seed. The result was that the cotton came up very scattering and has not made a very good stand though what there is of it is about a foot high and looks fine. The ground was overrun by sheep in the spring giving it a hard surface, and the light rains that came after it was plowed were insufficient to fit it for cotton culture. On the sandy spots the seed came up perfectly, and on sixty acres belonging to Dr. Ray, which had been thoroughly cultivated by him for corn, which was destroyed by squirrels, the land being afterwards seeded to cotton, the stand is uniform and fine.

The crop made rapid growth and shows no want of irrigation, though a portion of the land is like the rest of our plains and as dry as any at this time of the year from which we judge that little if any irrigation will be found necessary on such soil, when once the cultivator understands the business. The grasshoppers have done some damage on a portion of the field which adjoins the uncultivated plains. This enterprise is being watched with considerable interest by many of our farmers who have been waiting for someone to demonstrate the adaptability of our land to the cultivation of this crop.[7]

The next year Joseph Spear and Stephen Barton shipped five tons of cotton from the county to the Oakland gin. For a few years no mention of cotton has been found, probably because citrus, deciduous fruits and alfalfa were the glamour crops. Planting went on in Kern County. In 1884 Haggin and Carr put in a large planting but made no profit because of a labor shortage. In an attempt to remedy that problem, F.M. Owensby was sent to St. Louis to recruit Negroes to work on the Haggin and Carr ranches. The wage scale promised was $12.00 a month for men, $8.00 for women, $6.00 for boys and girls, plus keep. After the recruits reached California, they found they could make much more in other kinds of ranch work, so they left for greener pastures—literally!

Plot experimentation in cotton culture reached the Tule River section in the 1890's. For instance, in 1892 Jacob Gardner of Porterville raised cotton of excellent yield and quality. Today Poplar, Cotton Center, Woodville, Earlimart, Tipton, and adjacent areas to the west produce much of the county's $97,811,000 (in 1986) from cotton.

Although small planting continued, little progress was made because of a shortage of labor. World War I focused attention on cotton, which was needed for war material. The need coincided

Cotton field near Poplar.

with experiments the United States Department of Agriculture was making with Durango cotton in the Imperial Valley. Fortunately, W.B. Camp was sent to conduct experiments. His work led to the establishment of the now world-famous Shafter Research Station in Shafter in 1922. It also led to the development of a strain called Acala. That variety had originated in Mexico and was brought into the United States for study by the Department of Agriculture. In Mexico it was developed into strains called Acala 5 and 8. Mr. Camp brought Acala #5 and worked with it at Shafter until 1934, when George Harrison came to Shafter. He also worked with the strain until 1949, when the now famous Acala A 4-42 evolved.

Experimenters and farmers recognized the possible returns from growing just one strain of good cotton. In 1925 the California Legislature passed the One Variety Law. That law prohibited planting of cotton other than Acala in the counties of Riverside, Kern, Kings, Tulare, Fresno, Madera, Merced, San Joaquin, and Stanislaus.

Cotton culture in the valley may be measured in decades. It was established commercially in the 1920's. In 1920 census figures show 297 acres were planted in Tulare County. That same year cotton was listed for the first time as a major crop in California.

By 1925, 5,925 acres were planted. The Poplar Gin was built, and the area around Poplar and Woodville became the "cotton center" of the county with two more early gins, C.A. Webb Gin and the Anderson Clayton Gin. Cotton and labor were interdependent. For many years inquiring minds had been trying to make a practical mechanical picker. John Rust produced the first such picker, utilizing moistened spindles, in the South in 1931. The mechanical picker could harvest a bale a day. It produced mixed reactions because it appeared during the Depression, and the possible loss of thousands of jobs was not exactly relished.

The 1930's were years of trouble and turmoil. Over 64,000 acres were planted in Tulare County. By the middle of the decade planting had dropped to 46,866 acres. The Depression was one factor, but the main problem was verticillium wilt, which almost wiped out the fields. Thousands of migrants from the Dust Bowl were in the valley looking for any kind of work, and the 1930's were marked by labor problems and strikes. The going price for picking cotton was 60 cents for 100 pounds. Farmers were having difficulty getting enough money to operate their ranches. Part of the drop in acreage was due to the Cotton Acreage Adjustment Program of 1933. The Federal Government called for reduction in staple crops in order to bring prices to pre-war parity of about 12 cents a pound for cotton. In 1934 California's quota under the Cotton Adjustment Program was 209,205 bales. Of that quota, Tulare County was allocated 42,578 bales.

The 1940's brought tremendous changes in all phases of agriculture. The Federal Government extended crop insurance to cotton. (Tulare County was not included until 1962.) The war years increased the demand for fibers. Few people at the time, and fewer now, knew that 400 German war prisoners were brought into Tulare County to help harvest cotton. The group first picked peaches at the Tagus Ranch, for which they were paid nominal wages.

A most important event in Tulare County was the arrival of the first mechanical picker. It was bought in 1945 by C.R. Shannon, who farmed between Tulare and Visalia. The second mechanical picker was bought two years later by Maurice Henderson of Porterville. It was an International Harvester

Cotton picker unloading into trailer near Poplar.

and cost $8,000. It picked a bale in one hour and 15 minutes and was capable of doing the work of 30 to 35 people. The 1940's saw many changes instigated by the Commodity Credit Corporation in order to stabilize prices. Allotment and Land Set Aside programs were used to stablilze the market.

In the 1950's farmers had a huge carry-over and competed in a world market against the growing use of synthetic fibers. The 1956 Soil Bank Act provided for long-term land retirement for basic crops. Cotton, like the rest of the basic crops, became dependent upon Federal subsidies. Large corporate farms emerged, and it was not unusual for those corporations to receive millions of dollars in subsidies.

By the 1960's cotton was an almost mechanized crop. After years of testing a new variety, SJV-1, was released. In 1967 there was a very small crop. Prices rose, but in order to fill their commitments, manufacturers turned toward synthetic fibers. Many cotton farmers planted alfalfa instead of cotton.

Adverse reaction toward the payment of huge subsidies to corporate farms increased. The Triple A Legislation of 1970 initiated a Crop Set Aside policy for participating farmers in wheat, feed grains, and cotton, and set a ceiling payment of $55,000 annually to producers of those crops. Only farmers who signed up were eligible for price support. In substance, acreage limitations were removed; farmers were allowed to sell or lease their allotments and to collect cash.

The 1970's also brought problems. In spite of constant research and preventative measures, verticillium wilt, lygus bugs and air pollution began to take their toll. Then the dreaded pink bollworm was found to have invaded the valley. Drastic measures are taken in the constant battle of man versus insects and diseases. What air pollution will do to all phases of agri-business is under constant study. One thing is certain; if air pollution is not controlled, the productivity of the valley will certainly suffer.

1. Page 241.
2. *Transactions of the California State Agricultural Society,* 1872, page 249.
3. *Visalia Weekly Delta,* May 6, 1866.
4. *Visalia Weekly Delta,* June 1, 1867.
5. *California state Agricultural Society,* ibid.
6. *Tulare Times,* February 22, 1873.
7. *Visalia Weekly Delta,* June 25, 1874.

CHAPTER 13

HIGH ADVENTURE

The awesome Sierra Nevada, whose towering peaks form the eastern backdrop of Tulare County, may be described in terms of climatic and geographical barriers. The climatic barrier is vital; without it the valley would be a desert. Winds and storms deposit rain and snow in the mountains, and rivers bring the water to the valley floor. Modern highways give no inkling of the tortuous trails followed by pioneer emigrants who sought to break the geographical barrier.

Pedro Fages saw the mountains in 1772, and Father Garces saw them again in 1776. Father Pedro Font's map, drawn in 1776, gave them the descriptive name "una gran sierra nevada," the great snowy range. The Spaniards felt safe behind the geographical barrier until Jedediah Smith shattered that illusion in 1827.

The first inhabitants were Indians, whose arrival is shrouded in time. When white men came, they found two tribes living along the inhospitable eastern side and three tribes on the western side. The tribes on the east were the Washoe and Mono. The latter people spent most of their time gathering food, so they lived a mobile life without permanent villages. The western tribes were the Yokuts, Miwok, and Maidu. These people lived on the valley floor and along the foothills. Food was plentiful, so they had permanent villages. In the summertime valley Indians went to the mountains to escape from the valley heat and to gather different kinds of food such as pinon nuts.

Lumber played an important role in the history of the mountain area. Before the gold rush there had not been much need for lumber in California. The Spaniards and Mexicans preferred adobe as a building material. Hand-hewn beams were used to join or support structures, and tiles were used as roofing material. The Russians built the first sawmill in California in 1820 on Bodega Bay. This was on property later sold to John Sutter. The people who came during the gold rush created an unprecedented demand for lumber, which was so scarce that most people lived in tents or canvas shelters. By 1855, however, there were an estimated 80 sawmills in California and most of them were in the lower foothills. Nevertheless, lumber still had to be imported from the eastern coast and Australia.

Miners needed lumber to shore up shafts and tunnels. People needed lumber for houses and stores. Railroads needed lumber for trestles, track ties, and fuel for the engines. These needs led to a rapacious invasion of the Sierra Nevada.

Settlers found plenty of timber in Tulare County, but of course no sawmills. The early structures were made from brick as this advertisement indicated:

BRICKYARD; One half mile south of the Courthouse in Visalia. I can make brick better, cheaper, or on shorter notice than any other in this part of the country.
COLUMBUS MAJORS[1]

The first sawmill of record showed up in a $15,000 claim submitted in 1856 after the Tule River Indian War.[2] The claimant, Orson K. Smith, sawed oak and cottonwood and said the Indians had burned his mill and 100,000 board feet of lumber. There is no record of payment of that amazing claim.

In 1856 the firm of Smith and Hatch[3] built the first sawmill east of Visalia in the pinery on Mill Creek, later the Whitaker ranch. A difficult but passable road was built to the sawmill, which was powered by a flutter wheel in the creek. Smith and Hatch sold to Joseph H. Thomas in 1857. He replaced the flutter wheel with steam power and moved the sawmill a mile up the creek. Thomas did well and by 1862 employed 12 men. He advertised for teamsters and urged people to buy lumber at the mill. As an inducement, lumber at the mill sold for

$25.00 a thousand board feet. The same board feet sold in the valley for $50.00. The flood of 1868 completely washed away the sawmill and 40 large trees. Mr. Thomas returned to Visalia and began experimenting with deciduous fruit culture.

There were literally dozens of sawmills in the Kaweah and Kings River watersheds. They were sold and re-sold, named and renamed, mortgaged and redeemed, moved, and destroyed by fire. It is difficult to describe or locate them, but they all had one thing in common: the slaughter of the forest without regard for future needs.

The Tule River watershed was intensively invaded in the 1880's, but James Hubbs had built the first sawmill on the north fork of the Tule River in 1864. He kept records and estimated that it cost him $10,000 to equip the mill, build a wagon trail, hire men, and dig ditches. He sold the sawmill to Nathan Dillon, whose name is commemorated in Dillonwood.

The sawmills in the Tule River area, like those in Converse Basin, were eventually bought and operated by large lumber companies. Much of the Tule River timber area is now within Mountain Home State Park, Sequoia National Forest, and Balch Park.

The early sawmill era is well described in Hank Johnson's *They Felled the Redwoods,* Floyd Otter's *Men of Mammoth Mountain,* and Elaine Egenes' *Dauntless Dillons.*

Few early lumbermen made much money, but the industry they created has provided controversy, history, and profits.

The rather primitive wagon roads made it easier for people to get into the higher mountains. They went in the summer to find work in the sawmills, to buy lumber, or to camp. As time went on, going to the mountains in the summertime to escape the valley heat became a way of life for valley folk. Then there were men who went to fish, to hunt, or to drive stock to summer pastures. Before long, camping places, summer resorts, and inns were established to take care of summer visitors. The larger places were California Hot Springs, Pine Flat, Camp Nelson, Springville, Doyle's, and Camp Wishon, Summer Home, Mountain Home, Camp Lena, Silver City, and Mineral King.

The trip into the mountains was arduous. Wagon roads were steep, narrow, and twisting. The road bed was marked with chuckholes and ruts. The trip took several days and food for both the people and the stock was either taken along or bought along the way. On steep upgrades passengers walked to help the team. On steep downgrades brush was cut

John J. Doyle (1844-1915)
His Summer Home resort is now in Balch Park.

and dragged behind the vehicle to aid in the descent. When the travelers met a loaded lumber wagon on a narrow strip, they got out, unhitched the team and lifted their vehicle off the road so the lumber wagon could pass. People so anticipated the high adventure awaiting them that they ignored such inconveniences.

Three well known summer resorts in the Tule River country were directly connected with the lumber industry. They were Mountain Home, Camp Lena, and Summer Home, now either in or near Balch Park.

In 1885-86 L.B. Frasier built a sawmill in the northeast one-quarter of T19 S35 R30 (within Balch Park). He also built a controversial road from Bear Creek to the sawmill. Andrew J. Doty and his sons worked on the road. They took up a homestead near the sawmill and built a large cabin on the homestead. Frasier's mill had an output of 40,000 board feet a day and was a busy place. First the lumbermen and then the travelers to the back country asked Mrs. Doty to serve meals, and so Mountain Home Resort came into existence. Mr. Doty cleared a camping area, set up tents, and built a few cabins. Campers enjoyed music, croquet, dances, and hikes to see Centennial Stump, Battle Mountain, and the Indian Bathtubs. Fishing and hunting provided both food and recreation. A summer school was provided for the children, and

This hollow log at Summer Home was discovered by Clinton Brown of Porterville in 1870.

sometimes classes were held on Centennial Stump. Many of the men worked at the sawmill or made shakes, posts, and shingles for themselves.

Jesse Hoskins, a well known Lindsay rancher, took up 80 acres of timberland in order to save the trees from Frasier's logging crews. He built his summer home in the hollowed out trunk of a redwood which he called Hercules Tree.

Mr. Hoskins loved the forest giants and named them for friends or for Biblical or historical people such as Adam, Methuselah, Napoleon, Anne and Anthony, and the Seven Sisters. After his death the property was sold, and in the 1950's most of the trees, with the exception of the named trees, were cut down.

Summer Home was developed by John J. Doyle. Mr. Doyle was one of the men involved in the 1880 Mussel Slough Tragedy and spent eight months in prison. In 1885 he filed on Talbott Meadows about a half mile from Mountain Home, and developed it into Summer Home Resort. People enjoyed the usual summer activities. One of the attractions was the Hollow Log, first seen in 1870 by Clinton Brown of Porterville. Another attraction was the Sawed Off Tree. That redwood had been sawed through but did not fall, and it kept on living.

In 1905, Mr. Doyle sold his property to the Mt. Whitney Power and Electric Company, which planned to build a power house and flume. Mrs. John Hays Hammond, one of the principal stockholders, was shocked to learn that redwood trees were to be used. She persuaded the company to wait. Fortunately, the Southern California Edison Company bought the Mt. Whitney Power and Electric Company and scrapped those plans.

Mr. Doyle had heard that Mr. and Mrs. Allan Balch of Los Angeles were interested in buying property to donate for public parks. He told them about Summer Home, which they bought in 1923. They offered to donate the land to the County of Tulare if the county would build a road to the property. The county complied and accepted the property in 1930 as Balch Park.

There are many magnificent trees in the park. Two have been selected to bear memorial plaques. One is the Jordan Tree, whose plaque is self-explanatory:

John Jordan, 1807-1862

This giant redwood tree is dedicated to the pioneer spirit of John Jordan, drowned in Kern River May 22, 1862. He initiated the trail project leading across the Sierra from Yokohl Valley to the southern end of Big Owens Lake.

Jordan Tree in Balch Park. (Courtesy of Harold Schutt)

The other selected tree was dedicated in the fall of 1976 by the Tulare County Bicentennial Commission as the official Tulare County Bicentennial Tree.

Two-thirds of Tulare County is mountainous. Much of the mountain area is now preserved as Sequoia and Kings Canyon National Parks, Sequoia National Forest, Mountain Home State Park and Balch Park. The lengthy struggle to save the redwoods and the watersheds of the Sierra Nevada is indeed a tale of high adventure. It is the story of conservationists pitted against railroads and lumber companies. It is the story of the Federal government's policy "to get rid of public land as fast as possible." It is the story of the western myth of superabundance of natural resources.

The first white man of record to see the Sequoias was Hale Tharp, who came to Tulare County in 1856 and settled near present-day Three Rivers. Mr. Tharp was a stockman who owned more horses than cattle. He was looking for summer pastures when his friend, Chief Chappo, invited him to visit his tribal headquarters.

Judge Walter Fry, who recorded so much park history, interviewed Hale Tharp in 1910 and preserved his remarkable story.

I first located on my ranch where I now live in the summer of 1856. There were about 2,000 Indians then living along the Kaweah River above where Lemon Cove now stands. The Indian chief was named Chappo and he was a fine man. The Indians told me that I was the first white man that had ever come into their country.

Chief Chappo sent down two Indian young men to pilot me in, as there were no trails in the country, just Indian footpaths. I went on horseback, and it took me about eight hours to work my way in, the distance being about eighteen miles from my Three Rivers ranch.

When I arrived at the camp, Chappo and his men extended me a cordial welcome and gave me the best his camp afforded. He called out every individual in the camp and with much dignity and very long ceremony introduced me to all. There were over 600 Indians then living in the camp....

On the following morning Chappo showed me all through his camp and explained its advantages over that of others. It was the cleanest camp I have ever seen. He showed me the houserock, the spring, the river, the sweathouses, and what extra stores of food, clothing and other supplies he had. The supplies were all nicely stored under the rock,[4] leaving just enough space for two beds. In one of the beds was a woman with her leg broken, and in the other a woman with a very young baby...There was no smoke on the room ceiling then. That has been caused by the whites camping in there after the Indians left. He showed me the paintings on the rock and asked me to tell him what they meant. He said none of his people understood them, or knew from what material they were made...

I do not remember the dates when we were there, but I carved with my knife on the big hollow redwood log[5] my name and the date the same day that we got there...I had two objects in making this trip. One was for the purpose of locating a high summer range for my stock, and the other was due to the fact that the stories the Indians had told me of the "Big Trees" forest had caused me to wonder, so I decided to go and see.

I made my second exploration trip into Giant Forest during the summer of 1860 and by the same route that I went in the first time. On the second trip I took with me John Swanson. We camped one night at Log Meadow, then went on over into the Kings River Canyon returning again to Log Meadow after a period of about two weeks...A few days after our return we took a trip up the East Fork to Mineral King and back down the South Fork by way of Hockett Meadow. So far as I am aware, I am the first white man who ever visited either the Sequoia National Park or the Three Rivers region.

From the year 1861 up to 1890 when the park was created, I held Giant Forest country as my range, and some of my family went up there every year with stock. When the land up there was thrown on the market, with other men we bought large holdings, some of which my son, Nort, still owns.[6]

Dedication of restored Tharp's Cabin in 1923. Many of the people are from the Three Rivers Woman's Club which aided in the restoration of the landmark.

Tharp's Cabin as it looks after restoration in Giant Forest. (Courtesy of National Park Service)

The Sequoia *sempervirens* of the coast and the Sequoia *gigantea* of the Sierra Nevada are leftovers from the era of brobdingnagian reptiles. Sequoia *gigantea* grow at elevations of 4,000 to 8,000 feet and the groves that escaped logging extend from Placer County to Tulare County. Their slaughter began as soon as sawmill equipment could be packed into the higher elevation. Stark, mutilated stumps testify to man's disregard of future needs. The waste was appalling, for the trees were cut 10 to 12 feet above ground. When the brittle redwood fell it not only crushed everything in its path but shattered into chunks. The logging machinery of the time could not cope with those chunks, which were either sawed into smaller sections or dynamited. As a result, much of the tree was cut into fence posts,

Enjoying the High Country

Typical stage for people going to mountain resorts.

McFarland family leaving Mt. Home for Porterville after camping in the mountains all summer, 1895.

Hercules Tree in Camp Lena. This was the summer home of Jesse Hoskins. The people are not identified.

There are several "Centennial stumps" in the Sierra Nevada. This tree near Summer Home was supposedly cut in 1876, but the stories concerning its disposal are open to controversy.

Left: Colonel George Stewart inside Tharp's Cabin. Right: Colonel George Stewart (1857-1932) is recognized as the "Father of Sequoia National Park." (Courtesy of National Park Service)

shakes, and shingles. Big Stump Basin is a ghostly reminder of early logging practices. Another reminder is Converse Basin, where only the Boole Tree is still standing.

Pioneers who pushed westward suffered from what has been called the myth of superabundance. They naively believed that natural resources were inexhaustible. Federal land policies abetted that idea. People could obtain land under the Swamp and Overflow Act, by pre-emption, by using school and military warrants and, after 1862, by homesteading. Railroads obtained millions of acres of land through Federal subsidies. In 1878 the Timber and Stone Act was passed, whereby a person could take up 160 acres of land without living on the land or making improvements. A fee of $2.50 an acre was involved and supposedly the land was to be used only by the claimant. However, lumber interests began to use dummy entrymen to get the timberland of the Sierra Nevada.

In 1878, the year the Timber and Stone Act was passed, Colonel George Stewart, editor of the *Visalia Delta,* began a series of articles urging preservation of the mountain watersheds. Within a few years he was joined by such well known Tulare County men as Frank Walker, John Tuohy, Tipton Lindsey, J.D. Hyde, William B. Wallace, J.W.A. Wright, and Frank Wales. They were aided by nationally known John Muir and Gustavus Eisen.

This handful of men began the long and oft-times bitter fight to save the trees and watersheds so essential to the valley's expanding agriculture.

George Stewart was born in Placerville, California in 1887. His parents moved to Tulare County in 1866 and farmed near Tulare. George Stewart had what education the country school provided, but men of his caliber never stop learning. He went to work in a Tulare print shop and, when he was 19 years of age, worked for the *Visalia Delta.* Two years later he was city editor of that newspaper. Early-day newsmen moved about, and Stewart was no exception. He went to San Francisco to edit the *Mining and Scientific Press,* and then went to Honolulu where he worked on the *Saturday Press.*

In 1884 he came back to Visalia as editor of the *Visalia Delta.* George Stewart loved the outdoors and spent as much time as possible hunting and fishing in the mountains. His papers and articles on the geology of the Sierra Nevada, its glaciers, its volcanoes, and the Indian Rock Basins are still the best in their fields. He co-authored a book on the Big Trees which is a standard reference. He was a realistic conservationist. George Stewart was one of the architects of the national park system, and will always be remembered as the Father of Sequoia National Park.

In 1929 Colonel Stewart[7] was honored in a way that moved him deeply. Mt. Stewart in Sequoia National Park, as towering and outstanding as the man himself, was named for him. Three years later

High Timber Falls

Frazier Mill - 1890 - located in present Mt. Home, State Forest.

Above: Falling redwood is the Mark Twain Tree cut in 1891. The stump is near the entrance to Grant Grove. Upper right: Coburn Mill, 1892. Bull team hauling a section of a redwood tree to be exhibited at the World Columbian Exposition in Chicago in 1893. Lower right: Cut redwood at Mt. Home, 1892.

he was dead. His ashes and those of his wife are buried at the base of Mt. Stewart, in the mountains he deeply loved.

Colonel Stewart and his fellow conservationists began their campaign in the late 1870's, but the actual story of Sequoia National Park began with the Kaweah Cooperative Colony. The story of that socialistic colony is one of the controversial pages of Tulare County history.

Times were hard in the latter part of the nineteenth century and various "isms" were offered to cure society's ills. California has always been pictured as a utopia, so it is little wonder that by 1900 some 20 utopian colonies had been organized in the state. Some died in infancy; few lived to maturity. The Kaweah Cooperative Colony (locally the name was shortened to Kaweah Colony) located on the North Fork of the Kaweah River was the most pretentious and controversial of the utopian groups.

The idea originated in San Francisco in 1884. The leaders were men who were involved in labor unions. They structured the colony on the books of Bellamy and Gronlund, which pictured an industrial colony in which the people would control production and be rewarded according to the results they produced.

The leaders were Burnette Haskell, a brilliant attorney, orator, writer, Marxist, and dreamer; James J. Martin, a merchant and a writer and a leader of workingmen's unions; and John H. Redstone, also an attorney and a labor leader. The promotional literature was written by Haskell, who stated the purposes of the colony thus:

..the underlying purposes are, to insure members against want or the fear of want by providing comfortable homes, ample sustenance, educational and professional facilities, and to provide and maintain harmonious social relations on the solid and grand basis of liberty, equality, and fraternity.[8]

In order to provide for this utopian existence, it was necessary to find and use a natural resource. By accident or intent, the leaders chose timber as the natural resource.

Charles Keller was a member of a "cell" which Burnette Haskell had organized in Traver. He had heard of the timber in the mountains, and he hired Nort Tharp to guide him into the back country. Keller lost no time in reporting his discovery.

On October 5th, 1885 a group of men arrived in Visalia and by October 8th 53 claims had been filed, for 160 acres each, on land in and adjacent to Giant Forest. The men had 60 days to raise the required price of $2.50 per acre under the Timber and Stone Act.

Group of men ready to leave California Hot Springs for the high country.

The claimants were an interesting group. Some were from Traver, some were from Visalia, but most of them came from San Francisco. George Stewart's curiosity was aroused as he set type for legal notices. Seven of the men used the same address in San Francisco. More inquiries revealed that 14 of the men were not then citizens of the United States. The local land officials notified William Sparks, Commissioner of the General Land Office in Washington. Commissioner Sparks was aware of the misuse of the Timber and Stone Act, and he suspended the claimed four townships plus 14 adjacent townships from entry. He stated his reason for the suspension as fraudulent entries and irregularities in the surveys. The claimants welcomed the suspension, for they believed their claims were legal, and the delay gave them more time to raise money.

The Southern Pacific Railroad was a hated institution in spite of the benefits it brought. Rumors began to spread that the railroad was somehow involved in the land grab. The leaders of the Kaweah Colony unwittingly helped spread the rumor by filing incorporation papers for the Tulare Valley and Giant Forest Railroad. That grandiose scheme proposed building a railroad from a sawmill in Giant Forest to connect with the mainline railroad in the valley. The idea was so impractical that it was soon forgotten and a wagon road, the Giant Forest Wagon and Toll Road, was incorporated and work began on the Colony Road October 8, 1886.

The Colony Road was built under almost insurmountable conditions. There was not enough money to buy proper equipment or blasting powder, so the road was built with pick and shovel, back-breaking labor, and something akin to religious fervor. By the time the road reached Colony Mill in June 1890, the men were living on mush, beans, and acorn coffee.

The 18-mile road wound around hills and canyons. It had a grade of eight feet per 100 feet and reached an elevation of 6,000 feet. It was built so well that the Colony Road was the only road into Sequoia National Park until 1927. Parts of the road are still used as a fire road. The Kaweah Colony raised $50,000 through subscription to build the road. The harshest critics of the Kaweah Colony believed the Federal Government should have reimbursed the group for that road, but the last appeal for such a payment was denied in 1934.

Kaweah Colony had resident and non-resident members. Resident members (this included a family as a unit) paid $500.00. When a resident member paid $100.00 down he could move to the Colony. The remainder could be paid in monthly installments, worked out, or paid with machinery or supplies. Non-resident members paid a small fee and were urged to make liberal donations. There were two outside offices. One was in San Francisco, and one was in Visalia. Members were recruited all over the world.

Members came from all walks of life. They were a cross-section of artisans, tradesmen, and professional people. Their political beliefs were as varied as their occupations. The majority were well educated people who hoped to create a better way of life for their families. There were socialists, Marxists, anarchists, nihilists, and just plain dreamers. People in the Three Rivers country and Visalia liked the colonists, even though they looked askance at the communal experiment.

Haskell and John Redstone spent much of their time in San Francisco, while James Martin took care of the Visalia office. Haskell sought new members with alluring descriptions of Kaweah such as these excerpts:

The Giant Forest and its beautiful green meadows and crystal pools, surrounded by the giant, lofty trees, whose tops seem to touch the sky, is a sight to be seen nowhere else...In the springtime the hills are literally covered with beautiful and delicate flowers in endless variety. Orioles and wild canaries take possession of the trees and fill the air with melodies. The various grades of altitude embraced in our territory, together with the salubriousness of our climate, make it possible for any but tropical productions to be grown in Kaweah.

We shall have schools there, not for the children alone,

Building the Colony Road by the north fork of the Kaweah River, 1886. Note blacksmith in foreground. (Courtesy of Bancroft Library)

but for youths and maidens, for the babes, and for men and women. We big ones want to know something of literature, of science and art. We shall have songs and a band, and the music of tinkling guitars under summer stars by the rushing waters of the North Fork.

We shall tell our children of the heros of the world, not the butchers, of the moralists, not the priests; we shall have the choral music and the measured dances of the Athenian days to teach them grace; the quaint ceremonials of the middle ages to teach them beauty; the modern wonders of light and electricity to teach them truth; the tales of old Rome to plant the hearts of men within their breasts; the songs of old Sparta to move them to valiant deeds; the cruelly pitiable histories of the modern wage slave to stir their souls to heroic ire and bind their wills to Freedom's cause and creed alone.

We shall teach each other the courtesies of life and it well may be that among us alone of all the people of the earth shall be taught courage as a creed, fidelity as a dogma, truth as a commandment, love as a law, and purity as a truth. Here shall we hitch our wagons to the stars and not block their wheels with stones and mud.

We shall have painters and sculptors, I hope in time, although it will be enough for us to be humble students. Great poets and orators, writers and thinkers shall be cradled between our mountains. Upon one of the flats by the river we shall build out of the colored marble of Marble Canyon, a temple and a theater for ourselves alone, and here we will pursue the Beautiful, the True, and the Good.

Photograph of the Colony Road building crew. (Courtesy of Bancroft Library)

Advance was the principal camp for the colonists while the Colony Road was under construction. It was located on a flat about five miles above the present Kaweah Postoffice, on the North Fork of the Kaweah River. There were other temporary camps, but Advance and then Kaweah, nearer the present post offices, were the permanent "towns."

The government of the communal colony was detailed and intricate. Colonel Stewart described it as a visionary scheme, "as impractical as the spectacle of a locomotive's powerful machinery balanced upon a bicycle for which it is intended to supply the motive power."

Kaweah was years ahead of the time as far as labor relations were concerned. Everyone was paid a minimum 30 cents an hour wage. There was an eight-hour day, and men and women had equal pay and equal job opportunities. The unique concept used by the colonists was the substitution of time for money. A minute took the place of a cent. The rate of exchange for United States currency was fixed at one half cent per minute. Thus a 200-minute time check could be exchanged for a dollar. Haskell urged members to think of money as crystallized labor. Time checks were used to buy supplies at the colony store and meals at the communal dining hall. The leaders soon found out that the outside business world was not interested in exchanging money for time.

It is not necessary here to detail the collapse of the Kaweah Colony. It lacked three essential requirements. The Colony did not begin with enough money to meet immediate needs. The leaders were inexperienced in practical business methods. Members were not willing to put theory into practice. More time was spent in prolonged meetings discussing personalities and procedures than in producing goods to sustain the Colony. As the dissention increased, people moved away. Others took up homesteads and stayed in the Three Rivers area. About 40 families stayed until the scheme collapsed.

The Colony sawmill was built at what is now the Colony Mill Ranger Station. The road reached the mill in June 1890, a few months before Sequoia National Park was established.

The output of the sawmill was negligible, and it was on park land. The remaining colonists leased Atwell's sawmill, which was on patented land. The trustees were arrested and charged with cutting timber on government land. The case was tried in Los Angeles, and the men were convicted. The decision was appealed and reversed.

In spite of its failure, Kaweah Colony contributed to Tulare County history. It precipitated the formation of Sequoia and General Grant Parks. The Colony Road served as the entrance road to Giant Forest for years. The Colony newspaper, the *Kaweah Commonwealth,* was one of the Colony's real achievements. Haskell had a fine steam press which he brought to Kaweah. It is thought to be the first steam press used in the county. The newspaper was well written and edited by Haskell, and Mr. and Mrs. Fred Herschede did the press work. Many members contributed essays, poems, and letters. The *Kaweah Commonwealth* was both a sounding force and a unifying force.

The tangible landmark left by the colonists has achieved national fame. It is the tiny Kaweah Post Office on North Fork Road. The office was

Kaweah Post Office and State Historical Marker No. 389, located about three miles north of Three Rivers.

granted to Advance December 22, 1890 and moved several times to accommodate its patrons. It is still in use and is said to be the third smallest post office in the nation.

The fight to save the trees and watersheds of the Sierra Nevada began before the arrival of the Kaweah colonists, but when they filed on Giant Forest, conservationists realized "it was now or never." Perhaps the creation of the park is best told chronologically.

The 1870's were years of exploration and exploitation in the mountains. The Jordan and Hockett Trails, built in the 1860's, expedited travel. Each summer thousands of cattle, horses, and sheep were taken to summer pastures. Exploration centered around Mineral King. Harry O'Farrell was credited with the discovery of that mining area, but stockmen had been there before. The rush to the Mineral King mines began when James Crabtree of Porterville located the famous White Chief Mine in 1873. At the peak of that mining excitement, at least 3,000 people were in Mineral King and Silver City during the summer months.

In 1873 three men on a fishing trip climbed the peak now known as Mt. Whitney, named for Josiah Whitney, Chief of the State Geological Survey.

In 1875 a tree near the General Grant Tree was cut, and a section was sent to the Centennial Exposition in Philadelphia. It was so large that the section was cut into pieces for transportation and re-assembled for the exhibit. Most people who saw the tree scoffed, saying that nothing could grow that big.

In 1879 James Wolverton, a trapper and the first permanent resident of Giant Forest, found and named the General Sherman Tree in honor of his commanding officer, General William Sherman. That was also the year Tom Fowler built a road into Mineral King to exploit his Empire Mine.

The population of Tulare County tripled in the 1880's as subdivisions, land colonies, and expanding agriculture drew people in the lower valley. The dry years of the 1870's emphasized the need for irrigation on a larger scale. The 1887 Wright Act made it possible to set up local irrigation districts which could tax themselves to build canals and ditches. The need for irrigation water was predicated upon preservation of mountain watersheds.

In 1880 the Surveyor General of California requested that Sections 5, 6, 7, 8 of Township 14 Range 28 be suspended from entry because of the big trees growing there. J.D. Hyde, Frank Walker, and Tipton Lindsey convinced him that the trees were on Sections 31 and 32, so those sections were also suspended from entry. The next year United States Senator J.F. Miller introduced a bill to establish a national park extending from the Middle Fork of Kings River to the North Fork of the Tule River. The bill failed.

In 1889 the Patrons of Husbandry of Tulare County and the Tulare Grange held several meetings with representatives from like groups from Fresno and Kern Counties. Memorials asking for preservation of the Big Trees were sent to Congress. By the time the memorials reached Washington, Sequoia National Park was a reality.

It is interesting to note that the area the local groups wished to preserve was set aside in the National Forest Act of 1893.

In July 1890 Congressman William Vandever introduced HR Bill 11570, and Sequoia National Park was established September 25, 1890. The townships, including Giant Forest, were left out because of the still unresolved claims of the Kaweah Colonists. (The claims were declared fraudulent in 1891.) There was little local opposition to the creation of the park, although there were a few dissonant voices. One such was the *Tulare County Times,* which had always been sympathetic toward the colonists. Here is a typical comment:

> The great timberland in this County has been set aside as a Park by an act of Congress and named Sequoia National Park. This park will become accessible only when wild goats are trained to work in harness and carry pack saddles. But it will preserve our wonderous snow belt and give some forester a lucrative office. The government in this case awaited the stealing of the horse and then locked the stable door.[9]

The name, Sequoia National Park, had been suggested by Colonel Stewart and endorsed by Secretary of the Interior John Noble. The omission of Giant Forest was not opposed locally because by 1890 many felt the Colonists were entitled to their claims.

Even conservationists were stunned to learn that another bill had been signed October 1, 1890, adding five townships to Sequoia National Park. General Grant National Park, so established, included Giant Forest. The creation of General Grant National Park was a mystery for many years. Local people suspected that the Southern Pacific Railroad was involved, and words like "mysterious influence" appeared many times in newspaper editorials. Recent investigation shows that the railroad was involved, but the connection was neither sinister nor mysterious.

Daniel K. Zumwalt (see pages 85-87) was in Washington in 1890 as the guest of Congressman Vandever. Zumwalt was attorney and land agent for the Southern Pacific Railroad. He owned land in Tulare County, was an officer in the 76 Land and Water Company, and held stock in several irrigation companies. Undoubtedly he told William Vandever about Giant Forest. Vandever had sponsored a bill to preserve the watersheds of Yosemite Valley, and the provision to set aside Giant Forest was tacked on to that bill. It was understandable that Mr. Zumwalt, with his railroad connection, did not publicize his part in the legislation.

There is little doubt but that the Southern Pacific Railroad was interested. Tourism was becoming a lucrative business. The railroad owned and was selling land in the valley, and the company had investments in Northern California lumber operations. If timber was cut in the unprotected mountain townships, the railroad stood to lose money on the long haul freight of lumber into the valley. Recently, the first map showing the boundaries of Sequoia and General Grant National Parks was found. It was on stationery of the Southern Pacific Railroad dated October 10, 1890, just ten days after the area was set aside.

General Grant Grove was first seen by Joseph H. Thomas in 1862. At the same time the grove covered an estimated 2,000 acres. It was later heavily logged, and only four square miles were left to be preserved in 1890.

John Muir named Giant Forest in 1875. The General Grant Tree (and later the General Grant Grove and Park) was named in 1867. Judge Fry's papers include material revealing the origin of the name.

In 1867 a party of people from Porterville and Visalia camped in the mountains near a giant redwood tree. One of the ladies in the group, Mrs. Lucretia Baker, was an admirer of General U.S. Grant, and she named the tree for him. Her son, Henry Ford of Porterville, let Judge Fry copy the letter from General Grant.

Headquarters, Armies of
The United States
Washington D.C.
October 4th, 1867
My dear Madam;

Your favor of the 5th of September by express, accompanying a box containing branches, etc., from the largest tree in California, and no doubt in the world, which too partial friends have done me the honor to name after me is at hand. Please accept my thanks for thus remembering me and also for the kind expression of regard contained in your letter.
With great respect
Your Obt. Svt.
U.S. Grant

No provision for administration of the parks was contained in the legislation of 1890, so supervision was turned over to the Army. Captain J.H. Dorst and soldiers from the 4th Cavalry rode from the Presidio in San Francisco to the Park, arriving in June 1891. Captain Dorst soon requested that the park boundaries be surveyed and marked. He also requested that the boundaries be extended to include Mt. Whitney and the Kings and Kern River canyons. Conservationists endorsed both requests

Left: Captain John H. Dorst, 4th U.S. Cavalry, was the first administrator of Sequoia National Park, 1891. Dorst Camp and Dorst Creek were named for him. (Courtesy of National Park Service) Right: Ernest Britten (1862-1943) and Mrs. Britten. He was the first ranger in Sequoia National Park, 1900.

but it would take many years to accomplish enlargement of the parks.

Captain Dorst found an immediate problem. He estimated that half a million sheep were feeding within park boundaries. He reported that the situation had reached the point where it was almost impossible to find feed for the horses. The fight to exclude sheep from the park was a long and bitter battle, but they were finally banned after 1898. After 1930 no livestock was allowed to graze on park land.

The Army continued to administer Sequoia and General Grant National Parks until 1913. The soldiers built trails, and improved facilities in many ways. However, they were only there during the summer. In 1900 Ernest Britten was appointed winter Park Ranger.

Ralph Hopping and John Broder started the first stage line into the park in 1900. They also provided camp accommodations at Giant Forest. Stage fare plus a week's stay at the camp cost $35.00. The stage stopped to change horses several times along the way, and meals were served by Mrs. Redstone at Redstone Park. The stage stopped at Colony Mill, where travelers backpacked into higher elevations. John Broder also operated the first commercial pack train service out of Mineral King.

In 1900 Congress made the first appropriation, $10,000, to operate the park. In the next decade members of the Mt. Whitney Club, the Sportsmen's Association, the Tulare County Board of Supervisors, the County Chamber of Commerce, and civic groups from all county towns raised money to help build trails, roads, bridges, and fences in the parks. In 1903 the Colony Road was extended into Giant Forest.

The new-fangled automobiles were being tested in many ways by their happy owners. Mountain driving was one of those tests. In 1904 Mr. and Mrs. W.G. Luper from Vallejo succeeded in driving the first automobile into Sequoia National Park. Three years later Conrad Alles from Three Rivers drove the first automobile into Mineral King. Logging was still going on where land was privately owned. Park roads were posted for non-commercial use to stop passage of heavily loaded lumber wagons. When Walter Fry was appointed full-time Park Ranger in 1905,[10] one of his onerous duties was to enforce the stiff driving regulations. At times, automobiles were banned entirely. It was not until 1913 that the park really was opened to automobile traffic.

Mountain driving was a thrilling experience. Drivers had to sound the horn at each turn in the road. Teams had the right of way, so automobiles had to slow down or stop. Cars were backed up steep hills. Sometimes the passengers got out and pushed the car uphill. Night driving was dangerous because the lights dimmed or went out when the car slowed down for a curve. Service stations were nonexistent, so when the family went out for a "spin," someone had to remember to bring kits to fix flats

Soldiers on a redwood log in Sequoia National Park. (Courtesy of National Park Service)

and patch inner tubes, extra gasoline and oil, shovels, ropes and boards in case the car was bogged down in dirt, mud, or deep holes.

Private ownership of land within park boundaries was a pressing problem. Logging went on, and so did grazing. Much of the privately held land was bought in 1890 when several townships were reopened to entry. Several bills were introduced in Congress to appropriate money to buy the land, but they met so much opposition they did not get out of committee.

The Visalia Chamber of Commerce and county civic groups raised money to pay the expenses of Congressmen to visit the parks to personally see the need to enlarge the boundaries and to buy privately owned land.

In 1915 Stephen Mather was named assistant to the Secretary of the Interior and placed in charge of all national parks. He reorganized the office, and in 1916 Congress established the National Park Service to administer the national parks. Mather was named Director of the Service.

Stephen Mather was a Californian and familiar with the mountains. In 1915, at his own expense, he brought a group of Congressmen and leaders in the conservation movement to Tulare County. They camped in the parks and saw the problems as outlined by Director Mather. One member of the group was Gilbert Grosvenor of the National Geographic Society. Later Congress appropriated $50,000 to buy privately owned land, but that was not enough. The National Geographic Society donated $20,000, the County of Tulare donated $10,000, and Mather gave thousands of dollars. By the mid-1920's the National Geographic Society had donated $96,330 toward land purchases to save the big trees. By 1927 enough money had been raised by many agencies to buy 2,836 acres. Today a few privately owned tracts are still within park boundaries.

In 1926 Congressman H.E. Barbour succeeded in getting a bill passed which took in the entire upper Kern River Basin and Mt. Whitney. The fight to include the Kings River Canyon was not over until 1940 when President Roosevelt signed legislation creating Kings Canyon National Park. That park absorbed General Grant Park, and although the two parks are separate they are administered as Sequoia and Kings Canyon National Parks.

Today millions of people visit the parks, which offer unrivaled all-year recreational activities. Names of the small group of men who fought so long to save the big trees and the watersheds are remembered in Mt. Stewart, Mt. Eisen, Mt. Vandever, Muir Grove, Muir Trail, Zumwalt Meadows and Founders Grove. Tharp's Cabin, Atwell Mill, Colony Ranger Station, and Hospital Rock are all reminders of past history.

Left: Walter Fry (1859-1941) served in Sequoia National Park as Chief Ranger, 1912. He was appointed as the first civilian Superintendent in 1914 and in 1920 was appointed U.S. Park Commissioner. Right: Stephen Mather was appointed as first director of the National Park Service in 1916. (Courtesy of National Park Service)

Moro Rock was first climbed by Hale Tharp and his stepsons, George and John Swanson, in 1861. This monolith is 6,719 feet above sea sevel. The wooden stairs were built in 1917 and replaced by stone steps in 1931. (Courtesy of National Park Service)

1. *Tulare County Record & Fresno Examiner,* July 2, 1859.
2. Included in claims submitted to the State of California by Indian agents, Jennings and Campbell, in 1856.
3. Smith of Smith and Hatch was not Orson K. Smith.
4. Hospital Rock, a park landmark.
5. Tharp's Log, another park landmark. Hale Tharp lived in this log house each summer. His friend, John Muir, called it a noble den. It was restored by the National Park Service and the Three Rivers Woman's Club.
6. These excerpts are taken from Judge Walter Fry's papers in the Tulare County Library Historical Collection.
7. Mr. Stewart was a Colonel in the National Guard.
8. Excerpts from material written by Haskell were taken from brochures in the Tulare County Library Historical Collection.
9. *Tulare County Times,* October 2, 1890.
10. In 1914 Walter Fry was appointed first civilian Park Superintendent, and in 1920 was appointed United States Park Commissioner for the two parks.

CHAPTER 14

TOWNS OF THE COUNTY

To understand why a town is where it is, one must know something of its geography, climate, location on a route of travel, and its accessibility to water from rivers, lakes, or wells.

In Tulare County many towns were created by railroads. Many were promoted by real estate companies during the period 1880 to 1910, when the land use pattern in the valley was undergoing a rapid change. Some communities were planned by people who had much to do with the community's history.

The derivation of the community name tells something of its origin. Railroads were liberal with place names and favored Spanish names. Some towns were named for their founders. Early settlers sometimes thought of their own home town and used it for a new community. Miners had a wry sense of humor, and so we find names like Dogtown, Rag Gulch, and Shirttail Canyon.

Railroad towns started as either loading platforms or depots. All communities tried to identify themselves as soon as possible by applying for a post office and building or organizing a school and church. The dates of these institutions tell us when the community had "arrived," and the dates of their transfer or diminution tell us that the community was not going to grow. Many a once-busy community is remembered only as a name for a road or a school district.

ALLENSWORTH was the fullfillment of a dream. The dreamer was Allen Allensworth, born a slave and twice sold on the auction block.

He eluded his master and enlisted in the Union Army. He served through the Civil War and, after a religious conversion, he returned to the Army as a chaplain in the all-black 24th Infantry. He saw service in the Spanish-American War and the Philippine Insurrection and left the Army as Lieutenant Colonel Allensworth, the Army's highest ranking black soldier.

Colonel Allensworth dreamed of an all-black community where people could prove their worth. He interested some friends in this project, and they formed the California Colony and Home Association. In 1909 they bought several thousand acres in southwest Tulare County by the Santa Fe Railroad. Colonel Allensworth named the projected community Solita, but his associates insisted that it be named for him.

The group published a newspaper, *The Sentiment Maker,* which had wide circulation in the 24th Infantry and the all-black 9th and 10th Cavalry. Prospective buyers were promised small down payments and easy terms, and by 1912, 2,000 acres had been sold. The community grew rapidly, and 1,000 acres were cultivated. By 1909 there was a post office; the next year the Zion Methodist Church was organized; and in 1912 the school was established. Education was an integral part of Colonel Allensworth's dream. Mrs. Allensworth served as a trustee and donated a well-stocked library. In 1914 Allensworth had its own judicial district with Oscar Overr, thought to be the first black judge elected in California, presiding.

Water was and still is a problem for Allensworth. Around the turn of the century, artesian water was found on the dry west side of the county. Water from that source is pushed to the surface by gas pressure and has a strong sulphur taste and smell. The Allensworth Rural Water Company also bored wells and stored water in four reservoirs. For a few years the town and surrounding farms were lush green spots. Alfalfa, sugar beets, and truck gardens did well. Dairies and poultry farms brought in money.

The same water that produced crops began to kill them as irrigation percolated alkali to the sur-

Colonel Allen Allensworth (1842-1914) and Mrs. Allensworth (nee Josephine Leavell). Pictures courtesy of Mr. Cecil Berkley and Mrs. Katherine Green)

face of the land. The water table in the valley was lowering, and wells had to be deepened. For no apparent reason, the flow of artesian water in the lower valley stopped.

In 1914 Colonel Allensworth was killed in a vehicular accident in Southern California. Mrs. Allensworth stayed in the community for about a decade, but the combination of Colonel Allensworth's death and the dearth of water doomed the community. Families drifted away, land went for back taxes, and the Depression took its toll. The one unifying force over the years has been the school, which has remained open.

For years the few families who stayed hauled water for their household use. In 1968 a water system was built with the help of interested county people, federal money, and labor contributed by the people of Allensworth, and for the first time households had running water.

In 1969 measures were begun to restore Allensworth as the only all-black community in California. Legislation provides for a 240-acre State Park which will be an historical, cultural, and interpretative center for black studies. It seems that Colonel Allensworth's dream will emerge greater than anything he could have imagined.

First church	Zion Methodist, 1910
First school	February 8, 1912
First post office	September 25, 1909, moved to Earlimart, 1933

ALPAUGH is really an island in Tulare Lake. When the lake was full, the island was two or three feet above water. When the lake water lowered, the island was five to ten feet above water. It was covered with vegetation and known to the Indians as Chaw-loo-win. In 1859 Allen Atwell and Isaac Goldstein from Visalia bought the island and ferried hogs there to fatten on tule roots. It became known as Hog Island, Root Island, and Atwell's Island.

In 1906 a Southern California company headed by J.O. Brubaker bought land in the fertile lake bed to subdivide into small farms. The planned town was named Alpaugh for John Alpaugh, one of the company's men. It was located six miles west of the Santa Fe Railroad, with Angiola as the nearest depot. Eight years later the railroad built a spur into Alpaugh. The tract was divided into 96 business lots, 708 residential lots, and church and school sites.

W.W. Wilbur owned and farmed 8,000 acres surrounding Alpaugh, and he incorporated the Second Home Extension Colony and sold small farmland acreage.

Alpaugh also had water problems, which were solved by digging canals to Smyrna, ten miles to the south. Artesian wells produced almost as much natural gas as water, and the gas was used for both cooking and illumination. In 1915 the Alpaugh Irrigation District was voted in, and a complicated canal system, based on the original ditches, brings water to the area. Grain, sugar beets, and cotton are the principal crops.

In 1920 the Shell Oil Company discovered a large gas field near Alpaugh, and in 1934 the Trico Oil and Gas Company tapped a field where the three counties of Tulare, Kings, and Kern meet.

First church	Lutheran, 1909
First school	February 10, 1906, High school, 1913
First post office	February 16, 1906

ANGIOLA and its neighbors, Allensworth and Alpaugh, were all land colonies, and they all had the same problem — insufficient water.

In 1897 C.W. Clark, Elias Jacob, T. Bacigalupi, Susman Mitchell and the Santa Fe Railroad bought 160 acres of land to subdivide. The town was to be named Angela for Mrs. Bacigalupi, but the post office spelled it Angiola instead. The Santa Fe Railroad built a depot and warehouse to handle the rapidly expanding grain crop of southwestern Tulare County. Cattle and sheep grazed the drying bed of Tulare Lake, and as it got drier, grain and barley were planted there. The future of Angiola seemed assured, but it has not grown and remains a small farming community.

First church   Services held in the schoolhouse
First school   April 4, 1898,
      absorbed by Westside Union District, 1946
First post office   February 3, 1898,
                                moved to Corcoran, 1927

AUCKLAND, northeast of Orosi on Cottonwood Creek, was named by Phillip Sweet, who came from Auckland, New Zealand. He built a general store which he sold to Strachey Phillips when he returned to England. Mr. Phillips later sold a half interest to Lucius Uniacke.

Auckland was an important overnight stop for teamsters on their way to sawmills in the high country.

First school   Cottonwood, 1866,
          merged with Ash Mountain School in 1946
First post office   August 24, 1899,
                                  moved to Orosi in 1912

BADGER, high in the mountains east of Dinuba, was named in 1879 by Myron Woodard, who came from Wisconsin, the Badger State. The chief occupations in the Badger area have been cattle raising and lumbering. Badger was a favorite summer camping resort for valley people.

First school   Ash Springs, May 14, 1877,
                     now in Sierra Joint Union District
First post office   August 14, 1879

CALIFORNIA HOT SPRINGS, 22 miles east of Ducor, is a year-round resort famous for its medicinal hot springs. It has also been called Deer Creek Springs, which is a translation of *del venado*, the Indian name for the creek.

The Witt brothers, Henry, Napoleon, and Thomas, took up land for their cattle range in 1886. They were soon followed by other cattlemen and a few farmers who found that apples and vegetables grew well in the area. The Witts sold their property, and it went through several ownerships until 1900, when valley folk started coming to Hot Springs to use the medicinal mineral water. The year 1902 marked the beginning of the resort when a hotel, cabins, store, tents, and campgrounds were built.

In 1906 L.S. Wingrove, Susman Mitchell, Joseph Mitchell, and J.H. Williams bought the property, and in the next 20 years they developed it into one of the state's best-known health and summer resorts. Most mountain resorts began to decline as automobiles came into general use. Instead of staying in one place for several weeks, tourists could visit many places in the same length of time. People still come to use the mineral water, but

Street scene in California Hot Springs in the early 1920's. On the left are the offices, store, bathhouse, plunge and dancehall.

Passenger stages in front of Hotel Del Venado in California Hot Springs.

Hotel Del Venado - built in 1902.

Plunge, California Hot Springs - built in 1920.

John Milton Nelson (1831-1909), his daughter Emma Nelson Smith and his grandson, Nelson Smith. Taken in 1905.

Camp Nelson Hotel in 1904.

California Hot Springs is no longer a crowded summer resort. The principal industry is cattle raising, the same as it was a century ago.

First school	March 6, 1896
First post office	May 1, 1900

CAMP NELSON, east of Porterville on the Tule River, is a well known mountain resort and starting place for pack trains into the high mountains. John Milton Nelson homesteaded in 1886. He built a small sawmill, made shakes and planted an apple orchard. Cattlemen and sheepmen came that way with their herds going to summer pastures, and hunters and fishermen camped overnight on their way into higher elevations. Mr. Nelson built a few cabins and enlarged his home into a two-story hotel. In 1922 a good mountain road was completed, making access much easier. People began to buy small lots there and build their own summer cabins. Today Camp Nelson has grown far beyond the original homestead and is open all year.

CUTLER, southeast of Orosi, is a small community but an important shipping point for grapes, citrus, vegetables, and wine. Cutler has several large packing sheds. The Santa Fe Railroad came through that section in 1897, and Dr. John Cutler deeded some land to the railroad, which named the new community for him. Dr. Cutler was one of the county's prominent pioneers. In 1919 his son donated Cutler Park, east of Visalia, in memory of John and Nancy Cutler.

First school	February 8, 1915
First post office	May 7, 1910

DINUBA is the largest community in northern Tulare County. It is ideally located for both industry and agriculture. The area went through the cattle to grain raising phases typical of the county, but since both underground water and water from the Alta Irrigation District were available, grapes, deciduous fruits, field crops, vegetables, and cotton were planted early.

Dr. John Cutler (1819-1902) for whom Cutler Park and the town of Cutler were named.

Corner of L and Tulare Streets in Dinuba in 1920.

L Street in Dinuba in 1920.

Dinuba is a creation of the eastside Southern Pacific, built to tap the grain fields of the east side of the county. James Sibley and W.D. Tuxbury deeded the townsite to the railroad in 1888, and its name was first Sibleyville, then Sibley. When the railroad published its timetable, the name listed was Dinuba. Although several derivations have been suggested for the name, none have been entirely accurate.

When Dinuba was created, nearby Traver, once the largest grain-shipping point in the nation, began its decline. Families and businesses moved to Dinuba, and the final blow for Traver came when the offices of the Alta Irrigation District were moved to Dinuba.

Dinuba incorporated as a City of the Sixth Class on December 30, 1905. The first city officials were:

Chairman	R. F. Dunn
Clerk	J. T. Boone
Treasurer	J. R. Clotfelter
Marshal	J. W. Harper
Attorney	Leroy Smith
Trustees	F. H. Wilson, G. M. Dopkins, W. C. Hauser, J. H. Ramm

Farming in the Dinuba area is widely diversified. The major crops are raisins, many varieties of table and wine grapes, fresh fruits, citrus, vegetables, field crops, livestock, and poultry.

Agriculture-related industries include box companies, canneries, packing houses, two large poultry processing plants, and the Zellerbach Paper Converting Plant, which makes materials for agricultural processing. The largest industry is Sequoia Forest Industries, a sawmill and wood processing plant which is one of the West's largest manufacturers and distributors of lumber and specialty products.

First church	Methodist Episcopal, 1871, in Wilson Schoolhouse
First School	Wilson School (3 miles southeast of Dinuba), May 17, 1879
	Dinuba Grammar School, 1889
	Dinuba High School, 1899
First post office	February 9, 1889

DUCOR, 11 miles south of Porterville, is served by both the Santa Fe Railroad, Minkler Division, and the Southern Pacific Railroad. The usual

Ducor Hotel built in 1907 by Ducor Land Company.

Ducor Mercantile Company and Post Office, about 1911. Mail cart used to pick up and deliver mail to the train is on the left. Hitching rack is in left foreground. Pool hall at right, called The Irrigator, was owned by Foster Doty. Left to right are: Claude Hornsby, Bill Anderson, Wilbur Dennis, Ed Crail, Clarence Carlisle, Bert Long, Laurence Muller, Herman Muller, Roy Carter, Ed Hatch, Fred Carlisle, Bert Dennis, Fay Singleton, Mike Mitchell, Will Collins, Charley Hildreth and Charles Tibbens.

economic progression of sheep, cattle, and grain farming marked the settlement of that end of Tulare County.

Ducor is a contraction of Dutch Corners, the town's original name. Four Germans, Chris Joos, Ben Spuhler, Fred Schmidt, and Gotlet Utley (or Etley), took up adjoining homesteads in Section 34, Township 23, Range 27. They dug a common well where the four corners of their homesteads met. When the Southern Pacific Railroad came through in 1888, the timetable listed the place as El Granado, but it was changed to Ducor.

The town is actually the creation of the real estate boom that started around 1908, when excursions were run into the county from Southern California. In 1909 the Ducor Land Company bought what is now the townsite of Ducor. The company included three local men, S.W. Braly, C.G. Tibbens, and John Dennis, and two men from the southland, S. Richard Shoup and J.W. Righter. A water system,

Teams wait in line to be unloaded at the Ducor grain warehouse, built in 1908.

Alila (Earlimart) in 1906. The Alila school on the far right was built in 1886.

Water tanks on the railroad right-of-way in Earlimart. These tanks, used by the railroads, were familiar sights in the Valley.

sidewalks, streets, and a place for a park were built or designated. A commodious hotel was built to accommodate people on their way to and from California Hot Springs, as well as people who came on real estate excursions. A busy community grew, but did not fullfill its growth potential. Today Ducor is surrounded by large grain farms, cattle ranges, citrus orchards, and vineyards. Water from the Friant Kern Canal has made it possible to use land once thought fit to use only for pasture.

First church	Baptist, 1908
First school	January 6, 1909
First post office	November 21, 1907

EARLIMART, south of Pixley, was first known as Alila, said to be Spanish for "Land of Flowers." Alila was settled in the 1880's and soon had a depot, warehouse, blacksmith shop, school, and large artesian well. Streets were shaded by eucalyptus trees, and the community thrived. The surrounding area was planted to wheat and barley. A series of fires, crop failures, and dry years almost ruined the town and surrounding farms.

In 1910-11 a group of Los Angeles real estate men bought land and started the town of Early Market, a mile south a a quarter mile east of Alila. The name was soon shortened to Earlimart, but the Earlimart Fruit and Alfalfa Company failed in its effort to get the Southern Pacific Railroad to build a spur track to its subdivision. In 1916 the fortunes of Alila brightened, and that community took the name Earlimart. Today it is the center of a grain and cotton area.

First church	Community Methodist, 1939
First school	Alila, April 6, 1886,
	Earlimart, March 6, 1922
First post office	Alila, November 11, 1885,
	moved to Pixley, 1899,
	Earlimart, March 6, 1907

EXETER did not attract early settlers because it was not near a natural source of water. The nearest settlers were on Deep Creek and in Yokohl Valley. Sheep and cattle grazed the plains, and then wheat and barley farms sprang up. In 1877 John Firebaugh settled on what is now Exeter. He deeded part of the 240-acre homestead to the Southern Pacific Railroad in 1888. He planned to call the new town Firebaugh, but that name could not be used since his uncle, Andrew Firebaugh, had applied it to Firebaugh's Ferry in Fresno County. D.W. Parkhurst, land agent for the railroad, substituted Exeter for his home in England.

Until 1898, when the Southern Pacific connected Exeter and Visalia, Exeter provided stages for people going into the mountains or to Visalia.

The community grew slowly until the 1890's, when men began to plant citrus and grapes, both of which did exceptionally well. The largest grape acreage was planted to Emperor grapes, and Exeter is well known as the Home of the Emperor Grape. Exeter has three railroads: the Southern Pacific (1888), the Visalia Electric (1905), and the Santa Fe (1912). The need for transportation grew as packing houses, cold storage plants and dehydrators were built. The light industry needed by the agricultural economy is also coming to Exeter.

Exeter was incorporated March 2, 1911 with George Waddell as mayor; C.R. McEvers, clerk;

Looking east on Pine Street in Exeter, 1925.

E.H. Miles, treasurer; Ed Awbrey, assessor; Charles Mackey, Marshall, and McDonald Twiehaus, recorder-judge. The trustees were W.P. Ballard, Dr. J.F. Dungan, J.G. Kirkman, and Horace Davis. Exeter is a prosperous, rapidly growing community surrounded by groves, orchards, and vineyards.

First church	Methodist, 1876, at Lewis Creek
	First Baptist, 1892, in Exeter
First school	Rocky View, April 6, 1886,
	as Exeter in 1896
	Exeter High School, September 11, 1908
First post office	June 17, 1889

FARMERSVILLE is the third oldest community in Tulare County. Its name is descriptive of its rich and productive land, first settled around 1860. John Crowley and his brother-in-law, Merrill Jasper, established a general store in 1866 and two years later sold it to Thomas Brundage, who applied the name Farmersville to the first post office.

In the 1880's and 1890's many tracts of land around Farmersville were planted to deciduous fruits, especially French prunes. Cutting, dipping, and drying fruit provided ample work during fruit season. The Farmersville area now produces citrus, grapes, vegetables, all varieties of fruit, walnuts and cotton, and the town is growing rapidly.

Farmersville was incorporated October 5, 1960 with James Turnow as Mayor, Carl Waddle as City Clerk, and Leroy McCormick as City Attorney. The Council members were James Stevens, Willie Freeman, Don Freeman, and Truman Qualls.

First church	First Methodist, 1902-03
First school	May 5, 1869
First post office	August 26, 1868

FOUNTAIN SPRINGS, seven miles east of Ducor, was a well known crossroads and a place for watering stock. The springs were about a mile and a half northwest of the present crossroads called Fountain Springs. At times several hundred head of

Ox team in front of Brundage Store in Farmersville, 1898. These teams hauled lumber from the mountains.

Site of Fountain Springs Butterfield Stage Station in 1858. The reservoir is modern. One of the springs is in left foreground.

Goshen on old Highway 99. The building in the background is the Goshen Hotel. On the right is Kiteley & Bock's garage. Taken in the 1920's.

Goshen Mounted Quadrille team practicing a square dance on the Stokes ranch near Goshen. Print Stokes and his orchestra are on the wagon bed.

stock watered there at the same time. A later stockman dynamited the springs in order to improve the flow of water but managed to do just the opposite.

The crossroads was an important stage stop on the Butterfield Stage road, and on the route to the White River and Kern River mines. Today it is remembered by a state historical marker. Cattle and grain are the principal crops grown in the area.

First school	May 2, 1876, annexed to Ducor in 1930
First post office	February 24, 1875, moved to Plano, 1888

GOSHEN, the biblical "Land of Plenty," was first called Goshen Junction. The Central Pacific Railroad reached and named the place July 4, 1872. At that junction the Southern Pacific Railroad took over construction of the line. In 1876 the Southern Pacific Railroad began the Goshen Division, which bypassed Grangeville and created Hanford, Lemoore, Huron, Coalinga and ended at Alcalde in the Coast Range Mountains.

Goshen Junction was a busy place and the community prospered, but its economy was and still is based on agriculture, not transportation. Grain, cotton, and cattle ranches surround the town. Now Goshen has potential as an industrial center because of its location — on a main highway, on a railroad, and near an airport.

First school	March 4, 1885
First post office	April 1, 1880

IVANHOE, a center for citrus, deciduous fruits, and early vegetables, is located three miles northeast of Tulare County's Election Tree. In 1888 the Southern Pacific Railroad named it Klink for George Klink, a railroad auditor. At the time the area was a cattle range with some grain farms.

The Venice Hills Land Company was organized in 1912 and sold lots and small tracts from what had been the Fisher Ranch. That company tried to change the name Klink to Venice Hills but did not succeed. The first school in the area (a mile east and a mile north of the present school) was named Ivanhoe for Scott's novel. In 1924 Mrs. Ellen Boas suggested that Klink be changed to Ivanhoe to conform to the name of the school district.

Ivanhoe is a prosperous growing community with packing houses, cold storage plants, and trucking lines to take care of the fruit and vegetables produced there.

First church	First Presbyterian, 1914
First school	April 5, 1886
First post office	Klink, January 24, 1895; changed to Ivanhoe November 17, 1924

LEMON COVE, nestled in the foothills between Woodlake and Three Rivers, was first called Lime Kiln from lime deposits found there in 1859. Lime Kiln Hill, an anchor point for Terminus Dam, was the dividing line between the Wuchumne and Potwisha Indians who lived along the Kaweah River.

The histories of Lemon Cove and the John W.C. Pogue family are congruent. The Pogues came to California in 1857 and to Tulare County in 1862, settling near Venice Hills. After the flood of 1868 they moved to Dry Creek, where Mr. Pogue planted oranges and lemons in the family orchard. Up to that time lemons were considered too tropical to grow in the valley. When the family moved to what is now Lemon Cove, the citrus trees were moved successfully. The Pogue home, built in 1879, served also as a hotel for many years and is now the home of the Lemon Cove Woman's Club.

In 1894 Mr. Pogue surveyed 15 acres of the ranch into town lots and named the new town Lemon Cove. The community is surrounded by cattle ranches, orange and lemon groves, and grain fields and is on Highway 198, the road to the unlimited recreational and scenic opportunities at both Lake Kaweah and Sequoia National Park.

First church	Presbyterian, 1907
First school	Lime Kiln, April 4, 1882, as Lemon Cove, 1897
First post office	Lime Kiln, July 14, 1879, moved to Lemon Cove, 1898

LINDSAY, south of Exeter and near the foothills, is an ideal location for diversified farming. The Butterfield Stage Road lies on the western outskirts of Lindsay. That entire section of the county was first used for rangeland and then planted to grain. John J. Cairns, G.S. Berry and

W.F Pritchard's store built in Klink (Ivanhoe) in 1911.

Above: J.W.C. Pogue home and store (at left) in Lemon Cove. Built in 1879, the house now serves as the Lemon Cove Woman's Club headquarters. Below: Lemon Cove in 1920. The large buildings in the foreground are packing houses. The Pogue home is in the right background.

Captain Arthur J. Hutchinson (1846-1926), founder of Lindsay. (Courtesy of Harold Schutt)

Sadie Lindsay Patton Hutchinson and her granddaughter Sally Post. Lindsay was named for her. (Courtesy of Harold Schutt)

Above: Lindsay in 1902. On the left is the Baptist Church built in 1894. At far right is the Washington School, built 1891-92. The stores in the foreground would now face Sweet Brier Avenue. Below: A panoramic view of Lindsay, 1920. Packing houses are in foreground.

East Honolulu Street in Lindsay, about 1920.

W.S. Berry, the Mehrten brothers, John Tuohy, L.C. Keeley, J.H. Keeley and Elias Jacob planted grain from approximately Exeter to the White River country.

Lindsay is the creation of both the Southern Pacific Railroad and the Lindsay Land Company. In 1888 the Lindsay Land Company (see page 70) bought several thousand acres on both sides of the tracks and planned to subdivide it into small farms. The original plans called for irrigation from the Kaweah River until John J. Cairns successfully demonstrated that water could be pumped from a water table underneath the plains. Captain A.J. Hutchinson, who headed the Lindsay Land Company, named the new community Lindsay for his wife's family.

Pumped wells made it possible for an almost unprecedented planting of citrus and deciduous fruits. Then olives were planted at an equally impressive rate. Dry years and overpumping depleted the underground water at an alarming rate and the Lindsay-Strathmore Irrigation District was formed October 16, 1915 to divert water from the Kaweah River through well fields at Rancho de Kaweah. The next year the District was sued by the Tulare Irrigation District *et al* in what was to be one of the longest and most bitter water cases in California history. The case was compromised in 1936, when the Central Valley Project was assured. That project was the dream of Colonel Robert B. Marshall, a prominent Lindsay resident.

Lindsay is world famous because it is the home of the Lindsay Ripe Olive Company, the largest olive processing plant in the world. Olives are not the only major crop, for Lindsay is surrounded by citrus groves and vineyards. There are many industries related to agriculture, and Lindsay has 15 large packing and processing plants for fruit.

Commercial Transfer hauling grain in Lindsay in 1910. The men are not identified.

Lindsay was incorporated February 28, 1910 with the following officers: W.B. Kiggens, president; W.H. Mack, clerk; William Gann, marshal; G.V. Reed, treasurer; and Allen McGregor, P.T. Ostrander, Basil Prior and Charles Cowles, council members.

First church	Baptist, 1894
First school	April 4, 1890, Lindsay High School, 1907
First post office	October 31, 1889

MONSON, southeast of Dinuba, was named in 1888 by the Southern Pacific Railroad, either for Monson, Maine or Monson, Michigan. It was on land owned by Adolph Levis and Henry Jerusalem, who subdivided into town lots and small farms with water rights. At that time Monson was the main shipping point for that section. Machinery for the sawmills in the Sierra Nevada was unloaded there, and lumber was shipped from the same place. Monson was soon overshadowed by Dinuba and Sanger

Orosi Hotel, built in 1894 by Hudson Barton. He sold it to John Weber who later sold it to A.B. Johnson. The building burned in 1905. The site today would be a block west of Lloyds Bank on Avenue 416.

Corner of Palm and El Monte Streets in Orosi during the 1906 flood.

The El Monte Inn in Orosi was built in 1911 and burned in 1922. It was operated by Fred Conkey. The site today is about a block west of Lloyds Bank on Avenue 416.

Pixley, about 1886-87. Left to right are the Bradbury Building, the Allen Building and the Artesia Hotel.

and has never really developed. It is a very small community, surrounded by diversified farms.

First church	First Christian, 1887
First school	Seymour, May 5, 1887, name changed to Monson in 1896
First post office	July 22, 1889, moved to Dinuba in 1920

OROSI, east of Dinuba, is in a section of the county which attracted people long before the Southern Pacific Railroad came through in 1888. It was an open cattle range for years; then the grazing land was planted to grain, which was hauled to Traver for shipment.

In the spring of 1888 a group of Tulare and Fresno County people, along with men from Southern California, formed the Smith Mountain and Orosi Development Company. On April 14, 1888, the company sold 100 town lots. The company was headed by D.R. Shaffer, with R.J. Wickham as general manager and A. McCallum as general superintendent. The derivation of the name is not clear. Supposedly it was given by Neal McCallum, who looked over the fields of California poppies and said, "oro si," for land of gold. The railroad and post office listed it as Orosi.

Orosi is a flourishing community surrounded by citrus, grape, and vegetable ranches.

First church	Baptist, 1892
First school	Smith Mountain, May 6, 1878, Orosi, 1891
First post office	December 13, 1888

PIXLEY was, in a sense, created by the Southern Pacific Railroad when the line came through the county in 1872. It had the usual land pattern use, first rangeland and then homesteaders who planted grain.

In 1886 the Pixley Townsite Company was incorporated by three men from San Francisco: Darwin Allen, William Bradbury, and Frank Pixley. Pixley, for whom the community was named, had been Attorney General under Governor Leland Stanford. He became a well known newspaperman as editor of the *Argonaut*. When the company was formed, Pixley had a loading platform by the railroad, but Frank Pixley persuaded the railroad to build a depot and a three-story hotel. Pixley prospered as hundreds of tons of grain were shipped from its warehouses. Artesian water was available for irrigation, and the future looked assured. Then a series of fires, poor crops, and low prices induced many families to leave. Pixley was almost a ghost town.

In 1908 the community received a needed economic boost. Two outside corporations brought hundreds of acres and planted groves of eucalyptus trees, to be used to make furniture and lumber.

Poplar Store, taken about 1900.

Sites for sawmills were located, and tracts of trees were sold for as much as $200 an acre. The sawmills were never built because the wrong variety of eucalyptus had been planted. Remnants of the groves are still growing along Highway 99.

In 1916 the price of eucalyptus soared and an attempt was made to extract the oil from the trees, but it was too heavy for commercial use, and the idea was abandoned.

Pixley is a growing, prosperous community whose principal crops are cotton and cattle. Water from the Pixley Irrigation District canals is making it possible to plant alfalfa and fruit trees as well.

First church	United Brethren, 1913
First school	Howe, April 6, 1886; Pixley, 1899
First post office	June 3, 1887

POPLAR, west of Porterville, derived its name from a clump of poplar trees which grew in front of the home of A.B. Carpenter, who submitted that name for a post office.

Poplar is in a rich agricultural area irrigated with water diverted from the Tule River. In 1900 the Ridgeway brothers opened their creamery northeast of the little community, and many dairy farms sprang up in the area. Now there are dairy farms, cotton, grapes, and a variety of irrigated truck and field crops.

First church	Methodist Episcopal South, 1900
First school	Nearest were Rockford, August 5, 1868, and Pleasant View, May 3, 1876

Royal Porter Putnam (1837-1889) as he looked when he came to the Tule River Butterfield Stage Station in 1859.

Mary Packard Putnam (Mrs. R. Porter Putnam)

First post office	March 15, 1880, moved to Porterville, 1907

PORTERVILLE was named for Royal Porter Putnam (1837-1889), who came in 1859 as agent for the Tule River Butterfield Stage Station. The station, which included an inn, was on the south slope of Scenic Hill near the Tule River.

Putnam, who preferred his second name, started west in 1857. He contracted plains fever on the way. After a long convalescence he reached Los Angeles, where he was advised to find work on the Butterfield Stage Line instead of going to the mines.

Putnam's store and home in 1866. Mrs. Putnam is on the porch and Mr. Putnam is in the front yard of the home. The other people are not known.

Magnesite was mined around Porterville from the early 1900's until about 1931. The peak of operations came during World War I. W. P. Bartlett probably had more to do with developing magnesite mining than anyone else. It has been estimated that half a million tons were mined in Porterville and Success Valley.

His first job was that of hosteler at Packwood Station, and in a few months he was sent to the larger Tule River Station. Along with his duties as agent, he began to trade with travelers, settlers, and the Indians. The stage line was discontinued when the Civil War broke out. Putnam moved south of the station and set up a general store. However, he had competition from the village of Vandalia, which was located on the Butterfield Stage Road near the foothills.

By 1859 there were enough settlers in the village to have a post office, and on February 5, 1861, a school was granted to Vandalia. Then disaster struck in the flood of 1862, which washed away much of the farmland. When the flood waters had subsided, the people in Vandalia had another shock. The Tule River had changed its channel from the north and was flowing a mile south, washing away more land in Vandalia. People began to move to higher ground, and in a few years Vandalia was only the name of a school, a bridge, and a cemetery.

Putnam's town grew very slowly because another community, Plano, was emerging south of the Tule River, on the stage road. Plano had an excellent location and was on high ground. The derivation of the name is not clear, but it is reasonable to surmise that it had some connections with the plains spreading below the hills. Plano had a post office by February 13, 1871, and was soon the largest community south of Visalia. There were four hotels, three stores, two churches, saloons, a blacksmith shop, a livery stable, a brickyard, a school, and a cemetery. The soil was rich, and crops flourished. The Moreland-Campbell Ditch brought water from the Tule River for supplemental irrigation.

In spite of its better location, fertile soil, and plentiful water for irrigation, Plano gradually ceased to exist and Porterville began to grow. The reason was Porter Putnam, whose energy and courage went into building a community. After the flood of 1862, he bought 40 acres of land between the station and Vandalia for $200. In 1864 he had it surveyed into town lots, which he offered to give away to anyone who would move there. That same year he went east to marry his childhood sweetheart, Mary Packard. He had built a substantial home for her and had enlarged the store, which today would be on the northeast corner of Main and Oak Streets. Both Mr. and Mrs. Putnam were civic-minded and over the years participated in many social and community affairs. During the terrible dry cycle of the 1870's, Porter Putnam gave credit to his customers because he had faith in them. He was one of the few merchants in the valley who helped in that manner.

Eventually, many people and most of the business houses of Plano moved to Porterville. Putnam managed to get the Tule River post office on his side of the river, and in 1870 a school district was formed. The Plano School was annexed to Porterville in 1925 and renamed Vandalia School.

Tulare County's multi-million dollar citrus industry started in Porterville and is still a principal source of income in that area. Today Porterville is the trading center for the southern part of Tulare County. Surrounding it are farms producing cotton, citrus, grapes, olives, deciduous fruit, nuts, alfalfa, and dairy products. Supplemental water for irrigation comes from the Friant-Kern Canal and a network of smaller canals. Eight packing houses give work to many people. While many of the in-

The Richgrove Store with a warehouse in the rear. The Richgrove Hotel, built in 1909, is at right.

dustrial plants are related to agriculture, Porterville's location is attracting a variety of manufacturing establishments.

The Porterville State Hospital for the mentally retarded is the largest employer in Porterville. It is located near old Plano and was dedicated May 12, 1953, by Governor Earl Warren.

Porterville's location puts it near year-round recreation. The headquarters of Sequoia National Forest are in Porterville. Lake Success provides fishing, boating, swimming, water sports, and camping. Murray Park and Bartlett Park add scenic beauty and picnic areas. East of Porterville in the mountains are several resorts where people own their own summer homes. Balch Park and Mountain Home State Forest are within easy driving distances, as are Sequoia National Park and Kings Canyon National Park.

Porterville's schools started with the Tule River School in 1861. Today there are seven elementary schools, two junior high schools, two high schools, and the Porterville Junior College. The district also offers a full adult evening educational program.

Porterville was incorporated as a City of the Sixth Class May 7, 1902, with these officers: Wilko Mentz, mayor, and Fred Ackerman, Dr. O.C. Higgins, J.N. Larsen, and Arthur Abbey, council members.

Opposite page top: Porterville's Main Street in 1876. Putnam's store is the building with the balcony. Upper center: Main Street in 1892. Left to right the buildings are: Pohlman's Saloon, Tailor Shop, restaurant, Wilko Mentz General Store and the Putnam Building. Lower center: Main Street in 1895. Right to left are the Mountain Lion Saloon, Scotty's Chop House, Zalud's Saloon and Putnam's Pioneer Store. Bottom: Main Street in 1905. Left to right are Buford's Store, Scotty's Chop House, Zalud's Saloon, the Chapman Building the P. O. Davis Building and the Pioneer Hotel. Note the one automobile on Main Street.

On October 8, 1926, Porterville adopted a charter form of government with these officers: mayor, Marcus E. DeWitt; city manager, Fred W. Pease; council members, Chester H. Doyle, J. Frank Halford, George O'Brien, A. Louis Stone.

First church	First Methodist, 1865
First school	Tule River District February 5, 1861
	Porterville, 1870
	High School, 1896
	Porterville College, 1927
First post office	Tule River, April 29, 1859
	Porterville, February 13, 1871

RICHGROVE. The history of Richgrove began when Harry Quinn and Archibald Leitch moved sheep onto their Rag Gulch land in the early 1870's. A decade later many of the sheepmen in the southern end of the county began to plant wheat and barley, and warehouses and depots were needed.

In 1909 Mr. Quinn sold 15,000 acres at $23 an acre to the Reid Land and Development Company, whose partnership included S. Richard Shoup, Joseph Reid, W. O. Platt, and James Hadley. That company planned a town, built a hotel and store, and put in streets, sidewalks, and a water system. The name given to the town was Richgrove. The derivation of the name possibly came from the citrus groves planted in rich soil.

The same company sold and planted citrus groves from Ducor to Richgrove, but the 1913 freeze killed most of the small trees. The Reid Land and Development Company sold to the Richgrove Land Company but kept large orange groves south of Ducor. The Richgrove Land Company included some of the same men who were developing Terra Bella.

The community of Richgrove did not grow, but the surrounding land produces cattle and grain and

Top: Springville in 1890. Livery stable is on the left and Jonathan May's house is at right. Center: Daunt Store in Springville in 1898. George Daunt is the man behind the counter on the left and his brother Fred is at right. Clinton Brown and his son Jay are facing the camera. Bottom: Springville Soda Springs beside the Tule River. Shown are the bath house and dance hall.

thanks to water from the Friant-Kern Canal, cotton, grapes, and field crops have been planted. Packing houses and cold storage plants process the crops grown in the area.

First church	Four Square Gospel, 1947
First school	Wildflower, 1886
	Richgrove, March 5, 1923
First post office	January 4, 1911

SPRINGVILLE, east of Porterville in the mountains, was named for the natural soda springs. Cattlemen, sheepmen, and lumbermen settled the area. The community was originally named Daunt, for William Daunt, who built a general store. His daughter Fannie married Avon Coburn, who really started Springville in 1889. He had a large sawmill in what would now be Mountain Home, and then built a planing mill and box factory in Daunt. People who moved into the region began to plant oranges and lemons, both of which grew well. In 1911 the Porterville Northeastern Railroad built a line into Springville to haul out lumber and citrus from the packing houses built along the railroad. In that same year the name of the post office changed from Daunt to Springville. The railroad was gradually abandoned, and the last of the tracks disappeared in 1957 in the waters of Lake Success.

Springville is world famous for the Tulare Kings Counties Joint Tuberculosis Hospital, built in 1918 with Dr. J. Tracy Melvin as the first director. He was followed in 1934 by Dr. W.W. Winn, whose work in the field of pulmonary diseases would bring him world-wide recognition. In 1950 the Martin Memorial Building was donated by Mr. and Mrs. Dan Martin in memory of G.J. Martin, an early resident of Porterville. Medical research has all but eliminated the scourge of tuberculosis, so the hospital gradually closed. At the present time it is being remodelled into a senior citizens' housing complex.

Springville is still a cattle center, and each year the old image is preserved with a rodeo and the Jack Ass Mail Run from Porterville. Logging is also an economic factor. Since Springville is a gateway to the Sequoia National Forest, with its many camping facilities, mountain meadows, and unsurpassed recreational activities, tourism is big business in Springville.

First school	Dennison, May 5, 1887
	Springville Union, 1922
First post office	Daunt, February 18, 1886
	Springville, January 24, 1911

STRATHMORE, like its neighbors Lindsay and Exeter, was first a cattle range and then a grain-growing region. It has had three names other than Strathmore—Roth Spur, Santos, and Filo. Each tells a bit of the town's history.

In 1878 John and Peter Roth came to the area, and in a few years they owned several thousand acres planted to grain. They were joined by their brothers, George, John, Bennett, and Henry, and their sisters, Mary (Mrs. John Limegrover) and Barbara (Mrs. Owen Flynn). Mrs. Flynn, who died in 1965 at the age of 103, was affectionately known as Strathmore's First Lady.

In 1888 the eastside Southern Pacific Railroad stimulated grain and citrus planting along the line. The siding and post office were called Roth's Spur. In 1900 the Roth brothers sold to a subsidiary of Balfour-Guthrie, an English-owned company which still does a large export-import trade.

That company platted a townsite and Mrs. Hector Burness, wife of the company agent, called it Strathmore, which meant "great valley." The railroad timetable first called it Santos but finally changed the listing to Strathmore. Later on the railroad called it Filo, but strong protests from Strathmore persuaded the railroad to return to the name Strathmore.

Strathmore's economy is based on grain, citrus,

Left: The Strathmore Store and Post Office, about 1905. Right: Strathmore looking east from the S.P. Depot. The large brick building on the right is the Keeley and Burdick General Store.

packing houses, and cold storage plants. Feed lots are nearby, and several trucking systems aid in transportation.

First church	St. Andrews Presbyterian, 1907
First school	Lewis Creek, May 5, 1876
	Strathmore, 1913
	Strathmore High School, 1919
First post office	Roth, October 7, 1896
	Strathmore, April 26, 1907

SULTANA, east of Dinuba, was known as Alta before the Santa Fe Railroad came through in 1897. The railroad named the town Sultana for the Sultana grapes grown in the region. Abner Fraser was one of the first ranchers to process the bleached Sultana raisin into what is known as the Valencia raisin. Sultana now produces citrus, grapes, and vegetables.

First school	May 5, 1901
First post office	May 23, 1900

SEVILLE is a small agricultural community east of Yettem. When the Santa Fe Railroad built the Minkler Branch Line from Cutler to Exeter in 1913, location engineers chose Spanish names for stations. Seville was one of those selected.

First post office	September 5, 1915, moved to Visalia, 1931

TERRA BELLA, eight miles south of Porterville on Highway 65, was first called Deer Creek Switch, and then Terrabella.* Deer Creek attracted sheep and cattlemen long before the country was planted to grain. Before the Southern Pacific Railroad came through in 1888, grain from what is now

*All one word until 1909.

Terra Bella and Ducor had to be hauled to shipping platforms at Pixley, Tipton, and Alila. In 1890 the McNear Warehouse Company put up a warehouse in Terra Bella, and a warehouse at Ducor made it possible to store and ship grain from both those points.

Land colonization and real estate promotions brought citrus to Terra Bella. In 1908 a group incorporated the Terra Bella Development Company with the Edward Silent Real Estate Company of Los Angeles as its agent. The next year, a group of men from Southern California took over the Terra Bella Development Company. These men were to have much to do with the community's history. They were George and Phillip Hart, Marco Hellman, F.J. Thomas, and Frank Ensign. They planned a townsite and put in streets, sidewalks, and a water system. The Hart brothers built a substantial two-story brick building, and the company built a hotel, a bank, and a depot. Seven thousand surrounding acres were subdivided into small farms. Excursion trains from Southern California brought in hundreds of prospective buyers. Citrus did well around Terra Bella, and many small orchards were planted.

Lindsay is the center of olive processing now, but the first olive processing plant was built in Terra Bella in 1907 by A. Adams, who owned a processing plant in Sunland. Olives must have been shipped in, for the first record of a grove planted in Terra Bella was 1911, when Frank Ensign planted 40 acres. That same year STOMA, the Southern Tulare County Olive Marketing Association, was established in Terra Bella.

Another long-forgotten business was the Terra Bella Cannery, which started canning tomatoes in 1915.

The first store in Terra Bella was built in 1909 and operated by J.C. Higgins who was also the first postmaster. The men are not identified.

Terra Bella in 1911. The 1st National Bank is on the left. At right are Higgins Store and Post Office and the Terra Bella Hotel.

In 1909 a tract of land northeast of Terra Bella was subdivided and sold to some German people. The Lutheran Colony has prospered and grown over the years. The Zion Lutheran Church and the Zion School were both built in 1909. In 1956 the first units of the Good Shepherd Lutheran Home for retarded people were built. Many additions have been made to this home, which is regarded as one of the outstanding institutions of its kind in the nation.

Terra Bella, like many small communities, has had its share of fires, but the major problem was dwindling water for irrigation. The Terra Bella Irrigation District was formed in 1915 and brought new hope. A series of dry years in the 1920's, followed by the Depression, brought disaster and bankruptcy to many people. Land was sold for unpaid taxes, and people were forced to move away. Self-sacrifice and good management finally pulled the Irrigation District through a painful period. The District has expanded and improved, and with water available for irrigation from the Friant-Kern Canal, Terra Bella's agriculture is prospering. The major crops are grain, citrus, olives, and vegetables. Other types of business related to agriculture have come in, but the major industry still centers around packing houses.

Above: Hart Block in Terra Bella, built in 1911. Below: Terra Bella Cannery, which canned tomatoes as early as 1914. The building is on the west side of the railroad tracks.

First church   Community Presbyterian, 1911
First school   Salem, May 10, 1876
                                   Terra Bella, 1911
First post office   May to October 1891,
    then discontinued until reinstated April 9, 1909

THREE RIVERS, which takes its name from the three divisions of the Kaweah River, is not only located in a beautiful mountain setting, but is a gateway to nearby Sequoia National Park.

Hale Tharp came to the area in 1856 and settled on Horse Creek. By the early 1860's there were many cattlemen in that part of the mountains. Apples grew well there, and became a substantial source of income for several families.

Mrs. Lorenzo Rockwell suggested the name Three Rivers in 1879, when application was made for a post office. The community remained small, but it was a stopping place for lumbermen, stockmen, and people who were going to the high country. After the Kaweah Colony collapsed, some of its members homesteaded around Three Rivers.

The creation of Sequoia National Park and General Grant Park in 1890 helped Three Rivers grow. Summer cabins appeared along the river, as did motels, camping sites, and summer resorts. People came to buy apples, and the apple cider for which Three Rivers is still famous.

The Three Rivers Store (above) and the Three Rivers Lodge (right) were both built before 1900 by Frank and Noel Britten on the Britten Ranch.

Three Rivers' picturesque setting, climate, and proximity to the high country attracted such people as Major Fredrick Burnham, Carroll Barnes, Edna Covey, Albert Marshall, Monica Shannon, Armine von Tempski, and Forrest Hopping. Today many well known writers, musicians, artists, and sculptors live in the Three Rivers area. There are art galleries and exhibits, concerts, music festivals, and dramatic presentations. Guest ranches attract summer visitors. Nearby Terminus Dam and Lake Kaweah provide boating, fishing, and water sports. Not only is the dam a source of controlled irrigation for the drainage basin of the Kaweah, but also it is a reminder that the movement to harness the power of the Kaweah River began almost a century ago in Visalia.

First church	Presbyterian
First school	Cove, Ceptember 9, 1873, changed to Three Rivers, 1909
First post office	December 23, 1879

Swinging bridge over the Kaweah River across from Slick Rock, 1920's.

TIPTON, south of Tulare, is a railroad-created town. In July 1872, construction of the Southern Pacific Railroad southward stopped there for several months. Newspapers at that time referred to the place as Tip Town. Tipton was also said to be the name of a surveyor for the railroad.

Tipton and Pixley were shipping depots for grain from the southern part of the county until the eastside railroad was built in 1888. It has been a center for dairies and, since 1895, a large creamery, and presently the area has diversified crops including cotton, wheat, and alfalfa.

First church	Congregational, 1888
First school	May 3, 1874
First post office	September 19, 1873

TRAVER, southwest of Dinuba, once shipped out more grain than any other town in the nation. Traver was a creation of the 76 Land & Water Company, which planned a vast irrigation project in the northern part of Tulare County. County men who were part of that company were Thomas Fowler, Daniel K. Zumwalt, Peter Y. Baker, and C.F.J. Kitchner, but the town was named for Charles Traver, one of the directors from Northern California. The 76 Land & Water Company planned to take water from the Kings River and eventually irrigate 30,000 acres. About 2,000 acres of the tract were west of the Southern Pacific tracks.

Early in 1884 the Company mailed 10,000 handbills announcing that it was prepared to sell land and deliver water. Excursion trains arrived to bring people to the auction April 8, 1884. The only building in Traver was the unfinished depot, but $65,000 was realized from the sale of property that day. Within a few months Traver was a bustling, prosperous, growing community. Saloons, gambling dens, and a red light district made it probably the rowdiest town in the valley.

Traver had three disastrous fires, but each time the town was rebuilt. The project that had created Traver, however, also caused its decline. Irrigation of the dry plains percolated alkali to the surface, just as it was to do in Allensworth. Farmers who raised alfalfa, grapes, field crops, and fruit began to move away. The eastside railroad built in 1888 created new towns with warehouses and depots, and Traver lost much of its shipping business. The Alta Irrigation District, organized in 1888, bought out the canals and water rights of the 76 Land & Water Company in 1890.

Traver Day, April 8, is still a day of celebration and reminiscence for descendants of those Traver pioneers. When Traver was a large town, hundreds of residents and friends gathered for Traver Day. The day started with blasts from a shotgun, each blast signifying the years Traver had been in existence. Sometimes an anvil salute was given. There were games, riding exhibitions, a barbecue, and a dance. The big drawing card was a rabbit drive, when thousands of the jackrabbits that devoured crops were rounded up and clubbed to death.

Traver is slowly coming back as a farming community for crops other than grain. Scientific soil management plus irrigation makes this possible.

First church	Christian, 1885
First school	March 2, 1885
First post office	Cross Creek, established 1874, moved to Grandview, 1876, moved to Traver, April 14, 1884

Hauling grain to one of the three warehouses in Traver, 1890.

TULARE, the dairy capital of California, was created by the Southern Pacific Railroad in 1872. Tulare, like most of the railroad-created communites along the 1872 line, had been bypassed by early settlers because there were no natural sources of water.

The area selected by the railroad for a townsite was on property owned by Isaac Wright, who had brought his family from San Jose in 1870. He sold to the railroad and moved a quarter of a mile south, where he built the first house in Tulare (South T Street). The train pulled into Tulare July 25, 1872, and the village soon had a population of 20 persons. In 1875 the railroad brought in its shops, round house, and division headquarters and the town boomed, for there was a monthly payroll of $30,000 to $40,000.

In that same year artesian water was found south of Tipton, and this water was used to irrigate the 40-acre Tree Ranch. In 1881 artesian water was found on the Paige & Morton ranch near Tulare by Professor A.P. Cromley, who used a water witch rod to locate the water. The well produced 800,000 gallons of water a day. By 1892 it was estimated that there were 300 to 400 artesian wells in the county. However, this source of water could not irrigate the orchards, alfalfa, and other crops that were planted. A series of canals was constructed, and in 1889 the Tulare Irrigation District was organized. That body planned to divert water from

Isaac Wright (1823-1910)

Sale of lots in Traver, April 8, 1884. (Courtesy of Los Tulares)

Tulare in 1883, looking northwest. The vacant lot in the left center is now Zumwalt Park. Directly across the street is the Wheeler and Zartman blacksmith shop. The spire in the distance is the Congregational Church.

the St. John's River through canals. The district bonded itself for $500,000. Much of this was traded for construction work. From one-half to one-third of the water was lost as it coursed through the unlined canals.

Tulare had water, but it also had trouble. In 1891 the railroad served notice that it was moving the shops and round house to Bakersfield and the division headquarters to Fresno. Not only did Tulare lose the large payroll, but the railroad people had invested in homes which were soon a drug on the market.

Tulare had recovered from previous disasters. The fire of 1883 destroyed 25 places of business. In 1886 another fire again wiped out the business district. Each time the community recovered, but the loss of the railroad shops came at a particularly bad time. The nation was in the first phase of a long business depression, and the farmers of Tulare were left with $500,000 of bonded indebtedness for the Irrigation District. People began to move away, merchants closed their businesses, and farm land went for back taxes. The Irrigation District had to default on its payments, and interest accumulated. Objectors sought legal relief from "those accursed bonds." Eventually the bonds plus the accrued interest came to $663,000, or $163,000 more than the original debt. Over a period of months formulas of payment were worked out, and the remaining bondholders bore a ruinous tax of 36 cents for each dollar of assessed valuation of their property. Somehow they found the money to pay the tax.

On October 17, 1903, thousands of people from all over the valley gathered in Tulare to help the town declare its independence from debt. There was a carnival spirit as Governor Pardee and other dignitaries rode in the parade to the Pavilion. Following them was a float on which was a large wire basket. District farmers and their families filed by and tossed their bonds into the basket. Tulare had a fire it really enjoyed as Governor Pardee took a torch and fired the basket full of bonds. In spite of all the rejoicing, Tulare's water problems were just beginning.

In 1914 the Lindsay-Strathmore Irrigation District was formed to pump water from a well field near the Kaweah-St. Johns Rivers. The district bought the 1,000-acre Rancho de Kaweah four miles north of Exeter and bored 37 wells. The water was conveyed in redwood pipes so there was little leakage as there had been in the Tulare canals.

In 1916 the Tulare Irrigation District headed a group of 17 water districts and filed suit against the Lindsay-Strathmore Irrigation District (See page 71), claiming that the latter district was taking water from underground sources which were part of their long-established water rights.

The case went on for 20 years and is the longest

PROGRAM

ANVIL SALUTE AT SUNRISE

GRAND BOND PARADE, ...W. W. COLLINS
Sheriff of Tulare County, Grand Marshal.

(Parade will form at 9 a. m. on north K street and move promptly at 9:40 a. m. Arriving at Pavilion Park at 10:15 a. m.)

MUSIC BY THE BAND

PRAYER ....REV. DANIEL STEWART
Pastor of Christian Church, Tulare.

ADDRESS OF WELCOME .... JOHN TUOHY
Mayor of Tulare City.

MUSIC BY THE BAND

ADDRESS ....ARTHUR J. PILLSBURY
Member of Bond Liquidation Committee

MUSIC BY THE BAND

ADDRESS ....HON. M P. SNYDER
Mayor of Los Angeles

MUSIC BY THE BAND

ADDRESS .... A. SBARBORO
President California Promotion Committee.

MUSIC BY THE BAND

GRAND FREE BARBECUE 11:30 A. M.

PROGRAM

BOND BURNING CEREMONIES 2:00 P. M.

HON. J. W. DAVIS, President of the Day.

MUSIC BY THE BAND

PLACING THE BONDS IN A WIRE BASKET............
....THE TAXPAYERS

ADDRESS .... HON. WM. H. ALFORD
Member State Board of Equalization.

MUSIC BY THE BAND

ADDRESS ....HON. GEO. C. PARDEE
Governor of California

APPLYING TORCH TO THE BONDS

SONG "AMERICA" .... ALL THE PEOPLE

GRAND DISPLAY OF FIREWORKS, 7:30 P. M. AT RAILROAD RESERVATION ON SOUTH FRONT ST.

GRAND FREE BALL AT PAVILION
Everybody Dance

Top: Tulare Avenue in 1886. on the right three stores are identifiable: L. E. Schoenemann's General Store, Tulare Drug Store and an oyster house. Center: Bond burning program. It was an occasion for community celebration on October 17, 1903. Bottom: Smith College was founded in Tulare in 1885 by Dr. William T. F. Smith. A branch of the University of Southern California, it was located near D Street and Elm Avenue and ceased operations in the late 1890's.

case of record in California. Seven different judges heard the case and all were loathe to render a verdict, for either district would be ruined if its water were cut off. In 1936, when the Central Valley Project was assured, a compromise solution to the long and bitter litigation was worked out.

Tulare's economy revived when creameries were started and farmers went into the dairy business. As that industry was stabilized, Tulare farmers were assured of a steady dependable income, which in turn encouraged new business in the community.

The dairy industry attracted Portuguese from the Azores Islands, where dairy farming had gone on for centuries. When the Portuguese migrated to the United States, and especially to the San Joaquin Valley, they worked as ranch hands. Hard work and the cooperation of the entire family made it possible to buy cattle and rent or buy land for a dairy. In Tulare County many Portuguese people have stayed in the dairy or creamery business. Others have become part of the business and professional life of Tulare and nearby cities.

For many years Tulare has had a sister city, Angra de Heroismo, on the Azorean island of Terceira, the original island home of many Tulareans. In 1972 a delegation came from Angra to help Tulare observe its centennial, and in 1974 Tulare people went to Angra to help celebrate its 500th birthday. Presently a two-block area in downtown Tulare is being developed as a tribute to the contributions of its Portuguese citizens. The outstanding structure is the Angra Clock Tower.

Tulare is host each year for two outstanding fairs. One is the Tulare County Fair, and the other is the more recent Tulare County Farm Equipment Show.

Each city in Tulare County held fairs before the first Tulare County Fair was held in Tulare in October 1893. There were many exhibits of farm produce and the arts and crafts of the homemaker, but the drawing card was horse racing. The Board of Directors for the first County Fair were Jasper Harrell, H.P. Perkins from Visalia, W.B. Cartmill, A.P. Merritt, E.D. Castle from Tulare, Jacob Hayes from Poplar, George S. Berry from Lindsay, and G.A. Dodge from Hanford. In 1916 ten Tulare businessmen bought four acres south of Tulare and formed the Tulare Livestock Association, which was later turned over to the Tulare Chamber of Commerce, which operated the Fair and over the years bought more land. On June 30, 1936, the 24th District Agricultural Association was formed, with a board of directors appointed by the State. Kings County was originally part of the 24th District but withdrew in 1947 to set up its own fair.

Alfred J. Elliott became manager of the Fair in 1931 and held that position until 1965, when he was succeeded by Alden Slinde, who is still managing the operation.

Since 1967 Tulare has been host each February to the Tulare Farm Equipment Show held on the fairgrounds. It has become the largest fair of its kind in the world, drawing exhibits and visitors from all over the United States and many foreign

Tulare Avenue looking west from K Street in 1904.

Frank Bryant landed this plane on the old Tulare Fairgrounds a mile east of Tulare on February 10, 1912. It was the first plane to land in the County. Roy Francis was the pilot of the other plane, and 4,000 people came to see the air show that the two men put on.

countries. Millions of dollars worth of farm implements and just about everything related to agriculture are displayed. In 1976, 114,102 people attended the show, and space for 1977 is already sold out.

Tulare is also the home of the Tulare County Hospital, just south of the main business section. Tulare County has operated a county hospital since 1873, when a ten-bedroom house was built in Visalia. It burned in 1889 and the Supervisors bought Oak Grove Manor, midway between Tulare and Visalia on the Visalia-Goshen Railroad. Its location was impractical in the horse and buggy days, and when it burned in 1894, the Supervisors let a contract for a brick building in Visalia that was used until 1920. At this time it became necessary to build a larger building, and Tulare offered to donate 18 acres for the new hospital. The Supervisors agreed, and although it has been enlarged many times since, the site south of Tulare is the same.

Tulare incorporated March 8, 1888, with these officers: mayor, C.F. Hall; assessor, H.A. Charters; marshal, Frank Wootten; treasurer, L.E. Schoenemann; recorder, E.W. Holland; trustees, A.T. Cotton, E.A. Braly, F.M. Schultz, Jacob Goldman.

On May 19, 1923, Tulare adopted a charter form of government with these officers: mayor, W.N. Brown; city manager, George S. Lewis; council members, A.W. Rumley, L.N. McCallister, C.N. Sisson, and C.T. Paxton.

Tulare is growing rapidly, with its principal income from dairies, creameries and related industries. Other major crops are cotton, grain, sugar beets, cattle, alfalfa, hay, and field crops. Because of its location on a main highway, variety of industrial plants is attracted to Tulare. Many of these are not associated with agriculture.

Tulare has two high schools, a junior high and seven elementary schools. Tulare was one of the first cities to develop programs for special education for hard-of-hearing, blind, and orthopedically handicapped children. The Tulare Regional Auditory Center has pioneered many programs that are now used in other parts of the state. Tulare is also part of the College of the Sequoias District.

First church	Congregational, 1872
	Formally organized, 1874
First school	Fitzgerald, April 18, 1868
	Tulare, 1885
	High School, 1891
	Smith College, 1885
First post office	December 31, 1872

VISALIA is the oldest town between Stockton and Los Angeles. Its history permeates the entire history of the lower valley as well as that of Tulare County.

Visalia had the first church, school, home, newspaper, store, and business establishments in the lower valley. In spite of its location off a main line road and railroad, Visalia has always been the trading center of a large surrounding area.

Its geographical location on the delta of the Kaweah River has provided an incredibly fertile soil where almost any crop may be grown. Water has never been a problem because many creeks crisscross the delta, and there is the large St. Johns River. Water for irrigation was diverted as early as 1853.

The movement to preserve the big trees, watersheds, and scenic beauties of the Sierra Nevada began in Visalia. So did plans to harness the power

Above: This picture, dated 1863, is probably the oldest photograph of Visalia. The town pump is now the intersection of Main and Court Streets. On the right, looking east, are: Vallee's Book store and Grog shop, Bostwick's tin shop, Fashion Saloon, Sweet's store and warehouse, a produce store and Dr. Baker's drug store. On the left are: Thomas' blacksmith shop, the Overland Hotel, Clarke's Saloon, Elias Jacob's store, Henry Green's store, Levi Mitchell's store and Visalia House. In the distance is Matthews' Mill. Below: The same Main Street scene — 60 years later.

of the Kaweah River for hydro-electric development.

Visalia was named in 1852 by Nathaniel Vise for his ancestral home in Visalia, Kentucky. The next year voters succeeded in moving the county seat from Woodsville to Visalia.

Visalia was governed by the Board of Supervisors until its first incorporation in 1864. The officers chosen in that election were: president, Nathan Baker; clerk, Tipton Lindsey; assessor, John Gill; marshal, J.W. Kennedy; treasurer, Horace Thomas; trustees, David R. Dougalss, Daniel

Little White Schoolhouse, built in 1857, was the first school in the lower San Joaquin Valley. The site is now occupied by the Visalia City Library.

Visalia's business district in 1864. This is now on the south side of Main Street between Garden and Church Streets.

Woods Jr., Joseph H. Thomas, James E. Denny.

Incorporation was a necessary step, for the gold rush to the White and Kern Rivers in the middle 1850's brought about 6,000 people into Tulare County. Visalia was the supply center for the mines. When gold was found in Owens Valley in 1860, Visalia merchants sent supply wagons to those distant mines. The same thing was to happen a decade later when the mines of Mineral King drew hundreds of people to the mountains.

The influx of people brought a variety of businesses to Visalia. Stages lines, lumberyards, brickyards, saloons, livery stables, saddle shops, harness shops, wagon shops, blacksmiths, gunsmiths, hotels, restaurants, barber shops, dry goods stores, and general stores were established. Attorneys and physicians opened offices in the busy community.

Efforts to persuade the Southern Pacific Railroad to come to Visalia failed, so Visalia businessmen financed two feeder railroads, the Visalia-Goshen Railroad and the Visalia-Tulare Railroad. Many years later local men planned the Visalia Electric Railroad, which was taken over by the Southern Pacific Railroad.

On February 27, 1874, Visalians voted to incorporate as a City of the Sixth Class with the following officers: mayor, Michael Mooney; tax collector, J.C. Hoy; assessor, Julius Levy; recorder, Abel Elkins; city clerk, J.A. Nowell; trustees, S.A. Sheppard, J.A. Samstag, W.B. Bishop, W.A. Owen.

The largest and most enthusiastic celebration Visalia ever had took place September 9, 1897, when the Valley Railroad sent a train into Visalia. Thousands of people came to welcome the train, hear speeches, see the parade, and partake of a free barbecue of 65 beeves. At long last, Visalia was on a main line source of transportation. The next year the Santa Fe Railroad took over the Valley line.

In 1923 Visalia adopted a charter form of government with a city manager. The officers selected for that plan were: mayor, Joseph Barboni; city manager, B.J. Pardee; council members, James

Burke, Isaac Clark, Dr. Gilbert Furness, W.P. Willimott.

Visalia is situated amost midway between San Francisco and Los Angeles. That location plus adequate transportation by air, truck, and railroad has attracted industry to Visalia, mostly to an industrial park area on the western edge of town.

Other attractions to industry, besides location and transportation, are the cultural, educational, and recreational features available in Visalia. The recreational facilities are unmatched. In a short time one may drive to the coast or to the Sierra Nevada. County parks, city parks, and national parks provide areas of enjoyment for picnickers, fishermen, campers, and sports enthusiasts. Nearby Lake Kaweah offers boating, fishing, and water sports. Golf clubs, skating rinks, swimming pools, and youth centers are part of the scene. Theatres, the Convention Center, and College of the Sequoias bring in dramatic presentations and noted lecturers.

Visalia Unified School District includes 20 elementary schools, three junior high schools, three high schools, and a junior college, College of the Sequoias. Special education classes are provided for orthopedically handicapped, mentally retarded, blind, deaf, and aphasic children. The District and the college both offer excellent adult education classes.

Visalia is growing rapidly in both size and population, but the environmental growth pattern is planned, not haphazard. The economy is a welding together of agriculture and industry, with the emphasis on agriculture and its related agri-business establishments.

Visalia's first high school building was ready in 1897. It was located in an oval park on North Court Street, now named Lincoln Oval Park. When the second high school building on West Main Street was built in 1911, this school became Lincoln Grammar School.

First church Methodist Episcopal South, 1852
First school   Visalia, May 4, 1857
        College of the Sequoias, 1925
First post office from Woodsville, October 12, 1853

WAUKENA, ten miles west of Tulare, was originally Buzzards' Roost, a boat landing on Tulare Lake. The name came from buzzards which roosted in a small grove of oak trees on Cameron

Visalia's first City Hall and fire station built in 1872. The second story was added in 1876. The building was used until 1909 when the new City Hall and fire station were built on the same site, East Acequia Street between Church and Garden Streets.

The Harrell building, built in 1888 at Main and Court Streets, was Visalia's first "skyscraper." The man in the dark hat is Jasper Harrell. The Visalia-Tulare train started near the building. Armory Hall, also built in 1888, is in the background.

TIME TABLE
Visalia Electric Railroad Company

Schedule of Train Service.   In effect Monday, October 25th, 1909.

FROM VISALIA.

Train No.		502	504	506	508	510	512	514	516
VISALIA	Lv.	....	5:50	8:06	10:20	12:04	2:40	5:20	7:52	10:40
AMBLER		....	5:56	8:12	10:26	12:10	2:46	5:26	7:58	10:46
FARMERSVILLE		....	6:01	8:19	10:32	12:16	2:52	5:32	8:04	10:52
GIANT OAK		....	6:03	8:21	10:35	12:19	2:54	5:35	8:08	10:55
EXETER	Ar	....	6:10	8:28	10:42	12:26	3:02	5:42	8:15	11:03
EXETER	Lv	....	6:12	8:30	10:44	12:28	3:04	5:44	8:17	11:05
MERRYMAN		....	6:20	8:38	10:52	12:36	3:12	5:52	8:25	11:13
YOKOHL		....	6:22	8:40	10:54	12:38	3:14	5:54	8:27	11:15
LEVINSON		....	6:26	8:45	10:59	12:43	3:19	5:59	8:32	11:20
LEMON COVE	Ar	....	6:33	8:52	11:06	12:50	3:26	6:07	8:40	11:27

TOWARDS VISALIA.

Train No.		501	503	505	507	509	511	513	515	517
LEMON COVE	Lv	....	7:08	9:28	11:15	1:40	3:58	6:52	9:20	11:28
LEVINSON		....	7:14	9:34	11:21	1:46	4:04	6:58	9:26	11:34
YOKOHL		....	7:18	9:38	11:25	1:50	4:08	7:02	9:30	11:38
MERRYMAN		....	7:21	9:41	11:28	1:53	4:11	7:05	9:33	11:40
EXETER	Ar	....	7:30	9:50	11:37	2:02	4:20	7:15	9:42	11:50
EXETER	Lv	5:20	7:32	9:51	11:38	2:04	4:22	7:17	9:44	....
GIANT OAK		5:27	7:39	9:58	11:45	2:11	4:29	7:24	9:51	....
FARMERSVILLE		5:30	7:42	10:00	11:47	2:14	4:32	7:27	9:54	....
AMBLER		5:36	7:48	10:08	11:53	2:20	4:38	7:34	10:00	....
VISALIA	Ar	5:42	7:54	10:12	11:59	2:26	4:45	7:40	10:06	....

Light Figures A. M., Black Figures P. M.
NOTE: Cars run to Terminus only for special parties.

Visalia Electric Railroad time table, 1909.

Looking east on Visalia's Main Street in 1911. Lone Oak Park, the "smallest park in the world," is by the Dudley home on the left. Visalia High School, now named Redwood High School, is on the right.

Dedication program of July 4, 1916, for Visalia Municipal Auditorium (above) on East Acequia Street. The building was razed in 1964 and replaced by the Convention Center.

Program

CHAIRMAN OF THE DAY .... N. F. Bradley

SELECTION, Columbia, Visalia Concert Band, John Weinert, conductor

INVOCATION .... Rev. A. O. Raber

VOCAL QUARTET, A Song of Welcome (Beach)—Edith Pell, Jessie Anderson, Dr. E. E. Selleck and Leroy G. Smith. Mrs. John C. Hicks, accompanist.

REMARKS .... N. F. Bradley, Chairman

VIOLIN SOLO, Hungarian Dance, No. 5 (Brahms)—Prof. Clyde Keener. Dorris Crittenden, accompanist.

QUARTET AND CHORUS, Star Spangled Banner (Francis Scott Key)—Pell, Anderson, Selleck, Smith and Audience. Mrs. John C. Hicks, accompanist.

DECLARATION OF INDEPENDENCE .... Hon. Fred C. Scott

VOCAL TRIO, Our Country's Flag—Oree May Seale, Florence and Ida Herni. Mrs. John C. Hicks, accompanist.

VOCAL SOLO, My Own United States (Edwards)—Miss Edith Pell. Mrs. John C. Hicks, accompanist.

ADDRESS .... Hon. Max. Phelan

AMERICA .... By the Audience
Accompaniment by Visalia Concert Band.

PRAYER AND BENEDICTION .... Rev. Clyde P. Metcalf

STAR SPANGLED BANNER, (Francis Scott Key) .... Visalia Concert Band

---

Creek. The first settlers were cattlemen, and as the waters of the lake subsided, homesteaders came in to plant grain.

In 1886 the Los Angeles and Pasadena Tulare Improvement Company bought 12,000 acres to promote the sale of farmland and town lots. A site a little west of Buzzards' Roost was platted and named Waukena, which is a phonetical corruption of the name Joaquin from San Joaquin Valley.

Water for the farms came from artesian wells and Cameron Creek, and farmers raised alfalfa, dairy cattle, grain, and poultry. The company did not sell much of its land, and it lost interest in Waukena.

The farming area and the town revived when the Santa Fe Railroad built its westside line in 1897. In 1902 the Baculuipi Land Company of San Francisco subdivided land on both sides of the track and sold most of it.

Waukena is a rich, diversified farming community producing cotton, alfalfa, fruit, cattle and dairies.

First church   Church of the Brethren, 1913
First school   Buzzards' Roost, April 14, 1882
                                  Artesia, May 9, 1883
                                 Aurora, March 11, 1898
                       Waukena Union District, 1920
First post office   June 4, 1889

WHITE RIVER, southeast of Ducor in the foothills, was the second community to emerge in Tulare County. It was better known as Tailholt when it was a prosperous mining camp started in 1856. Now it is a ghost town. Father Garces named the river Rio Blanco in 1776, and Lieutenant Williamson gave it the English equivalent during his 1853 survey.

Gold was found around the White and Kern Rivers in 1853, and by 1856 thousands of people were on their way to the new fields. The first camp

Ten-Stamp Mill in White River. David B. James is at left.

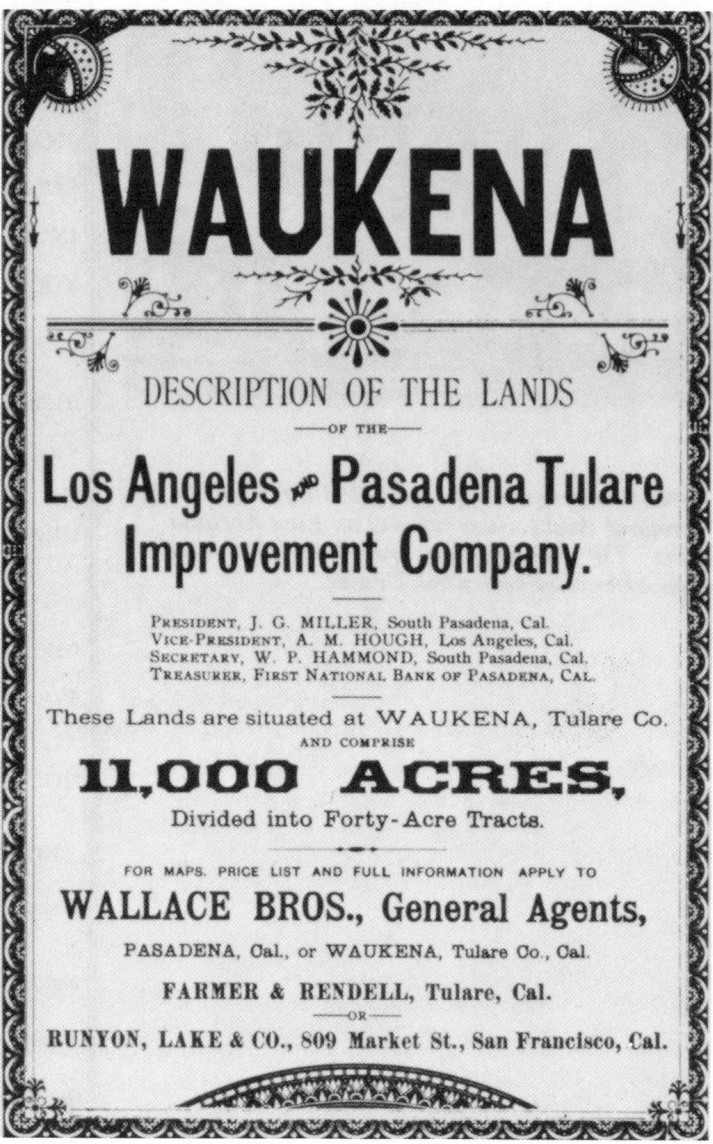
Waukena sales promotion advertisement, c. 1886. (Courtesy of Los Tulares)

Dedication of State Historical Marker No. 413 at Tailholt, 1949. Most of these people or their families lived in Tailholt at some time.

Stages in front of White River Hotel, which was built in the early 1860's.

Bald Mountain Mine. D.B. James is on the left. The others are not identified.

Four Tulare County pioneers — taken in White River in 1928. Left to right: Thomas Mayfield (1843-1929), Zachary Blankenship (1854-1929), Frank Bequette (1850-1929) and Michael Mitchell (1869-1930).

on White River was Dogtown, but when the trail to the mines bypassed Dogtown, its inhabitants moved up the Creek and started Tailholt. The derivation of that place name is anyone's guess.

A post office was granted June 10, 1862, and Levi Mitchell, the first postmaster, applied for it as White River. White River was the supply center for a large segment of the mining country during the half century that was important to mining. The price of gold dropped around 1900, and as mines closed, people left or went into the cattle business. There is little left of the mining town. On the north hillside is the community cemetery, and on the south hillside is obliterated Boothill, a dim reminder of the once boisterous mining camp.

First school   August 3, 1874
First post office   June 10, 1862,
              moved to California Hot Springs, 1933

Bravo Lake at Woodlake.

Visalia Electric Railroad car in front of Woodlake's first business building, built in 1910 on Naranjo Boulevard.

Woodlake business district, about 1915.

Woodville Ranch of Henry Hunsaker.

WOODLAKE was first known to early cattlemen as Antelope Valley. It takes its name from Bravo Lake (see page 38), along whose shore the early settlers established Stringtown. That small settlement was washed out in the flood of 1868, and the people moved to higher ground.

In 1907 Jason Barton, J.W. Fewell, and Adolph Sweet, all local men, bought and subdivided land on the east side of Cottonwood Creek and named it Elderwood. At about the same time orange and lemon groves and vineyards were planted in the sheltered valley. Redbanks Orchards, on the slope of nearby Colvin Hill, was started in 1894 and produced early peaches and other tree crops.

In 1910 Gilbert Stevenson, from Southern California, bought acreage south of Elderwood, built a "brick block" for stores, and platted a town which he named Woodlake. The community grew steadily and incorporated September 16, 1941, with Frank Howell as mayor and council members Kenneth Kress, J.M. Freeman, Rennie Brown, and Frank Vinton.

Water for agriculture comes from the Friant-Kern Canal, St. Johns River, Bravo Lake, Cottonwood Creek, and smaller creeks. Cattle are raised on the foothills, and grapes, citrus, tree crops, and early vegetables are the major crops. Woodlake has attracted light manufacturing plants as well as many packing houses and processing plants.

First church	Cumberland Presbyterian, 1866
First school	Antelope, May 12, 1870, as Woodlake, 1913
	Woodlake High School, 1914
First post office	January 30, 1908

Reverend James Slover, a long time Woodville minister who supposedly called the town Woodville when Sloverville was proposed as a name in 1871.

WOODVILLE, eight miles west of Porterville on the Tule River, is not to be confused with Woodsville, the first county seat of Tulare County, on the Kaweah River. Its name came from the profusion of trees growing there when settlers came.

Woodville has always been a farming and dairy

The Yettem Armenian Presbyterian Church was organized in 1911 with Reverend M. Jenanyan as the first pastor. The building burned in 1955 and was replaced with this church.

St. Mary's Armenian Apostolic Church at Yettem was organized in 1909 with Father Vahan Guldalian as pastor. The church burned in 1946 and was replaced with this building.

center. Now it also produces cotton, and three large cotton ginning plants are located in Woodville. There is also a prune dehydrator and a walnut drying plant.

First school	Woodville, June 5, 1878
First post office	June 5, 1871, moved to Porterville in 1908

YETTEM, south of Orosi, has had several names and a variety of crops, but it is really the story of the work and perserverance of Armenian people who have transformed plains into a "Garden of Eden."

The first settlers raised grain and called their village Cricketville. In 1881 Drew Dickey came from Woodville and built a general store. In that same year, Dave Churchill petitioned for a post office which the postal authorities called Churchill. Churchill never went beyond a store and post office because the ranches were widely separated.

In 1901 a few Armenian people began to farm. They raised tobacco, fruit, and vegetables, but principally grapes. Their largest source of income came from raisins. The golden bleached raisin industry, which now has a large export sale, started in Yettem when Krikor Arslanian hand-dipped the first sulphur-bleached raisins in 1909.

More Armenian people came to the area, and in the application for a post office Yettem, meaning "Garden of Eden," was selected from a list of names.

The two churches of Yettem have been a unifying force through the good and the very bad times its people have experienced. St. Mary's Armenian Apostolic Church was founded in 1909, and the Yettem Presbyterian Church in 1911.

Today the small community is surrounded by citrus, vineyards, grain and cotton fields, and large acreages of vegetables. Packing houses and sheds are adjacent to the railroad and truck terminals.

First church	St. Mary's Armenian Apostolic, 1909
First school	Churchill, May 5, 1887
	Yettem, 1912
First post office	Churchill, January 4, 1881, moved to Visalia, 1887
	Yettem, March 8, 1905

Bibliography

BOOKS AND PAMPHLETS

Alexander, Charles. *Battles and Victories of Allen Allensworth*. Boston, 1914.
Bain, Naomi. *Colonel Thomas Baker*. Kern County Historical Society, 1944.
Baker, John. *San Joaquin Vignettes*. Kern County Historical Society, 1955.
Bartlett, William P. *Happenings*. Boston, 1927.
Bartlett, William P. *More Happenings*. Boston, 1928.
Beasley, Delilah. *Negro Trailblazers of California*. Los Angeles, 1919.
Berg, Norman. *History of the Kern County Land Company*. Kern County Historical Society, 1971.
Berland, Oscar. "Giant Forest, The Legend and the Mystery." *Sierra Club Bulletin,* December 1962.
Bolton, Herbert E. *In the South San Joaquin Ahead of Garces*. Kern County Historical Society, 1935.
Boyd, William H. *Land of Havilah 1854-1874.* Bakersfield, 1952.
Boyd, William H. *A California Middle Border, The Kern River Country*. Bakersfield, 1972.
Brown, James L. *The Mussel Slough Tragedy*. Reprint, 1958.
Butterfield, H.M. "History of Deciduous Fruits in California." *Blue Anchor,* Vols. XIV and IV, 1937-1938.
California Fruit Growers Exchange. *The Story of California Oranges and Lemons*. Los Angeles, 1936.
Camp, Charles L. *Kit Carson in California*. Reprint, *California Historical Society Quarterly,* October 1922.
Carson, James H. *Early Recollections of the Mines and a Description of the Great Tulare Valley*. Stockton, 1852.
Chapman, Charles E. *A History of California: The Spanish Period*. New York, 1916.
Cleland, Robert G. *A History of California: The American Period*. New York, 1922.
Cleland, Robert G. *The Cattle On a Thousand Hills 1852-1870*. Huntington, 1941.
Cleland, Robert G. *This Reckless Breed of Men: The Trappers and Fur Traders of the Southwest*. Knopf, 1950.
Conkling, Roscoe and Margret. *The Butterfield Overland Mail*. 3 vols. Arthur Clarke, 1947.
Cook, Sherburne F. *Colonial Expeditions to the Interior of California's Central Valley 1800-1820*. University of California Anthropological Records 16.6, 1960.
Cook, Sherburne F. *Expeditions to the Interior of California's Central Valley 1820-1840*. Op cit. 20:5, 1962.
Coues, Elliott. *On the Trail of a Spanish Pioneer; The Diary and Itinerary of Father Garces*. New York, 1909.
Crowe, Earle. *General Beale's Sheep Odyssey*. Kern County Historical Society, 1960.
Cutter, Donald. *The Diary of Ensign Gabriel Moraga*. Early California Travel Series XL1, 1957.
Dalton, Emmett. *When the Daltons Rode*. Doubleday, 1931.
Derby, George H. *A Report on the Tulare Valley*. 32nd Congress 1st Session Sen. Doc. 110
Doctor, Joseph. *Shotguns on Sunday, The Story of Jim McKinney*. Great West and Indian Series XIV, Westernlore Press, 1959.
Egenes, Elaine. *The Dauntless Dillons*. Michigan, 1970.
Elasser, A.B. *Indians of Sequoia and Kings Canyon National Park 1962*. Sequoia Natural History History Association, Three Rivers.
Elliott, William W. *History of Tulare County 1883*. San Francisco.
Engelhardt, Father Zephrin. *The Missions and Missionaries of California*. 4 vols., 1908 to 1915.
Exeter. *Exeter 1911 to 1961*. Exeter Chamber of Commerce.
Farquhar, Francis P. *History of the Sierra Nevada*. Berkeley, 1965.
Farquhar, Francis P. "Walter Fry of Giant Forest." *Sierra Club Bulletin,* 1942.
Fenenge, Franklin. "Archaeology of the Slick Rock Village." *American Antiquity,* 1952.
Fremont, Charles. *Memoirs of My Life*. Chicago, 1887.
Frickstad, Walter N. *A Century of California Post Offices*. Oakland, 1955.
Fry, Walter. *Big Trees*. Stanford University Press, 1930.
Gayton, A.H. *The Ghost Dance of 1870 in South Central California*. University of California Publications in American Archaeology and Ethnology, 57-82, 1930.
Gayton, A.H. *Yokuts, Mono Chiefs and Shamans*. Op cit., Vol. 24 #8, 1930.
Gifford, E.W. and Schench, W.E. *Archaeology of the Southern San Joaquin Valley*. Op cit. Vol. 23 #1, 1926.
Grant, Blanche. *Kit Carson's Own Story of His Life as Dictated to Col. and Mrs. D.C. Peters about 1856*. Taos, 1926.
Griggs, Monroe C. *Wheelers, Pointers and Leaders*. Tulare County Historical Society, 1957.
Gudde, Erwin G. *California Place Names*. University of California Press, 1962.
Guinn, Joseph M. *Biographical History of the San Joaquin Valley*. Chicago, 1905.
Heizer, Robert F. *They Were Only Diggers 1851-1866*. Ballena Press, 1972.

Heizer, R.F. and Treganza, A.E. *Mines and Quarries of the Indians of California.* Ballena Press, 1972.
Heizer, R.F. and Whipple, M.A. *California Indians: A Source Book.* University of California Press, 1960.
Hine, Robert V. *California's Utopian Colonies.* San Marino, 1963.
Hine, Robert V. *Edward Kern and American Expansion.* Yale University Press, 1962.
Hurst, Harry. *Alta Pioneers 1924.* Re-edited and enlarged by his granddaughter, Mrs. Ernestine Burum Leas. Fresno, 1970.
Johnson, Hank. *They Felled the Redwoods.* Trans-Anglo Books, Los Angeles, 1966.
Kalfayan, Garabed. *Story of Yettem* (in Armenian). No date.
Kenny, Robert. *History and Proposed Settlement of the Claims of the California Indians 1944.* Sacramento.
King, Clarence. *Mountaineering in the Sierra Nevada.* London, 1872. Reprint 1911.
Kroeber, A.E. *Handbook of the Indians of California and Washington.* Bureau of American Ethnology, 1925.
Kroeber, A.E. *The Yokuts Language of South Central California.* University of California American Archaeology and Ethnology, January 1907.
Latta, Frank F. *Uncle Jeff's Story.* Tulare, 1929.
Latta, Frank F. *California Indian Folklore.* Shafter, 1936.
Latta, Frank F. *Little Journeys in the San Joaquin.* Tulare, 1937.
Latta, Frank F. *Black Gold in the San Joaquin.* Caxton Printers. Utah, 1949.
Latta, Frank F. *Yokuts Handbook.* Bakersfield, 1949.
Levick, M.B. *Tulare County, California. Sunset Magazine* for the Tulare County Board of Trade.
Lewis, Ruth R. "Kaweah: An Experiment in Co-operative Colonization 1948." *Pacific Historical Review,* Vol. XVII #4.
MacCurdy, R.M. *History of the California Fruit Growers Exchange.* Los Angeles, 1925.
Magruder, Genevieve. *The Upper San Joaquin Valley 1772-1870.* Kern County Historical Society, 1950.
Matthes, Francois E. *Sequoia National Park, A Geological Album.* University of California Press, 1950.
No Author. *Memorial and Biographical History of Fresno, Tulare and Kern Counties.* Lewis Publishing Company. Chicago, 1891.
Menefee, Eugene and Dodge, Frank A. *History of Tulare and Kings Counties.* Los Angeles, 1913.
Mitchell, Annie R. *King of the Tulares.* Visalia, 1941.
Mitchell, Annie R. *Land of the Tules 1950.* Reprint. Valley Publishers. Fresno, 1972.
Mitchell, Annie R. *Major Savage and the Tulareno Indians.* Great West and Indian Series VIII. Westernlore Press. Los Angeles, 1959.
Mitchell, Annie R. *Visalia: Her First Fifty Years.* Exeter, 1963.
Montgomery, Mrs. Nora Pogue. *Early Days in Lemon Cove.* Exeter, 1966.
Mora, Jo. *The Saga of the Hardworking Vaqueros.* Garden City Press, 1949.
Morgan, Dale. *Jedediah Smith and the Opening of the West.* New York, 1953.
Morrell, Ed. *The Twenty-Fifth Man.* New York, 1924.
Muir, John. *Our National Parks.* Boston, 1911.
Norris, Frank. *The Octopus.* New York, 1901.
Ormsby, Waterman L. *The Butterfield Overland Mail.* San Marino, 1954.
Otter, Floyd. *Men of Mammoth Forest.* Michigan, 1963.
Pietroforte, Alfred. *Songs of the Yokuts and Paiutes.* Healdsburg, 1965.
Pillsbury and Ellsworth. *Business Directory and Historical Descriptive Handbook of Tulare County 1888.*
Pogue, Grace. *Within the Magic Circle.* Visalia, 1943.
Pogue, Grace. *The Swift Seasons.* Visalia, 1956.
Porter, S. Thomas. *The Silver Rush at Mineral King.* 3rd printing. Visalia, 1966.
Priestley, Herbert I. *Franciscan Explorations in California.* Edited by Lillian Fisher. Arthur Clark, 1946.
Priestley, Herbert I. *A Historical, Political, and Natural Description of California by Pedro Fages.* 1775. Reprint, Ballena Press, 1972.
Purdy, Will. *Kaweah: An Epic Poem of the Old Colony.* Tulare County Historical Society, 1959.
Putnam, R. Porter. *The Journal of R. Porter Putnam. Farm Tribune.* Porterville, 1961.
Renovich, Stephen. "Visalia Electric Railroad." *The Western Railroader,* June 1959.
Ridge, John R. *The Life and Adventures of Joaquin Murietta,* Edited by J.H. Jackson. University of Oklahoma Press, 1955.
Rojas, A.R. *California Vaquero.* Fresno: Academy Library Guild, 1953.
Rojas, A.R. *Lore of the California Vaqueros.* Fresno: Academy Library Guild, 1958.
Secrest, William B. *The Gold of Old Hornitos as told by Francisco Salazar.* Fresno, 1964.
Sawyer, Eugene. *Life and Career of Tiburcio Vasquez.* Oakland, 1944.
Small, Kathleen. *History of Tulare County,* 2 vols. Chicago, 1926.
Smith, Wallace. *Garden of the Sun.* Fresno, 1956.
Smith, Wallace. *Prodigal Sons: The Story of Evans and Sontag.* Boston, 1951.
Spindt, H.A. *Life of Edward Kern.* Kern County Historical Society, 1939.
Stewart, George W. *Big Trees of Giant Forest.* San Francisco, 1903.
Stiner, Miss Ina. *Old Cemeteries of Southern California.* Porterville, 1954.
Stiner, Miss Ina. *History of Porterville.* Bound Typescript, no date.
Strong, Douglas H. *A History of Sequoia National Park.* Doctoral Dissertation, Syracuse University, 1964.
Templeton, Sardis W. *The Lame Captain: The Story of Peg-Leg Smith.* Westernlore Press. Los Angeles, 1965.
Thomas, Sister Mary. *Apostle of the Valley: The Story of Father Daniel Dade.* Fresno, 1947.
Thompson, Thomas H., *Atlas and History of Tulare County.* Tulare, 1892.
Tulare County Agricultural Commissioner. *Annual Reports.*
Tulare County Chamber of Commerce. *Tulare County Factbook.*
Tulare County Chamber of Commerce. *Tulare County Weather Facts.*
Tulare County Chamber of Commerce. *Tulare County Statistics.*
Tulare County Schools. *100 Years of Progress.* Compiled by Sigma Chapter, Delta Kappa Gamma.

Underhill, Reuben. *From Cowhides to Golden Fleece.* Stanford University Press, 1939.
U.S. Army Corp of Engineers in cooperation with the National Park Service. *Terminus Reservoir.*
Voge, Hervey H. *A Climber's Guide to the High Sierras.* Sierra Club, 1965.
Walker, Ardis. *Recollections of the Kern Frontier.* Kern County Historical Society, 1938.
Walker, Ardis. *The Rough and the Righteous of the Kern River Diggings.* Paisano Press, 1970.
White, John R. and Pusateri, Samuel. *Illustrated Guide to Sequoia and Kings Canyon National Park.*
Williamson, R.S., *Report of Explorations in California for Railroad Routes,* 1853. Pacific Railroad Reports V, 1856.
Wilson, Neill, and Taylor, Frank J. *Southern Pacific, the Roaring Story of a Fighting Railroad.* McGraw-Hill, 1952.
Wood, Raymund. *Agua Fria.* Academy Library Guild, 1954.
Wood, Raymund. *The Life and Death of Peter Lebec.* Fresno, 1954.

MANUSCRIPTS AND GENEALOGIES

Chatters, Ford and Chatters, Roy. *Chatters-Halleck Family History.* 1973.
Campbell, David. *Crossing the Plains in 1846.*
Dickey, Albert. *Reminiscences.* 1948.
Frost, Arba W. *Papers of Arba Frost.* Tulare County Library Historical Collection.
Fry, Walter. *Papers of Walter Fry.* Tulare County Library Historical Collection.
Higdon, Harriet Wright. *Isaac Wright Family.* 1939.
Homer, Rodney. *Balaams of California.* 1975.
Homer, Rodney. *Our Sperry Family.* 1968.
Homer, Rodney. *Mehrtens of the San Joaquin.* Family newsletter, 1964 to present.
Keagle, Cora. *The Hoskins Family.* 1945.
Lincoln, Thomas R. *The Fly Family.* 1958.
Madrid, Edith. *Romero-Salazar Families.* No date.
Moore, Raymond M. *Moore, Reynolds, Chatten, Cutler Families.* 1973.
McGee, Mrs. Lizzie. *Mills of the Sequoias.* 1952.
Peterson, Naomi Pursell. *History of the Frank Pursell Family.* 1975.
Richardson, Mrs. Mildred and Richardson, Mr. and Mrs. Kenneth. *Harry Quinn Family.* 1961 and 1976.
Reynolds, Edgar. *Diary.* 1852.
Roehl, Mrs. Kenneth. *Enoch Wright Family.* 1971.
Smith, Dr. Robert. *Edwin Storey.* 1964.
Stevens, Abner. *Savage-Springer Families by Lt. Colonel Howard Savage.*
Stewart, George W. *Papers of George W. Stewart.* Tulare County Library Historical Collection.
Turner, Wallace. *Thomas and Frances Towery.* 1970.

NEWSPAPERS

Kaweah Commonwealth *Tulare Advance Register*
Lindsay Gazette *Terra Bella News*
Porterville Enterprise *Visalia Delta*
Porterville Farm Tribune *Visalia Times*
Porterville Recorder *Visalia Times Delta*
Sentiment Maker *Woodlake Echo*

NEWSPAPER SERIES

Brice, Dorothy. "Pioneer Interviews." *Terra Bella News,* 1971-1972.
Mitchell, Annie. "Golden Memories." *Visalia Times Delta,* 1950-1952.
Mitchell, Annie. "Tales of the Tules." *Visalia Times Delta,* 1971-1973.

HISTORICAL SOCIETY BULLETINS

Fresno Historical Society. *Fresno Past and Present.*
Kern County Historical Society. *Historic Kern.*
Tulare County Historical Society. *Los Tulares.*
Delano Historical Society. *The Plow.*

Index

Abbey, Arthur A., 75,135
Ackerman, Fred, 135
Adams, A.H., 74
Advance, 111,112
Akers, Henry, 29
Alila, 50,52,69,124,138
Allen, Darwin, 131
Allensworth, 117,118,141
Allensworth, Mr. & Mrs. Allen, 117,118
Alles, Conrad, 114
Alpaugh, 118
Alpaugh, John, 118
Angiola, 119
Angra Tower, 145
Antelope Valley, 42,155
Anza, Juan Bautista de, 16
Arden Company, 89
Armsby, J.K., 79
Arslanian, Krikor, 156
Asbill, John, 38
Atwell, Allen, 118
Atwell's Mill, 111,115
Auckland, 119
Awbrey, Ed, 125

Baca, Santos, 92
Bacigalupi, T., 119
Bacon, Fielding, 37
Badger, 54, 119
Bailey, Fred, 74
Baker, Lucretia, Mrs., 113
Baker, Nathan, 29,32,34,147
Baker, Peter Y., 43,141
Baker, Thomas, 28,29,30,37
Balaam, Edwin, 40,59
Balch Park, 102,103,135
Balch, Mr. & Mrs. Allan, 103
Ball, J.M., 29,30
Ballard, W.P., 125
Baptismal site, 16,17
Barbed wire, 40
Barboni, Joseph, 148
Bardsley, L.W., 90
Barker, John, 29
Bartlett, W.P., 133
Bartoldus, Joe, 92
Barton, Enos, 11
Barton, Hudson, 130
Barton, Jason, 155
Barton, Stephen, 98
Basques, 91,96
Beale, Edward, 24
Bearess, T., 75
Bearss, J.B., 76
Beaver, Oscar, 53
Beinhorn, William, 63,68

Benware, William, 37
Bequette, Frank, 153
Bequette, Paschal, 79
Berry, George S., 64,65,66,68,70,71,74,127,145
Berry, William, 64,68,70,129
Bergstrom, Chris, 65
Best, Daniel, 67
Biggs, D.W.C., 39
Bishop, W.B., 148
Blain, W.H., 84
Blair, Jonathan, 40,77
Blankenship, William, 29,36
Blankenship, Zachary, 153
Blossom, Ira, 40,78
Boas, Mrs. Ellen, 126
Bond, Levi, 39
Bonneville, Benjamin, 22
Bonnie Brae Ranch, 71,74
Boone, J.T., 122
Borba, M.C., 88
Bossler, Simpson, 45
Bowling, John, 26
Box, Joe, 39
Bradbury, William, 131
Braly, E.A., 146
Braly, S.W., 123
Bravo Lake, 38,77,154,155
Brey, Hiram, 75
Bridger, Jim, 23
Briggs, Frank, 79,81
Briggs, George, 79
Briggs, George, 79
Briggs, John, 79
Briggs, Joseph, 79
Britten, Ernest, 114
Britten, Frank, 140
Britten, Noel, 140
Broder, John, 114
Brooks, Joel, 27,28
Brown, Clinton, 103,136
Brown, Rennie, 155
Brown, Samuel C., 37
Brown, W.N., 146
Brumfield, Dr. F.M., 75
Brundage, Thomas, 125
Bryant, Frank, 146
Bubal, 18
Burke, Harry, 57
Burke, James, 149
Burness, Mrs. Hector, 137
Burnett, Peter, 13
Burrough, Henry, 30
Buswell, C., 75
Butterfield Stages, 38,126,127,132
Buzzard's Roost, 149,151
Byrd, Molly, 51

Byrd, Perry, 50

Cabot, Father Juan, 18
Cairns, John J., 68,69,70,71,74,75,76,127,129
Cairns, Walter, 76
Caldwell, George, 39
California Hot Springs, 102,109,119,120
Callison, Ezekial, 39
Cameron, Alex, 30
Camp Babbitt, 73
Camp Lena, 102
Camp Nelson, 102,121
Camp Wishon, 102
Camp, W.B., 99
Campbell, David, 39
Campbell & Pool Ferry, 25,26,27,30
Campbell, William J., 25,26,27,29,34
Carmelita, 22
Carmen, Richard, 42
Carothers, Sam, 68
Carpenter, A.B., 132
Carson, Kit, 22,23
Carter, Joseph, 75
Cartmill, W.F., 85,89,145
Cartmill, William, 85,86
Carver, Joel, 39
Castaic, 36
Castle, E.D., 145
Central Pacific Railroad, 42,126
Central Valley Project, 42,124,129,145
Ceres Holdup, 50,52
Charters, H.A., 146
Chatten, Richard, 34,37,80
Chief Chappo, 10,40,104
Chief Francisco, 28
Chief Watoka, 25
Churchill, 156
Churchill, Dave, 156
Clark, Isaac, 149
Clarke, C.W., 119
Click, Martin, 87
Clotfelter, J.R., 122
Coburn, Avon, 108,137
Coffeeville, 51,57
Coker, Henry, 39
Collis Holdup, 51,52,53
Colony Mill, 110,111
Colony Road, 109,110,111
Cotton, A.T., 146
Court of Sessions, 29,30
Cow, Henry, 10
Cowles, Charles, 129
Crabtree, James, 37,44,112
Cramer, 49
Crespi, Father Juan, 1,15
Cromley A.P., 142

Crowley, John, 125
Curtis, S.Z., 74
Cutler, 121
Cutler John, 30,121

Dalton, Bob, 49,50,51
Dalton, Emmett, 49,50,51,56
Dalton, Gratton, 49,50,51
Dalton, William, 49,50,51
Danner, Nathan, 39
Darwin, Andrew, 42
Daunt, 136,137
Daunt, William, 136,137
Davidson, M., 75
Davis, Horace, 125
Davis, James, 30
Davis, Tom, 42
Dean, Gilbert, 29
Dean, Wiley, 50,51
Deep Creek, 37,124
Deer Creek, 18,39,138
De Masters, David, 12
De Masters, Foster, 37
Denny, James, 147
Dennis, John B., 123
Deputy, W.C., 29
Derby, Lt. George, 28
DeWitt, Marcus, 135
Dickey, Albert, 42
Dickey, Drew, 156
Dill, William, 26,29
Dillon, Nathan, 37
Dinuba, 43,121,141
Dodge, G.A., 145
Dominguez, Jose, 24
Dopkins, G.M., 122
Dorst, J.H., 113,114
Doty, A.J., 102
Douglass, David R., 147
Doyle, Chester, 135
Doyle, John, 102,103
Ducor, 64,122,135,138
Dungan, Dr. J.F., 125
Dunlap, John, 39
Dunn, R.F., 122
Dusy, Frank, 64

Earlimart, 50,124
Echeandia, Jose de, 21
Edmunds, E.P., 30
Ehrmann, Mrs. Freda, 71
Eisen, Gustavus, 107,115
El Camino Real, 26
El Camino Viejo, 41
Elderwood, 155
Election Tree, 26
El Granada, 123
Elk Bayou, 37,39
El Tejon Grant, 36
Elkins, Abiel, 148
Elliott, Alfred, 145
Ellis, Rad, 39
Ellis, Sam L.N., 54
Ely, Joe, 12
Emeterio, Francisco, 7
Empire Mine, 42,112
Ensign, Frank, 138
Escudo, Father Jaime, 18
Eshom Valley, 11,13
Eshom, John, 37
Estanislao, 19
Estrada, Manuel, 46
Estudillo, Lt. Jose, 18
Evans, Chris, 51,52,53,54,55,56,57
Evans, Eva, 52,55
Evans, James, 84

Evans, Tom, 56,57
Everton, Alfred, 40,74
Ewing, John, 40
Ewing, W.H., 29
Exeter, 124,125

Fabregat, Narcisco, 18
Fages, Eulalia, 15
Fages, Pedro, 1,7,15,16,24,36,101
Falconer, Mrs. Mary, 93
Fancher, John, 29,37,38
Farmersville, 13,40,79,123
Ferguson, E.C., 42
Fewell, J.W., 155
Figueroa, Jose, 19,23
Filo, 137
Finley, William, 30
Firebaugh, John, 124
Fisher, Jim, 42
Flanders, C.H., 75
Flemming, Charles, 79
Flemming, George, 79
Flynn, Matt, 40
Font, Father Pedro, 101
Ford, Henry, 113
Fort Miller, 28
Fort Tejon, 23
Fort Visalia, 32,34
Four Creeks, 25,26,28,29,32,33
Fountain Springs, 39,68,125,126
Fowler, Thomas, 38,40,42,43,44,112,141
Frankenberger, L.C., 30
Fraser, A.B., 29,30
Fraser, A.H., 38
Fraser, Abner, 138
Frasier, L.B., 102
Freeman, Don, 125
Freeman, J.M., 155
Freeman, Willie, 125
Fremont, John C., 22,23,24
French, Dr. Erasmus, 25
French, D.W.C., 30
Fresno Scraper, 64
Frost, A.W., 33
Frost, George, 70,74
Fry, Walter, 104,113,114
Funston, James, 116
Furness, Dr. Gilbert, 149
Futrell, W.W., 87

Gann, William, 129
Garces, Father Francisco, 16,101,151
Gard, George, 54,55,56
General Grant Park, 111,112,113,114,139
General Grant Tree, 3,113
General Sherman Tree, 3,112
George, Dr. S.G., 71
Ghost Dance, 11
Giant Forest, 40,104,109,110,112,113,114
Giant Oak Ranch, 79
Gibbons, Mrs. Deming, 73
Giddings, E.O., 75
Gill, John, 147
Gilliam, S.T., 84
Gilmer, Rufus, 79
Glenn, Richard, 29,30,34
Godey, Alexis, 23,24
Goldman, Jacob, 146
Goldstein, Isaac, 29,118
Goodburn, Robert, 30
Gordon, Aneas B., 29,30
Gordon, Jack, 37
Goshen, 42,50,126
Grand Island, 26,33
Grand Jury, 30
Grasshoppers, 75

Graves, Roy, 90
Green, W.E., 90
Grimsley, J.H., 87
Grosvenor, Gilbert, 115
Guldalian, Vahan, 156
Guthrie, John, 39

Hadley, James, 135
Halbert, Edward, 92
Halford, J. Frank, 135
Hall, C.F., 146
Hambright, James, 40
Hamilton, Hugh, 40
Hardemann, Dr. J.E., 60
Harper, J.W., 122
Harrell, Jasper, 29,37,145
Harris, Joseph, 37
Harrison, George, 99
Hart, Edwin, 92
Hart, George, 138
Hart, Phillip, 138
Hartley, Henry, 29,37
Harvey, Walter, 25,27,30
Haskell, Burnette, 109,110
Hastings, Warren, 68
Hatch, J.B., 29,30
Hauser, W.C., 122
Hayden, Charles, 30
Hayes, F.C., 90
Hayes, Jacob, 145
Haynes, Daniel, 29,30
Hazelton, William, 29
Hellman, Marco, 138
Henry, Albert, 74
Henry, Oliver, 74
Henry, Wilshire, 74
Herbert, Phillip, 26
Hercules Tree, 103,106
Herrera, Alsalio, 45,46
Herschede, Mr. & Mrs. Fred, 111
Hewey, John, 39
Hidalgo, Father Miguel, 18
Higdon, W.F., 90
Higgins, Dr. O.C., 135
Hilliard, Abraham, 28,30
Hockett, John, 39
Hockett Trail, 112
Holland, E.W., 146
Hollister, William, 35
Holt, Benjamin, 67
Homer, Joseph, 40
Homestead Act, 107
Hopping, Ralph, 114
Hossack, John, 92
Hospital Rock, 8,40,115
Hoskins, Jesse, 103,106
Howeth, Luke, 92
Hoy, J.C., 148
Hubbs, James R., 102
Hudgins, John, 28
Hudson Bay Trappers, 21,22,23
Hunsaker, Henry, 39,155
Hunt, I.W., 30
Hutchinson, Mr. & Mrs. A.J., 66,70,71,74,75,76
Hyde, J.D., 107,112

Ichow, Mr. & Mrs. Henry, 10
Indians, 4-14
Inyo County, 3
Iturbide, Augustin, 18
Ivanhoe, 42,126,127

Jacob, Elias, 66,68,69,119,129
Jacob, Morphew, 80
Jacob, Thomas, 80,82
James, Frank, 49

James, Jesse, 49
Jasper, Merrill, 125
Jenanyan, Reverend M., 156
Jennings, Sam, 30
Jerusalem, Henry, 129
Jewett, Philo, 97
Jewett, Solomon, 35,91,97,98
Joos, Chris, 123
Jordan Trail, 112
Jordan Tree, 103

Kaweah Colony, 109,110,111,112,113,139
Kaweah Post Office, 111,112
Kaweah River, 17,28,70,102,104,109,127,139, 146
Kay, Eugene, 50,51,53,55
Keeley, John, 68,129
Keeley, Lewis, 68,129
Keener, Henry, 79
Keener, John, 36,37
Keller, Charles, 109
Kennedy, J.W., 147
Kern County, 3
Kern, Edward, 23
Kern River, 16,18,28,102,147
Kiggins, W.B., 129
Kinder, Henry, 30
Kings Canyon National Park, 3,115,135
Kings County, 3
Kings River, 17,21,25,28,43,141
Kingston, 57,58
Kirby, Seth, 39
Kirkman, J.G., 125
Kitchener, C.F.J., 141
Klein, Bruno, 39
Klink, 126,127
Knox, John, 79
Knudsen Food Products, 90
Kress, Kenneth, 155
Kukus Cult, 11

Labachotte, B.G., 92
Labor, 69,79,82,111
La Dolorosa, 16
Laguna de Tache, 36
Lambert, Jacob, 29
La Marche, Joe, 90
La Marsna, Joe, 87
Larsen, J.N., 135
La Salve, 16
Latta, Frank, 13,36,38
Lawrence, A.J., 30
Lawrence, Mr. & Mrs. Henry, 10
Lebec, Peter, 23
Leitch, Archibald, 135
Lemon Cove, 40,74,77,104,127
Levis, Adolph, 129
Levy, Julius, 148
Lewis, George, 39,146
Lewis, J.S., 75
Lewis, M.B., 26,28,29
Lime Kiln, 127
Lindsay, 8,69,70,71,76,127,128,129,143
Lindsey, Tipton, 40,107,112,147
Logo, Samuel, 30
Lone Oak Cemetery, 28
Los Angeles-Stockton Road, 28,32,34
Love, Tom, 11
Lovelace, Joseph, 40
Loverin, Si, 57
Lubking, Henry, 40,67
Lumley, Aubrey, 74
Lumley, Gerald, 74
Luper, Mr. & Mrs. W.G., 114
Lynchings, 58

Mack, W.H., 129
Mackey, Charles, 125
Magnesite, 133
Majors, Columbus, 101
Majors, John, 34
Mariposa, 17
Marshall, Robert B., 129
Martarell, Juan, 45,46
Martarell, Pete, 45
Martin, Mr. & Mrs. Dan, 137
Martin, G.J., 137
Martin, James, 39,78
Martin, James J., 109,110
Martin, Father Juan, 16,17
Martinez, Father Luis, 18
Marvin, John, 26,27,28
Mason-Henry Gang, 49
Mather, Stephen, 115,116
Matthews, Cecil, 32
Matthews, Osee, 32
Matthews, Reuben, 32,67
Matthews, Warren, 30,32
Mattley, Ricardo, 45,46
Mayfield, Thomas, 153
Mayfield, William, 29,37
McCall, Abijah, 64
McCall, Dan, 57
McClosky, Mr., 79
McCormic, Thomas, 29,30
McCormick, Leroy, 125
McCrory, Jim, 58,59,60,62
McCullum, Neal, 79,131
McEvers, C.R., 124
McGee, David, 39
McGregor, Allen, 129
McIntyre, John, 92
McIntyre, Tom, 92
McKevitt, F.B., 79
McKinney, Jim, 59,60,61,62
McLaughlin, John, 21
McMillen W.W., 9,26
Meadors, Charles, 89
Meckley, John, 29
Mehrten, William, 40,63,68,129
Melcaldie, 22
Melvin, Dr. J.T., 137
Menne, John, 40
Menne, Lorenz, 40,92
Mentz, Wilko, 135
Merced River, 17
Merritt, A.P. 145
Merritt, H.C., 80
Merryman, A.C., 74
Merryman, R.C., 74
Miles, E.H., 125
Miller, Zachariah, 74
Milligan, Reverend John, 62,74
Millinghausen, August, 74
Miner, James, 87
Minkler Railroad, 42,122
Mineral King, 42,43,44,102,104,112,114,148
Mineral King Ranch, 78
Mitcham, Jonathan, 30
Mitchell, Joseph, 119
Mitchell, Levi, 153
Mitchell, Michael, 153
Mitchell, Ozoro, 40
Mitchell, Susman, 119
Monroe, J.B., 39,87
Monson, 129
Mooney Grove, 37,80,82
Mooney, Michael, 148
Moore, Andrew, 65
Moore, Hiram, 65
Moore, Orlando, 65
Moraga, Gabriel, 1,17,18

Moraga, Jose, 17
Moro Rock, 40,116
Morrell, Ed, 55,56
Morrow, Almerin, 29,30
Motherall, N.W., 81
Mount Whitney, 3,112,113
Mt. Whitney Power & Electric Company, 71, 77,103
Mountain Home, 102,108,137
Mountain Home State Forest, 102,135
Muir, John, 40,91,107,113,115
Munoz, Father Pedro, 17,18
Murphy, Dan, 39
Murphy, J.F., 29,90
Murray, A.H., 34
Murray, Commodore, 34,39
Murray, J. Patrick, 39,40
Mussel Slough, 49,103

Neilson, George, 90
Nelson, John M., 121
Newman, Emil, 75
No Fence Law, 40,42
Norton, Peter, 40,92
Nowell, J.A., 148

Oak Forest, 4,17
O'Brien, George, 135
O'Farrell, Harry, 112
Ogden, Peter S., 22
Olives, 71,72,129,138
O'Neal, J.C., 29,33
Orosi, 79,130,131
Orr, J., 74
Ortega, Juan, 18
Orton, Julius, 29,37,39,70,72,74
Osborn, Bill, 12
Ostrander, P.T., 129
Overr, Oscar, 117
Owen, John D., 84,87
Owen, Richard, 23
Owen, W.A., 148

Packard, Jeff, 62
Packwood, Elisha, 29,36,37,38,39,83,133
Packwood, Samuel, 38,39
Paige & Morton Ranch, 78,142
Palmer, Joe, 40
Pardee, B.J., 148
Parkhurst, D.W., 124
Patrons of Husbandry, 112
Patterson, John, 29,34
Payne, Dr. Thomas, 25,26,28
Payeras, Father Mariano, 18,19
Paxton, C.T., 146
Pease, Fred, 155
Peppers, Shelby, 39
Perkins, Elijah, 54
Perkins, Henry P., 79,145
Persian, James, 37
Peterson, Henry, 75
Peterson, W.A., 29
Phillips, Perry, 92
Phillips, Strachey, 119
Pico, Jose, 18
Pictographs, 10
Pike Lawless Station, 38
Pine Flats, 102
Pinkham, Eben F., 79
Pioneer Land Company, 74
Pixley, 49,50,68,131,138
Pixley, Frank, 131
Plano, 73,133
Platt, W.O., 135
Pogue, J.W.C., 40,74,77,127
Pohut, Mr. & Mrs. Joe, 6,10

163

Pool, John, 25,27,30
Poplar, 98,99,131,132
Porteous, James, 64
Porterville, 32,44,60,74,77,132,134
Porterville Co-operative Creamery, 89
Portillo, Pablo de la, 19
Portola, Gaspar de, 15
Pratt, Dan, 74,87
Prior, Basil, 70,129
Pritchard, W.F., 127
Prothero, Anastacio, 39
Prothero, Joseph, 36.37,38,39
Pumped Wells, 70,71,129
Putnam, Mr. & Mrs. Porter, 132,133

Qualls, Truman, 125
Quinn, Harry, 40,92,93,94,95,96,135
Quinn Family, 93

Rag Gulch, 93,117,135
Ragle, E.T., 40
Rainbolt, P.A., 29,30
Ramm, J.H., 122
Rancho de Kaweah, 71
Real Fresh Milk, 90
Redbanks, 78,80
Redstone, John, 109,110
Reed, G.V., 129
Reid Land Company, 135
Reid, Joseph, 135
Reynolds, Edgar, 32
Rhodes, Daniel, 29
Rice, J.O., 37
Richardson, Mrs. Mildred, 93
Richgrove, 93,135
Ridgeway, Christopher, 89,132
Ridgeway, Edward, 89,132
Righter, J.W., 123
Robinson, Tod, 79
Rockwell, Mrs. Lorenzo, 139
Rodeos, 37
Romero, Mrs. Edith, 47
Roth, 68,137
Roth, John, 68
Roth, Peter, 68
Rouse, Martin, 79
Ruiz, Francisco, 16
Rumley, A.W., 146

Sacramento Valley, 1,17
St. John's River, 29,143,146
St. John, Loomis, 29
Salazar, Jesus, 46,47
Salsa, Frank, 92
Sampson's Flat, 54
Samstag, Joseph, 45,145
San Emigidio, 19,24,36
San Joaquin River, 1,17
San Xavier del Bac, 16
Sanbourn, E., 81
Sandlappers, 40,70
Santos, 137
Sarthou, Alex, 92
Savage, James, 25,26,27,28
Sayre, C.A., 90
Schmidt, Fred, 123
Schmittou, Sterling, 74
Schoenmann, Louis, 146
Schultz, F.N., 146
Sequoia National Forest, 3,102,107
Sequoia National Park, 3,41,107,110,111,113,
    114,115,135,139
Serra, Father Junipero, 15,71
76 Land & Water Company, 42,43,87,141
Seville, 138
Shaffer, D.R., 131

Shafter Research Station, 99
Sheppard, Samuel A., 148
Shoufler, Reuben, 29
Shoup, S. Richard, 125,135
Sibley, James, 122
Sibleyville, 122
Silver City, 102,112
Sinarle, Gabriel, 92
Sisson, C.N., 146
Skiles, Harvey, 97
Sky Farmers, 40,70
Slinde, Alden, 145
Slinkard, Solomon, 39
Slover, James, 155
Smith, Billy, 29
Smith College, 144
Smith, Elijah, 83
Smith & Hatch Mill, 78,101
Smith, Jabes, 36,38,39
Smith, Jedediah, 21,22
Smith, Leroy, 122
Smith, Orson K., 29,32,38,101
Smith, Peg-Leg, 23
Smith, Will, 52,53,54
Smith, W.L., 92
Smith's Ferry, 27
Solita, 117
Sontag, George, 50,51,52,53,54,55,56
Sontag, John, 50,51,52,53,54,55
Sorrels, Samuel, 39
Southern Pacific Railroad, 42,49,50,52,109,113,
    122,124,126,129,131,137,141,142,148
Stoma, 72,138
Spangler, Daniel, 92
Spear, Joseph, 98
Spier, Joseph, 78
Springville, 77,102,136,137
Sprott, W.E., 75
Spuhler, Ben, 123
Stanford, F.H., 26
Stevenson, Gilbert, 155
Stewart, George, 107,109,111,113,115
Stiner, Miss Ina, 38
Stockton Gang Plow, 63
Stokes, Yancy, 37
Stone, A.L., 135
Stone Corral, 54,55,56
Strathmore, 137
Sultana, 138
Summer Home, 102,103
Sum Tache, 16,18
Sunflower Creamery, 89
Swall, William, 89
Swanson, George, 40,104,116
Swanson, John, 40,104,116
Sweet, Adolph, 155
Sweet, Phillip, 119

Tagus Ranch, 80
Tailholt, 151,152
Talbott, Theodore, 23
Tarabel, 16
Tehachapi Pass, 16,21
Tejon Pass, 1,18,25
Telamne, 17,18
Terra Bella, 24,67,72,77,135,138
Tharp, Hale, 10,37,40,105,107,115,116,139
Tharp, Nort, 40,104,109
Thomas, Isaac H., 78,79,80,85,92,101,147
Thomas, Joseph H., 78,113,147
Thomas, Mark, 79
Thompson, A.O., 87
Thompson, Peter, 92
Three Rivers, 40,104,111,139
Tibbens, Charles, 123
Tibbetts, Bert, 62

Tibbetts, Mrs. Luther, 73
Tibbetts, Will, 62
Tilton, J.E., 80
Timber and Stone Act, 107,109
Ting, Peter, 74
Tipton, 69,98,138,141,142
Tipton Creameries, 87,89
Tisto, Bob, 11
Townsend, Homer, 45
Traver, 42,43,69,109,122,141,142
Traver, Charles, 43,141
Traver Hold-up, 57
Tulare, 64,69,142,143,144
Tulare Co-operative Creamery, 86,89
Tulare County Grange, 112
Tulare Lake, 1,5,17,25,36,37,43,68,118,149
Tule River, 1,17,18,36,39,102,132
Tule River Indian Reservation, 3,5,81
Tule River Indian War, 101
Tuohy, John, 68,79,92,107,129,144
Turner, Josiah, 30
Turnow, James, 125
Tuxbury, W.D., 122
Twiehaus, McDonald, 125
Tyler, John D., 39

Udell, David, 87
Uhl, Fred, 45
Underwood, Wesley, 63
Uniacke, Lucius, 119
Utley, Gotlet, 123

Vandalia, 133
Vandever, William, 87,113,115
Van Gordon, Ira, 40
Vasquez, Tiburcio, 57
Van Tassel, Louis, 30
Venice Hills, 77,126,127
Vera, Jose, 13,95
Vigilantes, 34,59
Vincent, Samuel, 39,87
Vinton, Frank, 155
Visalia, 32,33,34,36,44,146,147,148,149
Visalia Creamery, 84
Visalia Electric Railroad, 77,148,150,154
Visalia Saddles, 45,46,47,48
Viscaino, 15
Vise, Abner, 30,33
Vise, Mr. & Mrs. Nathaniel, 29,32,33,147
Vossler, Joe, 87

Waddell, George, 124
Waddle, Carl, 125
Wagy, Phillip, 32
Wales, Frank, 107
Walker, David, 45,46,47,48
Walker, Frank, 107,112
Walker, John, 84
Walker, Joseph R., 22,23
Wardlaw, James, 74
Warner, Erasmus, 79
Watson, Wiley, 71
Waukena, 149,151,152
Weeks, Edwin, 47
Weisenberger, Joseph, 75
Weston, Austin, 78
White, Charles, 39
White Chief Mine, 44,112
White, Mr. & Mrs. Huffum, 73,74,92
White River, 16,18,39,147
Wickham, R.J., 131
Wiggins, Ellen Vise, 33
Wilbur, W.W., 118
Wilcox, Mr. & Mrs. Jim, 10
Wilcox, Sardis, 39,73
Williams J. Howard, 119

Williams, John W., 81
Willimott, W.P., 149
Wilson, F.H., 122
Wingrove, Lilburn, 119
Wingfield, Alfred A., 29
Wingfield, Charles R., 29,30,37
Winn, Dr. William, 137
Wirt, John, 76
Witt, Clifford, 39
Witt, Henry, 74,119
Witt, Napoleon, 74,119
Witt, Thomas, 74,119
Witty, George, 50,52,56
Wolverton, James, 112

Woodard, Myron, 119
Woodlake, 40,42,154,155
Woodville, 42,87,98,99,155
Woods Cabin, 25,26,29
Woods, John, 28
Woodsville, 26,27,28,29,32,33
Works, Enoch, 40
Works, Hopkins, 40
Wotten, Frank, 146
Wozencraft, Dr. Oliver, 25,26,28
Wright, I.M., 81
Wright, Isaac, 142
Wright, J.W.A., 107
Wright, William, 79

Yettem, 156
Yoi-Mut, 13
Yokohl Valley, 9,57,103,124
Yokuts, 4,5,6,7,8,9,10,11,12,13,101,141
Yosemite Valley, 22
Young, Ewing, 22
Young, George, 30

Zalvidea, Father Jose, 16
Zion Lutheran Church, 139
Zimmerman, Adolph, 40,92
Zimmerman, Henry, 40,92
Zumwalt, Daniel K., 85,87,92,113,115,141
Zumwalt, Jacob, 87